THE
NEW THEATRE
OF EUROPE
3

Already published:

THE NEW THEATRE OF EUROPE
THE NEW THEATRE OF EUROPE 2

Edited by Robert W. Corrigan

THE
NEW THEATRE
OF EUROPE

3

Four Contemporary Plays
From the European Stage, Including

INADMISSIBLE EVIDENCE by John Osborne

THE SUNDAY PROMENADE by Lars Forssell

THE CURVE by Tankred Dorst

THE LAUNDRY by David Guerdon

Edited with an Introduction by
ROBERT W. CORRIGAN

A DELTA BOOK

For Janet and Jim

whose vision, courage, and friendship
have made so many things possible.

CONTENTS

THE
NEW THEATRE
OF EUROPE
3

INTRODUCTION

Introduction: THE DRAMA OF THE DISENGAGED MAN

Whenever any tendency in the arts catches on to the point that it becomes an attractive commodity to be packaged in formulas, labeled as avant-garde, and sold supermarket-style in paperbacks and college courses by those purveyors of new movements—the critics—you can be pretty sure that it is nearly dead or had been completely misunderstood. Such has been the case with the most recent fashion in dramatic literature, the "Theatre of the Absurd."

To hear most people talk, one would think that Beckett and Ionesco, and later Pinter and Albee, had read Camus' *The Myth of Sisyphus* and then had accomplished some kind of magical philosophic and aesthetic fusion between the content of absurdity and theatrical form. To think this way is to misunderstand both the theatre and absurdity (not to mention Beckett and Ionesco, Pinter and Albee). We tend to forget that these playwrights are using techniques as old as the theatre itself, and that absurdity and our awareness of it as an inescapable fact of the human condition are as old as life itself. The quality which characterizes so much of the serious drama of the past two decades is not absurdity but the despair that many writers have felt when confronted with the seemingly bleak fact that, as Simone de Beauvoir put it, "between birth and death there is absurdity." Despair is the only mortal enemy of art, and the lifelessness of so much of the contemporary theatre is not due so much to our playwrights' concern with absurdity as it is to their unnecessary capitulation to it. We are, after all, absurd

whether we know it or not, and the basic challenge of existence is
to live in spite of it, because of it. The same holds true for the
theatre; what is crucial is not absurdity, but what comes after it.

Looking back, one is almost immediately conscious of the fact
that the theatre—like the victims of Hiroshima—has gone through
some grotesque (although not uninteresting) permutations since
the close of the Second World War. But with very few exceptions,
there has not been an important play written during this period
which has not been either a violent protest against the forces of
dehumanization that seem to dominate our world, or else an attempt to reveal the isolated and alienated nature of the human
condition as it exists amongst such hostile forces. Until very re-
cently, most playwrights have had a tendency to renounce the public forum and have recoiled to the innermost privacy of unsharable
moments of existence. At best, their plays have been little more
than rebellious gestures; more often, they were the violent graphs
of a cornered man. These writers may cry out in anguish, "Where
oh, where, can we find 'a man for all seasons' in an age of the common and dehumanized man?", but they have, in fact, denied the
validity of any season but the winter of their discontent. The central actions of the contemporary theatre have been protest and
retreat. It has been, as I pointed out in the introduction to the
first volume in this series, a theatre which has revealed man detached from the machinery of society; one in which man is defined
by his solitude and estrangement, and not by his participation;
one in which man is left face to face with himself.

Now, in a way, such protests certainly seem justified. The problems of our times are so numerous, complex, and immense that the
mind—not to mention the imagination—is overwhelmed if not
paralyzed by them. Samuel Beckett, in an interview, stated that
human suffering has reached such colossal proportions that it is
impossible for him to write about it anymore. Duerrenmatt, in
Problems of the Theatre, expressed his fear that our world has
grown too big for the theatre.

> For only what the eye can take in can be made visible in
> art. . . . Today art can only embrace the victims, if it can
> reach men at all; it can no longer come close to the mighty.
> Creon's secretaries close Antigone's case. The state has lost

its physical reality, and just as physics can now only cope with the world in mathematical formulas, so the state can only be expressed in statistics. Power today becomes visible, material only when it explodes as in the atom bomb, in this marvelous mushroom which rises and spreads immaculate as the sun and in which mass murder and beauty have become one. The atom bomb cannot be reproduced artistically since it is mass-produced. In its face all of man's art that would recreate it must fail, since it is itself a creation of man. Two mirrors which reflect one another remain empty.

How do you dramatize the war in Vietnam? Or the starvation in India? Or the poverty and overcrowding in Harlem? Or? Or? Or? In short, the central problems of our times. As far as I know, there hasn't been a single play of national or international reputation which attempts to deal directly with any of these problems. It can be argued, and often is, that such issues, while they may be important to the artist as an individual, should not be the concern of his art. Perhaps. But the theatre, if it is to be vital, must be what Herbert Blau has called "The Public Art of Crisis." By its very nature it involves a social context, and if it is to be meaningful, it must deal with the world as it is now; it must celebrate the conflicts and crises of the individual in his life with other men. There is no question that these conflicts are difficult to cope with, but if dramatists retreat from them, our theatre has had it. They cannot renounce the dimensions of the twentieth century just because in certain respects adjustment to them is not achieved without distress. We may suffer from exposure to the new scale, but it is necessary for us to meet it. For only complete acceptance of the world that is developing can make our lives genuinely acceptable and our art genuinely meaningful.

Generally, the artist's failure to establish an *entente* with the living present is defended on the grounds that the world which has developed over the past century is either inhospitable to art or unworthy of being celebrated by the artist. And when this defense is pushed, invariably technology and its two monster children, industrialization and collectivity, are indicted as the mortal enemies of the arts. Read the critics, read the cultural historians, read many of the artists themselves (read even my own introductions to the first two volumes in this series), and it will be the exception who does not agree with the late theologian, Paul Tillich, when he argues that "technical society is the great threat against the person and the arts."

Very briefly, the anti-technology case is built something like this: Our industrial collective society is, for the most part, based on technology and technological change. Technology has as its first principle specialization. Industrialized specialization inevitably leads to functionalism, standardization and interchangeability, the manipulation of people as objects, a sense of personal anonymity, and ultimately a condition of total alienation. Since specialization does not make demands upon the individual as a human being, but is only concerned with his functional qualities, his specific technical ability, the individual's human qualities quickly tend to atrophy as he is increasingly absorbed into the industrial collective. Soon his personality begins to undergo severe psychic and even moral changes; and eventually the individual comes to lose all sense of his own identity. Our highly industrialized technological society has standardized man so completely that he has come to be nameless, faceless, and readily interchangeable. So the argument goes. And for the past two decades most serious dramatists, both in Europe and America, have been dedicated to the task of revealing the depersonalized nature of this kind of society. They, like the students at Berkeley, have been protesting against the increasing IBM-ization of our world.

All right, fair enough; so this is true. So we are alienated and estranged. So we feel like victims of a system which we weren't responsible for creating. So robotization seems to be the cause and effect of every facet of modern life from supermarket packaging to the most horrifying totalitarian atrocities. This has become a pretty fashionable position for people to take. In fact, one of the most acceptable intellectual postures of our time is to bemoan the loss of selfhood in an age of technology. And no one has assumed this position more readily than myself. *But maybe we are all wet?* Maybe those of us in the theatre who strike such doomsday poses harm the theatre more than we ever help it?

Fortunately, today attitudes seem to be changing, and with increasing frequency our artists—even in the theatre—are asking: What's wrong with an age of technology? Why must it be the

enemy of art? Perhaps it is wrong to make technology our twentieth-century whipping boy? And as these questions are asked, our
views about alienation begin to change.

We have become aware, for instance, of how naïve much of
what has been written about our contemporary alienation really is.
Invariably the well-known authors on this subject tend to contrast
the fragmented twentieth-century citydweller with the whole man
of some earlier paradise of togetherness. But alienation—the loss
or voluntary surrender of self—has been a feature of all historical
societies. More important, and the arts reflect this with increasing
frequency, we are discovering that that sense of alienation which
technology is supposed to have created is not so widespread as our
cultural commentators maintain that it is. For most people there
is no basic incompatibility between one's sense of self and the
many social masks which each of us must also assume. In fact, for
the majority of us, the capacity to fit oneself into roles (and hence
enter into a condition of alienation) is seen not as an unavoidable
necessity, but as a highly desirable talent to have. We do not despair over the plurality of our condition, but rather we are in-
trigued, if not absorbed, by the possibilities of it. Alienation, then,
is a fact of life. And thus to identify it as a universal evil characteristic of this age is neither accurate nor useful. It supports an
ideology of despair; it is a sham profundity that repudiates the
present and its possibilities. *The present and its possibilities.* That's
what I believe a vital theatre has always been interested in. Rather
than joining Tillich in insisting that "technical society is the great
threat against the person and the arts," perhaps we ought to recognize the fact that the spirit of our industrial and electronic technologies has brought to man the possibility of a maturity and a
larger measure of freedom than he has ever known before in history. Actually, I believe most Americans recognize this fact; it is
an awareness that is central to our national character. For most of
us, and this has been true from the beginning of our history, frontiers—whether geographical, industrial, or cultural—are not
thought of as limits of the possible, but rather as challenges to be
overcome. The frontier spirit and its capacity for adaptation is a
part of the technological spirit; it has brought with it the qualities
of freedom and dynamism which characterize our nation; and it is
something which we as a people know instinctively. (Perhaps this

characteristic explains, at least in part, why not one important American playwright of the past twenty years has followed the various paths forged by his Continental counterparts. American audiences have not been wildly enthusiastic over most of the "significant" post-World War II European plays either. Only our "serious" critics, usually under the influence of Continental intellectuals, have been uniform in their acclaim of the diverse achievements of the new theatres of Europe).

I know it is not fashionable these days for critics of the arts to refer to C. P. Snow, but he made an observation about the kinds of freedom that our technologies have produced which cannot be overlooked.

> We cannot avoid the realization that applied science has made it possible to remove unnecessary suffering from a billion lives—to remove suffering of a kind, which, in our privileged society, we have largely forgotten, suffering so elementary that it is not genteel to mention it. For example, we *know* how to heal many of the sick; to prevent children dying in infancy and mothers in childbirth; to produce enough food to alleviate hunger; to throw up minimum shelter; to insure that there aren't so many births that our other efforts are in vain. All this we *know* how to do. [*The Two Cultures: A Second Look*]

Obviously, knowing how to do these things doesn't necessarily mean we do them. Disease, starvation, poverty, and overpopulation are still major problems in most parts of the world. But the fact is —and this both because of and in spite of the bomb—we have at hand the knowledge and the resources to free people from the terrible absolutistic preoccupation with survival so that with increasing frequency they can turn their energies to building a culture in which men can more nearly fulfill their greatest potentialities.

Drama has always been preeminently concerned with choice. In earlier ages kings, princes, and other personages of noble status were the fit subjects for drama because their choices were most free of the forces of necessity. As W. H. Auden has pointed out, when a king decided to steal another country—for whatever his reasons—it was without question a moral decision.

But when a poor man with a starving family stole a loaf of bread it was almost certain to be an act of physical necessity with little, if any, moral dimension to it. One of the reasons that the naturalistic movement of the nineteenth century is thought to be such a revolutionary period in the history of the theatre is its radically different view of necessity and its relationship to choice. Largely because of Darwin's theories of evolution and the discovery of new genetic laws, many writers came to be convinced that man's existence, including his personality, was a phenomenon that could be explained in terms of scientific laws. As a result, increasingly, man's complex biological needs rather than his capacity to make moral choices were thought to be his most significant characteristic. Once such a view was accepted, however, the exceptional man, who because of his position and power had the greatest freedom of choice, ceased to be the fullest embodiment, and therefore the best representative of the conflicts and choices that most clearly define the human condition. Instead, the lives of the poor —in whom the role of natural necessity is most readily observable —became the playwright's most suitable subjects. And lo, we have the drama of the common man.

But today this is changing. In widening the possibilities of our choices, widening the possibilities for us in ways that even our parents find it difficult to comprehend, technology has freed us into a fuller measure of our manhood and in so doing has, I believe, begun to restore the dimension of significant moral choice to the theatre. No one questions for a moment that our mass society is fraught with problems and limitations, but it is also developing a new kind of freedom which is peculiarly appropriate to drama. Perhaps an example will clarify what I mean. A few years ago, a UNESCO team was traveling about the Middle East, and, as UNESCO teams are wont to do, they were making a survey. The team went about the hillsides asking the shepherds if they had ever considered doing something else. The shepherds were completely baffled; it wasn't a matter of not being able to answer the question, they couldn't even comprehend it. It was like asking them if they had ever considered changing their age or their sex. The identity of those shepherds was so locked into a pattern of static conformism that their imaginations were incapable of conceiving the possibility of change. In our highly developed technological society, on the other hand, a man is able to realize his identity according to the many functional roles he plays. Strangely enough, I believe this gives us an elusive freedom to create a fuller destiny of our own. This freedom may be hard to bear, as Dostoyevsky's Grand Inquisitor pointed out; but such burdens must inevitably attend man's emergence into his most appropriate freedom.[1]

In addition to its power to enlarge the range of human choice, another of the most striking characteristics of technology is *play*. Ask any man working on basic research what he is doing, and he is likely to answer: "Playing around." This response has a profound meaning. It indicates a spirit of liberation and suggests that there is an unexpected element of humanity involved in technological research. One of the dominant characteristics of all scientific research is improvisation, and I do not believe it is an accident that all of the arts, including the theatre are moving more and more toward the improvised performance. In the past few years our artists seem to have come to a new awareness that technology is not something to be afraid of, but rather it is a great tool which the artist can use both in a technical way *and* in a spiritual way. And that quality of technology which captured the artist's attention first was its aspect of play. Play, the manifestation of delight and wonder in one's creative powers and the world that gives those powers scope. Play, that unself-conscious, ebullient homage to life itself, that uncalulated celebration of existence.

As I indicated earlier, the contemporary theatre has not, for the most part, celebrated the dimensions of the twentieth century. Rather it has tended to be in protest against them. In their mani-

[1] The difficulties that such freedom imposes was certainly one of the central elements in the recent student revolts at the University of California at Berkeley. Although I am well aware that the issues there were extremely complex, I cannot help but agree with former President Clark Kerr when he said: "The University is a disturbing place for many students but that does not mean it is devoid of meaning. One of the big advantages of a big city or a big university—as against a smaller and more monolithic closed community—is that people find those things which may mean something to them. They are given a choice. It would be terribly stultifying to find yourself in a place which has a single meaning, and that meaning is the same for everyone. The only kind of society that has only a single meaning is an authoritarian one. . . . Many tend to be overwhelmed by their opportunities; there are so many lectures to choose from, so many things to do, that they tend to become lost. They are torn too many ways and wind up condemning the whole structure."

festoes the playwrights of protest claim that they want to revitalize the theatre. But history shows us that whether we are talking about discrimination and civil rights, poverty and urban renewal, or the arts, protest is never enough. There must be an embrace as well as a protest. And this means the theatre must embrace this industrialized collective world which our technologies have played such a major role in creating. In the past, whenever it was most alive and most a part of people's daily lives, the theatrical performance was an act of celebration. We must never forget that a celebration— whether it be of a birthday or the Fourth of July, a momentous victory or some great achievement of the human mind and spirit —is a joyful response to an event; it is not the creation of the event itself. A celebration is always *ex post facto*. Thus, only by consciously and expectantly standing within the movement of history, only by standing *within* the technological enterprise, can our playwrights ever hope to be capable of celebrating it. The theatre in its greatest periods has always been concerned with man's capacities, and it seems to me that there has never been a time in history when there was a greater potential for human capacity than right now in our high-voltage electrical age.

However, in making this hopeful prognosis of the theatre's future, I have failed to discuss a very important kind of play. In the 1950s the theatre was unquestionably dominated by the Absurdist playwrights. The major theme was alienation, and in play after play man was revealed in a condition of helpless passivity, unable to communicate, unable to cope, incapable of altering a system which was transforming him in so many profound ways. Beckett's Gogo and Didi could only wait for an unknown Godot who might not come; Ionesco's recipe for salvation was delivered by an orator who turned out to be a deaf mute muttering something about angelfood cake; Osborne's Jimmy Porter could rail against the world with passionate rhetoric, but it all turned out to be futile anger; Max Frisch's contemporary man proved to be helplessly inept. One could continue this catalog, but it seems clear that the drama of the alienated man was as passive as it was pessimistic.

By 1965 there were signs of new vitality in the theatre. The emergence of the thrust stage as the dominant form of theatre architecture created a new kind of audience involvement. Happenings, games, and improvisations instilled a new spirit of spontaneity. A willingness to mix media—especially the film—has opened up all sorts of new possibilities both in form and technique. The theatre of the present seems to be in a very unpredictable stage, but there is no denying it is full of life.

However, what about the first half of the 1960s?

Generalizations seldom, if ever, hold up for very long; but as I look back at this five-year period just completed, the most significant characteristic which I discover in the theatre is the unflagging drive on the part of playwrights to deal, somehow, with absurdity. Quite interestingly, American writers approached this struggle in totally different ways than did their Continental counterparts.

Our playwrights seemed to leap-frog over (or in some cases go around) the Theatre of the Absurd. Tennessee Williams in his last important play, *Night of the Iguana* (1961), wrote a drama in which his tormented characters are able, at least briefly, to escape from the "continual rush of time" and achieve a state where a "little understanding" and communication between two people can exist. All of Edward Albee's plays beginning with *Who's Afraid of Virginia Woolf?* (1962) reveal that he has backed away from the spirit of alienation which dominated the theatre of the 1950s (and which was certainly the governing force of his earlier work) and has moved with increasing directness toward a theatre which, while ambiguous, nonetheless does tend to celebrate the possibility of enlarged human capacity. And I believe the same can be said of Arthur Miller's most recent plays, *After the Fall* (1963) and *Incident at Vichy* (1964), Robert Lowell's *The Old Glory* (1964), and Saul Bellow's fascinating but poorly received *The Last Analysis* (1964).

But most of the European dramatists writing during this period followed a different strategy. And this brings me directly to the plays in this volume. On the Continent the reaction against the Theatre of the Absurd was more subtle and at times more aggressive, although it was not so affirming and optimistic as the American reaction. In the fifties the protagonist in the European theatre was, as I said earlier, the alienated man. In the first half of the sixties he was the disengaged man. At first glance, the distinction between these types may appear too slight to have any significance. Certainly the behavior of both kinds is usually similar. The essential difference, I believe, is involved with a switch from the

Alienated
x disengaged

passive to the active voice, and this switch brought about profound changes in the kind of plays which were written. The image of man presented by the Absurdists was one of supine helplessness. The theatre of the disengaged man, on the other hand, while it ultimately had no solutions to man's victimized condition, refused to take it any more. The new playwrights seemed to be saying that if the dehumanizing forces which seem to dominate the world cannot be changed or overcome, then "let's cut out!" It is the same change of attitude which distinguishes the Diggers and the Flower People from the Beatniks. No longer is the slogan "We shall overcome"; it has become "Turn on, tune in, drop out." Alienation may be the unavoidable condition of mid-twentieth-century life, but if this is so, then an increasingly large number of people are insisting on their right to detach themselves from a society which perpetuates such a condition. Yet such a decision leaves these people in an ambiguous position which is as strange as it is new. Their decision to be disengaged, while it is a conscious and meaningful choice, is totally dependent upon the continuance of that world from which they would be detached. They may be "cutting out," but as they move away from the scene they have to be constantly looking back over their shoulders to make sure that the scene is still there. The disengaged man is a self-dramatizing personality, and his every action is composed of two elements: he must watch himself as he acts and he must always be conscious of how those people from whom he has detached himself are reacting to his actions. In a very real sense, then, for him to act is to be the voyeur to his own actions.

It is for this reason that I believe Jean Genet has been the most important single influence in the European theatre of this decade. Since Genet is not represented in this volume, it would be inappropriate for me to discuss his work here; but there is one quality essential to all of his plays which may help to illuminate the plays which I have chosen. All of these plays can be better understood if they are seen in terms of Genet's belief that the most effective strategy the individual can employ to deal with the absurdity of his condition is to allow the actor in himself to emerge. Each of us, Genet contends, must play all of life's roles; we must act furiously within the paradoxes of life in order to resist and withstand our consciousness of its absurd terms. In a sense, Genet urges each of us to become like Hamlet after he has learned the lesson of the players: we must become actors. This is the choice of the disengaged man. He has become an actor in an effort to accept, to tolerate, or to escape from the multiplication of paradox that defines him in his world. He has become an actor because it allows him to play at committed living within a context which provides a safe sense of definiteness and definition. It is a condition analogous to children's games or participation in a sport. In both instances there can be great passion and involvement, and in some cases, total identification; but there are also rules and we know it. Just as the child knows that his games are played in the realm of fantasy (in fact, he is insulted if adults ever feel the need to point this out to him), so adults know that to cheat in a game is to spoil the game. It is this paradox which Diderot described so long ago, and it further explains why the disengaged man acts and at the same time is the voyeur of his actions. And this capacity for voyeurism enhances his capacity to act meaningfully. However—and this is crucial to our discussion—to choose to be an actor as a life strategy is to create a fantasy world which, while it may be self-contained, is totally dependent upon the real world it would reject. No one described this ambiguity more clearly than Hazlitt in his definition of the actor written in 1817 in "On Actors and Acting":

> Players are "the abstracts and brief chronicles of the time"; the motley representatives of human nature. They are the only honest hypocrites. Their life is a voluntary dream; a studied madness. The height of their ambition is to be *beside themselves*. Today kings, tomorrow beggars, it is only when they are themselves that they are nothing.

The disengaged man, like the actor, succeeds as long as he is able to play at living in imaginary worlds. But the moment one of these is impinged on by the objective reality of our industrialized collective society he either reverts to his condition of helpless alienation or he is completely destroyed. Such is the fate of the disengaged man, and this is the fate of the protagonists of the plays included in this book.

John Osborne's (1927–   ) *Inadmissible Evidence* (1964) is a brutal judgment of the disengaged man. Many people feel that Osborne has never lived up to the promise of his early plays, *Look Back in Anger* and *The Entertainer*. This may be true—although I'm not sure just what such a statement means—but there can be no question that in the character of Bill Maitland he has created one of the towering roles of the theatre in our times. The most remarkable thing about this character is the fact that, while it is impossible to like him, he nonetheless always commands our attention. It is a strange sensation to be mesmerized by mediocrity. Bill Maitland is an inelegant lecher, an addicted personality who alternates between too much whiskey and too many pills, an insensitive and unprincipled lawyer who just barely survives on the petty wretchedness of others, and finally a failure in every human relationship in which he has participated. In an act of self-judgment in the play's courtroom prologue, he says about himself:

> I am almost forty years old, and I know I have never made a decision which I didn't either regret, or suspect was just plain commonplace or shifty or scamped and indulgent or mildly stupid or undistinguished. . . . I have depended almost entirely on other people's efforts. . . . And then, then I have always been afraid of being found out.

Except to the most morbidly curious, such a character should be monstrously dull. But he isn't, and one of the chief reasons we find him so compelling is Osborne's incendiary brilliance of language. There is no one writing in the theatre today who has a surer mastery of stage rhetoric than he, and I believe the secret of his success lies in his ability to deal with disturbing themes without resorting to cheap or eccentric tricks of language. Jonathan Miller, the British writer-director, made a penetrating comment about this capacity when he said in an interview:

> There is an essay by George Orwell about Salvador Dali in which he says that the mediocre talent can often attract more attention than it is worth by dealing in evil. Dali is a man with a rather mediocre imagination who attracts much attention by dealing in extravagantly eccentric sick themes. . . . The thing about Osborne which is so attractive is that he

doesn't have any need to resort to this sort of sickness in order to produce his effect. No one has his capacity for sustained pessimistic rhetoric, a scalding, absolutely nihilistic pessimism. Theatre of Disgust, if you like.

Many people have seen *Inadmissible Evidence* as a play in which the young and angry Jimmy Porter of *Look Back in Anger*, having just reached middle age, discovers his own spiritual bankruptcy and turns his seemingly limitless capacity for bitter disgust away from the world and now directs it toward himself. Certainly, this is true. In *Inadmissible Evidence* Osborne has written a drama of middle-aged withering away in which Maitland not only reveals his emptiness ("We are the hollow men") but judges his mediocrity as well ("Not with a bang, but a whimper"). But such a reading of the play doesn't explain why Maitland judges himself as he does. It seem to me that only when we recognize that from the beginning Osborne has been writing dramas of disengagement will the full import of this play become clear.

Jimmy Porter is angry because he has come to believe that everything about society is mean and hypocritical. In his disgust for the world he has consciously chosen to step outside it, no matter how this decision may affect his wife and friends. But Jimmy's whole angry existence is totally dependent upon the continued existence of that society which he rails at so bitterly. The judgment which Osborne makes on the life of Jimmy-Bill now that he has reached forty is not directed at his anger but at his act of disengagement.

The play opens with a courtroom scene which is, in actuality, taking place within Maitland's own mind. Acting as his own defense attorney he attempts to present his case. In his analysis of the existing social system, he sounds quite reasonable and his charges read like a liberal middle-class weekly journal of opinion. But the lawyer and the judge are the same person, and gradually the inadmissible evidence with which he ultimately indicts himself creeps into his defense-indictment. By the end of the prologue, he has acknowledged his failure and has judged himself guilty. The scene ends with him saying: "I should like to stand down if I may. I am not feeling very well. . . . I am not equal to any of it. But I can't forget it. And I can't begin again."

The main body of the play consists of a number of scenes in which the inadmissible evidence of Bill's life is presented to us directly. We see what it means to be the disengaged man. As a lawyer he sees the law as something to use to his own ends rather than as a body of social value which he is committed to serve. ("I don't think the law is respectable at all. It's there to be exploited. Just as *it* exploits us.") In his relationships with his office fellows he is brutish, cruel and insulting. In his dealings with his clients he is insensitive and inept. In a fascinating scene with his daughter—in which she says not a word—he reveals a blindness which is as staggering as it is pathetic. But it is finally in his relationship with women, particularly his wife and his mistress, that we see the failure of disengagement as a strategy for living. Because he has no awareness of human otherness he has only succeeded, as he says in his self-indictment, in "inflicting more pain than pleasure." He has not found love; he cannot stand the presence of any woman who loves him; and he is no longer capable of being satisfied by those indiscriminate sexual conquests which seem to have filled a good share of his adult life.

Bill Maitland (né Jimmy Porter) chose to detach himself from every claim which society can make on the individual. At the end of *Inadmissible Evidence*, as we see him broken and alone on the stage, we know he has at last succeeded in making the final cut. It has been a meaningless achievement, and John Osborne, who fathered the "angry" generation in the British theatre, has demonstrated most convincingly that, when anger over the failures of society becomes so extreme that it leads to disengagement from that society, the anger will eventually turn into a caustic self-disgust which can produce only isolation and impotence.

Bill Maitland is not an attractive character, but this does not mean that the disengaged man cannot be one. In fact, Justus Coriander, the protagonist of Lars Forssell's (1928–   ) *The Sunday Promenade*, is one of the most interesting and engaging characters to have been created for the European theatre during this decade. Forssell is a Swede with an American undergraduate degree. He is best known as a poet, but he has been writing plays since 1953. A number of them have received major productions in Sweden (the most important being *Mary Lou* in 1962 with Ingrid Thulin in the title role), but it was not until *The Sunday*

Promenade was produced by the Royal Dramatic Theatre in the fall of 1963 that Forssell came to be thought of as a man of the theatre rather than as a talented poet trying his hand at writing plays.

Forssell's play is particularly appropriate to this volume because everything he has ever written for the theatre has had disengagement as its central theme.[2] However, in dealing with the theme, he gives it a special emphasis: the disengaged man is ultimately a dehumanized man and hence a betrayer of humanity. The protagonist in each of Forssell's plays—and especially his last three, *Charlie McDeath, Mary Lou* and *The Sunday Promenade*—has lost all faith in anything outside of himself and is totally incapable of loving another human being. He sees that all ideologies have eventually betrayed humanity, and he believes that disengagement from all personal loyalties and commitments to values is the only strategy for coming to terms with the absurdities of existence. Forssell, in both his plays and his essays, asserts that this betrayer is the true representative of our times and should be treated sympathetically. In an interview in 1962, he is quoted as saying: "In our times the betrayer becomes a tragic person and consequently is not unsympathetic."

It is this sympathetic approach to the disengaged man which accounts for the radical difference in tone between *The Sunday Promenade* and *Inadmissible Evidence*. Forssell makes it clear in all of his plays that his hero is doomed from the start. Either the betrayer is himself betrayed by the world from which he would escape, or, what is even more painful, in his distrust of all tender feelings and responses, he will cut himself off from all human sensibility and will hence ultimately betray himself. But because Forssell is sympathetic to the impulse which leads to this disengagement and ultimate betrayal, his plays—and particularly *The Sunday Promenade*—seem to be driven by the excitement and heady energy of an impossible gamble with life rather than by

---

[2] In this regard, I am particularly indebted to Harry Carlson, Forssell's American translator, who not only brought the play to my attention, but has written most perceptively about Forssell's work and the theme of disengagement in his plays. See "Lars Forssell—Poet in the Theatre," *Scandinavian Studies*, 37:1 (February, 1965) and "The Anti-Hero in the Plays of Lars Forssell," *Players Magazine*, XL (November, 1963).

the energy of vituperative disgust which is the motive force of Osborne's drama.

The Sunday Promenade is Justus Coriander's play (although Harry Carlson is quite right when he points out that one of the chief reasons that this is Forssell's most successful play is that for the first time he has been able to orchestrate his theme through the interaction of several fully developed characters). The opening scene sets up his flamboyant entrance; the rest of the first act and the first scene of the second act develop his character through exposition and several peripheral episodes; the second scene of the second act and the third act are concerned with his involvement in the central action of the play; and the epilogue reveals his demise. Coriander is a grocer in a small provincial Swedish town. The people who live there are small of mind and spirit; conditions are really quite shabby, and everything about existence there is abysmally dull. No one could be blamed for wanting to escape its dreary confines. And Coriander attempts to do so by creating imaginative constructs. In the opening scene it soon becomes apparent that when he is not around life is pretty dull. He breaks all of the rules; he makes people laugh, he is a practical joker and a master put-on artist; he feasts outrageously on life. But the most important thing about him is his creative imagination. Such characterizing phrases as "Justus is a poet"; "Justus he *creates*, he does"; "You never know what to expect with Justus"; "He's an actor. Justus is a real rascal"; "Yes, I *know* I go to extremes. It's just that when I pretend to be a gypsy, I *become* a gypsy" make it clear that for life to be bearable Justus must continually turn every situation into a theatrical event for which he writes and directs the script and in which he plays the starring role. But he does this at the expense of others. To live his fictional life he must defile and humiliate the rest of humanity. As his son says: "Why must Father's fantasies always be at other people's expense? He says the world is beautiful, and you have to use your eyes, and you have to love. . . . And yet he does everything in his power to ridicule the world and defile the people in it!"

The central metaphor of the play is the promenade of the title. The only regular custom of the Coriander household is to take an imaginary trip on Sunday afternoons by walking around the dining-room table. They can go anywhere they choose, but once the journey has begun everyone must adhere to the rules of the game. These trips are filled with many exciting imaginary adventures, and Justus is always urging his followers to think up more exotic episodes. But the point of this game is that it is Coriander's way of conquering a shabby reality. He creates a fictional world which is governed by laws of his own making, and as long as he controls the game he not only has a stranglehold on life, but he also controls the feelings and lives of his family. The rest of the family humors him in this—in fact, they really quite enjoy it—but they, at best, take it only half seriously, and they certainly do not attribute the same powers to it that the master of the house does. For Justus this fiction is reality. Without it—like Hazlitt's actor—he is nobody. As Pastor Ruriksson says:

> No one is allowed to break the spell during the Sunday Promenade. Since we've come three laps, anyone who has to go back must return three laps. Those are the rules of the game. They must not be broken. Whoever breaks them is . . . dead, you might say.

During the promenade which occurs in the play, everyone is a member of an army sitting around the campfire on the eve of a battle. The spirit of the game is catching and we see how each character begins to reveal many of his true thoughts and hidden desires. Suddenly Coriander's invalid son, Carl Michael, has a real attack. A life situation has impinged upon the game and, as the family rushes to help the stricken boy, Justus struggles vainly to maintain control by keeping the fiction alive even at the expense of his son's life. He fails, because as one of the characters says: "This is no game now, Mr. Coriander," and the second act ends with Coriander weeping and apparently defeated.

It is fitting that Coriander's fictional world is shattered by the collapse of Carl Michael, for it was in the *agon* which just preceded the promenade that the traits of Coriander as a betrayer of life were revealed by his soon to be dead son. Although our sympathies are still with the energetic father during this scene, the boy says things to and about his father which we soon discover to be true. An idealistic student of Marx, Carl Michael sees the delusion of his father's isolated life within a world fabricated of dreams. "Just look at you!" he says. "You talk about Life. But you don't give a damn about the living. You talk about Death. But you've forgotten the dead. You talk about Love, but you can't love. The same is true of the poetry you read . . . drawn from a reality you talk about but have never seen. . . . And you . . . you dream in general! You don't want to hear about reality!"

The breakdown of the Sunday promenade proves Carl Michael to be right, but at just this point Forssell surprises us and this, I believe, is his greatest achievement in the play. Justus Coriander is a tenacious gambler and rather than acknowledge the collapse of that construct which symbolizes his whole way of life, he enters into the most impossible wager of all! He will defeat death. As Jesus did the daughter of Jairus, he will bring his now dead son back to life. And he wins. However, it is this apparent victory— for his son had not actually died—which sets him up for his final downfall: in his bargain with God, Justus has promised that if the boy's life is saved he will go to Outer Mongolia as a missionary to the barbarian hordes. He will leave his safe little world and will set out "to conquer the world." No more dreams, but reality. ("I've been a dreamer, now I'm going to face reality.") He goes, but as we learn in the epilogue, which takes place seven years later, he fails completely. Reality, it turns out, is dangerous and involves more than Coriander had bargained for. He is slain by the Mongolians, and his last words before they had significantly cut out his tongue—the source of his power over life—were "I didn't know the world was that big."

For Justus Coriander the only acceptable reality is the moment of here and now, which he attempts to shape and control with his extraordinary imaginative powers. The future is always to be feared because in its unpredictability it can always get out of control. Like all Romantics (and thematically the play has much in common with the poetry of Keats and Shelley), Justus attempts to conquer time: "Time is our enemy. Let's not talk about anything but *now*. *Now* we're alive, *now* we exist." And as are all Romantics, he is doomed to failure. His end is fittingly prefigured in the midst of the promenade. As the group sits around an imaginary campfire, Coriander asks his mother to tell him a story. She complies and relates the legend of "The Man Who Wanted to

Murder Time." In the story, for the man to succeed he must finally kill himself; then he is free of all time, he belongs to eternity. So, too, with Justus; when, in the midst of his struggle with reality, he is drawn into a situation which is too large for his imagination to control, he is bound to be destroyed.

In *The Sunday Promenade* the disengaged man is revealed as a betrayer who is ultimately betrayed. But there is something almost noble in his impossible quest. The only characters in the play who find love and some measure of contentment are Angelica, Coriander's deaf-mute daughter, and Abraham, his goodhearted but unimaginative clerk. In a long monologue in the third act, Abraham sums up the alternatives:

> Mr. Coriander seems to be living in a dream. He can't see how shabby and dirty and ugly life really is. He doesn't *want* to see it. The others . . . they seem aware of the shabbiness, like I am, and they live with it. That's why they're wiser and *happier* than he is, because he *wants* to be happy, he *has* to be happy, no matter what! . . . That's why he cries sometimes . . . he cries. Did you know that? Once you realize how . . . shabby everything is . . . then you can be happy in the midst of the shabbiness. Then you're wise, Angelica. Otherwise, you're not. But I guess all this is depressing, isn't it?

Depressing, indeed! If the acceptance of life's shabbiness is the only recipe for salvation, then there will always be Justus Corianders who will search for the strategies to transcend such narrow limits even if the search ultimately leads to self-destruction and the betrayal of the human condition.

There are, however, other forms of betrayal, and one of the most interesting of them is the central theme of *The Curve* (1960). Since the death of Bertolt Brecht in 1956, the German Theatre has been in a state of great ferment and experimental activity. It is almost as if the Master had to die before the numerous lesser lights of the stage could be seen. Unquestionably, one of the most interesting of these new writers is Tankred Dorst (1925——). The writer of several plays and numerous stimulating essays on the theatre, Dorst is best known on the Continent for his long one-acter, *The Curve*, which appears here. In some respects this play will seem tangential to the central theme of this essay—and here I believe the date of its composition is significant —but it does reveal symptoms which I believe were instrumental in prompting writers to become concerned with disengagement; and, more important, it is built upon that kind of irony which is essential to the drama of disengagement.

The Curve is a dramatic parable on the theme: "Is one justified in killing in defense of one's way of life?" Like all parables, the play seems quite simple; but this simplicity is deceptive. The parable is an evocative and open-ended form, and as the play's simple story unfolds it brings to mind everything from the war in Vietnam and the recent Arab-Israeli war to racial incidents in Mississippi and Michigan. The case for killing always appears so carefully reasoned and is supported by such unshakeable claims to justice and morality.

The play has a pared-down directness in its means. Two brothers live at the foot of a murderous mountain curve. The road is narrow and badly marked and at a certain time of day the sun blinds anyone who happens to be driving on the curve. The result is inevitably a crash which kills the people and wrecks the car. One brother repairs the car, which they then resell; the other buries the victims and writes protests to the Director of the Bureau of Highways. As the play opens they are awaiting the next accident— number twenty-five; it occurs, but the driver for some miraculous reason does not die. He turns out to be the Director of the Bureau of Highways. When he learns of the condition of the curve, he vows to take immediate steps to correct it. After an increasingly menacing debate, the brothers kill the Director and prepare to write another letter to the Director's successor protesting the horrible conditions of the curve.

The aspect of *The Curve* which I find so fascinating, and at the same time so terribly disturbing, is the fervor with which the two brothers, Anton and Rudolf, talk about change while at the same time they do everything possible to perpetuate the old conditions. They are the diehards who succeed by posing under the liberal banner. The deaths caused by the curve are both their way of life and the source of their livelihood. Since this goes against their avowed moral principles, they seem to be doing everything possible to change things. The sinister quality of the play is that we soon

become aware that, while they are active in this protest, they do
only those things which are certain not to have any effect whatsoever. They complain that their protests go unread in the bureaucrat's office and they sound convincing. Then when the Director
crashes and has all twenty-four petitions in his briefcase, it appears
they were wrong. The Director had come to take action. Only
then do we see the situation shift, and the brothers prepare to
murder their victim. The double irony of this is that the Director
was not the least bit concerned about the curve and was actually
on his way to meet his mistress on the other side of the mountain.
The petitions in his briefcase were only window-dressing. So the
brothers' strategy was right all along.

As I indicated earlier, this play is not directly about disengagement; but it does nonetheless relate to the other plays in this
volume. The Curve dramatizes certain of those attitudes, which
our society tends to support, which disgust men of moral sensibility and prompt them to disengage themselves from the world.
What the other plays in this volume reveal, however, is the truth
that such moral corruption is not something we can blame on
society, but resides in the heart of every man—including those
who are most disgusted by it.

The Laundry (1962) by the French playwright, David Guerdon
(19——), is an example of still another way that the conflicts
of the disengaged man have been dramatized in the theatre of
the sixties. The play is based on the Cretan myth of the Minotaur,
and since it is quite likely that most contemporary readers and
audiences will not easily remember this myth, it might be helpful
to summarize briefly the legend before discussing how Guerdon
works with it in his play.

Minos is struggling with his brothers for the throne of Crete.
The god Poseidon sides with him and agrees to send a bull out
of the sea as a sign of Minos' supremacy, providing that Minos
then sacrifice the bull on Poseidon's altar. The bull appears, Minos
becomes the King, but he does not sacrifice the bull as he had
vowed he would, but rather substitutes a lesser animal in its place.
For a time the kingdom thrives (given the theme of the plays
in this book, I think it is significant that Minos is the first great
businessman king in Greek legend), but Poseidon will have his

revenge. The god instills in Queen Pasiphaë an uncontrollable
lust for the bull which she is driven to satisfy. The fruit of their
union is the Minotaur: a monster with the body of a man and
the head and tail of a bull. The Minotaur soon becomes a threat
to the community and Minos has Daedalus, the master artist-
craftsman, build a labyrinth as a prison for it. Locked in the labyrinth, the Minotaur is fed young men and women captured by
the Cretans as they expand their empire. Eventually, Theseus
comes from Greece and, with the help of Princess Ariadne and
Daedalus, enters the labyrinth and slays the monster.

The two most important aspects of the legend, at least as far
as our discussion is concerned, are: (1) Minos, himself the son of
Europa and Zeus disguised as a bull, is clearly the one responsible
for the monster's existence. The theme of the legend is public responsibility and Minos' failure to act as befits a true king. The
birth of the Minotaur does not connote a sexual crime, but is Poseidon's punishment of Minos for his original transgression of personal greed. (2) Theseus is the hero because he acts not for
himself but for the commonweal. He is the archetypal figure of the
culture hero, who because of his pure spirit (and the assistance of
a woman with equal purity of heart) is able to cleanse society of
the stain of sin and restore it to a condition of vitality and well-
being.

These are the elements of the legend which Guerdon uses
in the writing of his play. But the ways he changes both their
structure and incidents to create a contemporary parable of disengagement is what makes it so interesting. Everything in the legend
has been perverted; indeed, one can go so far as to say that perversion is the basis of Guerdon's theatrical style. The cause of the
monster's birth is sexual—Madame Yvonne's infatuation with another "bull" nineteen years earlier. (Her husband, the Minos
figure, doesn't figure in the play at all.) While this sexual cause is
used only to heighten the atmosphere of guilt in the play, the
ambience of the action is, nonetheless, one of perverted feelings in
a world in which love is considered a "disease." This ambience is
maintained throughout the play, and the dénouement is a homo-
sexually inspired murder. In developing this action, Guerdon uses
the labyrinth-laundry of the title and the setting as a grotesque
metaphor of the modern world. But again, there is a change of

emphasis: for while the laundry does indeed house a monster, it soon becomes apparent that the members of Madame Yvonne's household, and not Daniel the Minotaur, are the real monsters. Daniel is, in fact, a sensitive, gentle and loving soul whose chief delight in life is to take long walks in the countryside. On the other hand, Laurent, the contemporary Theseus, is a hero of hostility. With behavior ranging from the extremes of arrogance and submission, he is lazy, unfaithful, a crooked schemer, and a murderer. Driven by guilt and yearning for his lost innocence, he finally kills Daniel because the "monster's" purity of spirit makes Laurent's consciousness of his own monstrousness unbearable.

Guerdon develops the theme of disengagement in two parallel ways, one of them obvious, the other not so readily apparent and much more complex. On one level Daniel is the hero of disengagement who would prefer to return to his prison in the laundry rather than live as a hero-freak in a world which he has discovered to be tawdry and rapacious. While this is certainly a meaningful aspect of the play, I believe it is the development of the other level that is Guerdon's most significant achievement. On this level, Laurent (and to a degree all of the others in the family) is the disengaged person and his situation is revealed as the true condition of contemporary man.

The world which Guerdon shows us in *The Laundry* is one that perverts, and Laurent is its victim: he is the completely perverted man. But he, in turn, attempts to use perversion as a strategy of disengagement from that world. Whenever one discusses perversion he is plagued by the moralistic overtones which have become attached to the word in common parlance. But as psychologists use the word, perversion represents a compromise between the expression and inhibition of a forbidden wish. It is, as defined by the psychoanalyst Donald M. Kaplan, "the crime our guilt forbids and the deed that fulfills certain infantile ideals." It is in this sense that psychology refers to homosexuality as a perversion, and why to the neurotic personality the pervert is a hero. Herbert Marcuse explains in greater detail why this is so in *Eros and Civilization*:

> The perversions seem to give a *promesse de bonheur* greater than that of "normal" sexuality. What is the source of their promise? Freud emphasized the "exclusive" character of

the deviations from normality, their rejection of the procreative sex act. The perversions thus express rebellion against the
subjugation of sexuality under the order of procreation, and
against the institutions which guarantee this order. . . . The
perversions seem to reject the entire enslavement of pleasure
ego by the reality ego. . . . In a repressive order, which enforces
the equation between normal, socially useful, and good, the
manifestations of pleasure for its own sake must appear as
fleurs du mal. . . . [Perversions] are a symbol of what had to
be suppressed so that suppression could prevail and organize
the ever more efficient domination of man and nature—a
symbol of the destructive identity between freedom and
happiness.[3]

I believe this passage can help us understand Laurent's ambiv-
alent relationship to Daniel—not to mention all of the other
characters, and especially his wife—but it also helps to clarify both
the nature of Laurent's relationship with Tony many years before
and why he must murder Daniel. To see just how it does, I should
like to examine the play's crucial scene: the confrontation of Laurent and Daniel in the second act (beginning on page 286). When
they meet in the darkened laundry (at the heart of the labyrinth of
personality) the intoxicated Laurent is afraid and believes Daniel
wants to hurt him. Daniel knows it is the other way around and
quietly leads Laurent to reveal his true self: he is totally alone,
hates women, is filled with a lacerating self-disgust, and is haunted
by a monstrous guilt. As he tells his life story—especially of his
love for and murder of Tony when he was twelve—it becomes
clear that all of Laurent's memories and impulses are infantile.
Daniel begins to rock him as if he were in a cradle, and Laurent's
deepest wish emerges to the surface of his consciousness:

LAURENT: All this old blood came back up into my mouth
    when I saw you! . . . I'm afraid, Daniel! At night while
    I'm sleeping I sometimes start to cry and I wake up feeling
    awful. Then when I get to sleep again it's even worse and I

[3] The Beacon Press edition, pp. 49–51, as quoted by Donald M. Kaplan in
"Homosexuality and American Theatre: A Psychoanalytic Comment,"
Tulane Drama Review, 9:3 (Spring, 1965), pp. 33–34.

begin screaming. Lena has to wake me up, she feels sorry
for me. Yes! Now I know—I suddenly remember! It's just
like this—the way it is now. You're following me down a
hallway and the walls are all moldy, like these. I'm afraid.
You hold out your hand—and then suddenly there's . . .
nothing left. . . . Yes, that's it. . . . You catch me in the
middle of the hanging sheets, and instead of killing me,
you hold me in your arms and rock me gently back and
forth. I discover a terrible joy, a horrible happiness, and
I'm a little boy again. I'm a little boy and I'm back with
Tony.

DANIEL: I give you this peace?
LAURENT: You erase everything. You wash everything clean.
It's like the waves of the ocean washing the shore.

Laurent, in his guilt and fear of retribution, wants the monster
Daniel—whom he has completely identified with the monster of his
dreams—to destroy him so he can be washed clean and start over
again. Of course, Daniel cannot do this and wouldn't even if he
could. His refusal prompts this dialogue, which prefigures the
events of the final scene:

LAURENT: If you don't want to save me, it's because you don't
love me.
DANIEL: I don't love you.
LAURENT: Then I'm all alone.

With this, Laurent breaks down, begs Daniel for help, and passes
out.

When the others enter the laundry at this moment, they mis-
interpret the metamorphosis of Laurent and attribute to Daniel a
supernatural power to transform people's lives. This idea of Daniel
as a miracle-working god figure is developed throughout the re-
mainder of the play. Daniel at first resists it, but he is finally persuaded to accept the role and is about to face the huge crowd
which has been gathered, when Laurent reappears for their final
and fateful confrontation.

All of his adult life, Laurent has been waiting for the miracle
which Tony had promised him when he was a young boy: "The

two of us would share our lives together in the delights of the world." This miracle has never come to pass and he resents the world because of it. This explains both his sadistic treatment of women and his destructive self-disgust. Laurent sees in Daniel the embodiment of his dream (for him Daniel is the incarnation of the ideal described by Marcuse in the passage quoted above): he lives above morality. He is free from all societal restraints to seek his own destiny. We know, in fact, that Daniel cannot do this, but Laurent resents the fact that Daniel's very existence reveals such freedom as a possibility, but cannot provide him with the means to achieve it for himself. This resentment is clear in the following speeches:

> Daniel, you haven't the right to show yourself! You haven't the right to toss them into the boiling water of awakening, only to leave them later in their own mirror! Look at me—at what I've become: a worthless nobody! And I used to have such strength. . . . When you save people, you should save them completely—otherwise, it's better to leave them to their misery! . . . The Key! You have it, Daniel, and you must give it to me. Tell me why I've been tortured all these years by the vision of your face. You know and you're going to tell me!

As the action rushes to Daniel's murder, Laurent shouts, "You're my dream become reality—the reality must explain the dream." Of course, Daniel cannot do this and he turns to return to his attic prison rather than assume a role he could never play. Laurent chases him and kills him, and when he returns to the rest of the group, he says: "There—it's finished! The dream is over. . . . When a dream becomes a reality, it must be loved. . . . or destroyed. Nothing else is possible."

The murder, then, is a perversion of a perversion. Homosexuality is an act of perverse disengagement. However, like all the other strategies of detachment, it can never be a totally successful life solution. Daniel represents the embodiment of the perfect solution, but he is a figure of fantasy who can only make Laurent more conscious than ever of the impossibility of his quest. Dr. Kaplan expands on this in the article I've already referred to, as follows:

An important ideological derivative of homosexuality protests a supramorality: In submitting to neither of your sexual
choices, I exceed both. And in so doing, I fulfill my destiny,
not on your terms but on my own. The protest here is against
the Father who, on the most significant occasion in the
homosexual's life—sexual conception—was heterosexual and
procreative. "Psychoanalytic theory sees in the practices that
exclude or prevent procreation"—I am again quoting Marcuse—"an opposition against continuing the chain of
reproduction and thereby of paternal domination." The
homosexual, then, is a rebel.

But he is a rebel of a particular sort. "The freedom he demands," as Camus said of Sade, "is not one of principles, but
of instincts." Thus, as an ideologist, when he sides with the
victim against the oppression of God or society, the homosexual's ideologic style does not champion humanity, but
merely himself. Ideology, whose sole program is instinct, that
is, behavior without responsibility—a program ultimately
without action—is merely nostalgic for justice and reforma-
tion but is actually seeking restoration of the spoilt child, a bit
of which is lively in every victim, as well as oppressor. Intelligence, discrimination, and reason—the dawnings of the
post-Oedipal child and the neutralizers of defiling domination
—have little status in a homosexual ideologic style. . . .

Thus the homosexual gravitates toward the rebellious tradition of the anguished romantic and, like Sade, is susceptible
to a confusion between individuality and egocentricity, liberty and libertinism, freedom and lawlessness. The homosexual engages in—to use Camus' cogent phrase—the
"Dandies' Rebellion." [4]

[4] Kaplan, *op. cit.*, pp. 36–37. Mention of Camus' phrase underscores the
relevance of his definition of the Dandy to the central theme of this introduction. Particularly pertinent is the following:
"The dandy is, by occupation, always in opposition. He can only exist
by defiance. Up to now man derived his coherence from his Creator. But
from the moment that he consecrates his rupture with Him, he finds himself delivered over to the fleeting moment, the passing days, and to wasted
sensibility. Therefore he must take himself in hand. The dandy rallies his
forces and creates a unity for himself by the very violence of his refusal.
Profligate, like all people without a rule of life, he is coherent as an actor.
But an actor implies a public; the dandy can only play a part by setting

The Laundry, like the other plays in this volume, reveals the ulti-mate futility of disengagement as a life style. But it also indicates why it, like all romantic quests, haunts the human spirit—especially in times when other, more realizable possibilities seem so un-satisfying.

—*Robert W. Corrigan*

---

himself up in opposition. He can only be sure of his own existence by finding it in the expression of others' faces. Other people are his mirror. A mirror that quickly becomes clouded, it is true, since human capacity for attention is limited. It must be ceaselessly stimulated, spurred on by provo-cation. The dandy, therefore, is always compelled to astonish. Singularity is his vocation, excess his way to perfection. Perpetually incomplete, always on the fringe of things, he compels others to create him while denying their values. He plays at life because he is unable to live it. He plays at it until he dies, except for the moments when he is alone and without a mirror. For the dandy to be alone is not to exist." (*The Rebel*, Vintage Books, pp. 51–52.)

INADMISSIBLE EVIDENCE

John Osborne

CHARACTERS

Inadmissible Evidence was first performed at the Royal Court Theatre, Sloane Square, London, on September 9, 1964, by the English Stage Company. Directed by Antony Page, decór by Jocelyn Herbert, and with the following cast:

JONES	John Quentin
BILL MAITLAND	Nicol Williamson
HUDSON	Arthur Lowe
SHIRLEY	Ann Beach
JOY	Lois Daine
MRS. GARNSEY	Clare Kelly
JANE MAITLAND	Natasha Pyne
LIZ	Sheila Allen

Act One

The location where a dream takes place. A site of helpless-
ness, of oppression and polemic. The structure of this parti-
cular dream is the bones and dead objects of a Solicitor's
Office. It has a desk, files, papers, dust, books, leather arm-
chairs, a large, Victorian coat stand, and the skeleton of an
outer office with clerks, girls and a telephonist. Downstage is
a dock in which stands the prisoner of this dream, BILL
MAITLAND. *At back, high above the outer office, hangs the*
Royal Coat of Arms. In front of this are the green benches of
one of the High Courts of Justice, in which sits one of HER
MAJESTY'S JUDGES. *From centre a* CLERK OF THE COURT *reads*
the indictment. Before this there has been an air of floating
inertia before the three actors come to some sort of life out of
the blur of dream.

CLERK: William Henry Maitland, you are accused of having un-
lawfully and wickedly published and made known, and caused
to be procured and made known, a wicked, bawdy and scandalous object. Intending—
BILL: Object?
JUDGE: Proceed, proceed.
CLERK: Object. Intending to vitiate and corrupt the morals of the
liege subjects of our Lady the Queen, to debauch and poison
the minds of divers of the liege subjects of our Lady and to raise

and create in them lustful desires, and to bring the liege subjects into a state of wickedness, lewdness and debauchery. How do you plead? Guilty or Not Guilty?

BILL: Not guilty. [*Pause.*]

CLERK: Place your right hand on the book and repeat after me: I swear by Almighty God—

BILL: I swear. . . . My lord, I wish to affirm.

JUDGE: Very well.

CLERK: Do you swear and affirm?

BILL: I swear and affirm. . . . [*Pause. Then a hoarse rattle. Clearing his throat at intervals.*] I hereby swear and affirm. Affirm. On my. . . . Honour? By my belief. My belief in . . . in . . . the technological revolution, the pressing, growing, pressing, urgent need for more and more scientists, and more scientists, for more and more schools and universities and universities and schools, the theme of change, realistic decisions based on a highly developed and professional study of society by people who really know their subject, the overdue need for us to adapt ourselves to different conditions, the theme and challenge of such rapid change, change, rapid change. [*Flails. The* JUDGE *looks at him reassurringly and he picks up again.*] In the ninety-seven per cent, ninety-seven, of all the scientists who have ever lived in the history of the world since the days of Euclid, Pythagoras and Archimedes. Who, who are alive and at work today, today, now, at this time, in the inevitability of automation and the ever increasing need, need, oh, need for, the stable ties of modern family life, rethinking, reliving, making way for the motor car, forty million by nineteen; in a forward-looking, out-ward-looking, programme-controlled machine tool line reassessment. With, yes, with faculties of memory and judgement far beyond the capacity of any human grief, being. Or any group of human who has ever lived. [*Pause.*]

JUDGE: Yes?

BILL: In the facts, above all the facts, inescapable. Anna, my wife, Hudson, I mean my managing clerk, Hudson, Joy, the telephonist, the enrichment of our standard of living, I've lost my prescription, Jane, my father's too old to be here, thank God, the National Research, Research Development Council, the Taylor Report, the Nayler Report, failure report, and a projected

budget of five hundred thousand million, millions for this purpose, the practical dangers of pre-marital in the commanding
heights of our declining objects.

JUDGE: Objects?

BILL: Objects? I think so, my lord. I think that's what I meant to
be saying [*Continuing.*] Facing up realistically, the issues that
are important, really, central, social change, basic, burning
issues.

JUDGE: I think that is evident.

BILL: I wish I could see more clearly.

JUDGE: Very well. [*Pause.*]

CLERK: My lord, I have been retained by the defendant. However, after long discussion with myself, and my learned colleagues, he has expressed his intention of conducting his own
case.

JUDGE: I see. You have tried to dissuade him from this course?

CLERK: We have, my lord. He is quite adamant.

JUDGE: Mr. Maitland, you must be fully aware of the implication,
of your decision?

BILL: Yes.

JUDGE: It is my duty to warn you of the difficulties that may be
involved in discarding the services of learned counsel.

BILL: I see that. Except I wish I *could*.

JUDGE: And to warn you against taking an irrevocable decision
which will almost certainly . . .

BILL: But I'm incapable of making decisions.

JUDGE: Involve you in onerous difficulties, in view of the complexi-
ties we are faced with here. Even though, as a practising solicitor of, I believe, some standing and experience, you are no
doubt better equipped to conduct yourself than would ordinarily
be the case. [BILL *smiles.*] I put it to you now, once and for all;
do you persist in this decision?

BILL: [*looks at* CLERK.]: I do, my lord.

JUDGE: Very well. [*Pause.*] Proceed.

BILL: I beg your pardon?

JUDGE: Carry on, Mr. Maitland.

BILL: Me, my lord?

JUDGE: Yes. You, Mr. Maitland.

BILL: But what about them?

JUDGE: Are you—or are you not conducting your own case?

BILL: But them? What about them?

JUDGE: Mr. Jones will, I believe, lead for the prosecution.

CLERK: That is correct, my lord.

JUDGE: Come then. Do let us get on.

BILL: He was supposed to be defending me.

JUDGE: Mr. Maitland. Have we not, just a few moments ago, established that you had dismissed Mr. Jones.

BILL: Yes.

JUDGE: And that you have elected to conduct your own defence?

BILL: Well, it is. I did. But then it shouldn't be me.

JUDGE: Shouldn't be you?

BILL: No.

JUDGE: What shouldn't be you?

BILL: Well, if it is. Why isn't he starting off then?

JUDGE: Starting off?

BILL: Yes. [*Pause.*]

JUDGE: You have already started off. [BILL *ponders.*]

BILL: But—I seem to have made some sort of absurd. . . . Isn't it? I mean: he should have started off first. In the very first place. [*Pause.*]

JUDGE: That is true. However. . . . You have done so instead.

BILL: But what about the . . .

JUDGE: That is my ruling. It is possible that it may be reversed or re-interpreted at another time elsewhere.

BILL: What about the last word?

JUDGE: I suggest you begin.

BILL: I shouldn't be the one to have to start off.

JUDGE: Possibly not, but you have, and the ruling is quite clear.

BILL [*Bafflement. Tries to focus*]: I ought to; have; the last word.

JUDGE: No doubt, we shall see in the event.

BILL: What event? I'm here, aren't I?

JUDGE: You must be aware, with your training and background, that the law can often be very flexible in these matters.

BILL: As your lordship pleases. As you say, it probably makes very little difference.

JUDGE: Demonstrably.

BILL: Before I—

JUDGE: Yes?

BILL: May I have a glass of water? [*The* JUDGE *motions to the* CLERK, *who obliges.* BILL *tries to study his face.*] My lord— which one is Mr. Jones?

JUDGE: There. [*He indicates the* CLERK *a little impatiently. The* CLERK *hands him the glass of water.*]

BILL: Please forgive me. I have rather a headache. Perhaps that's why I'm here now. I had too much to drink last night, that's just the simple truth of it. Well, when I say that, I mean not much more than I usually have. Most nights. But that's well, I do drink quite a lot. Quite a lot? Oh, anyway, I'm what you'd call a serious drinker. That's to say, I just don't mess about once I get going—when I do. When I do? I nearly always do. I can drink a whole bottle of whisky. Can't be any good for the heart, can it? It must be a strain, pumping all that fire and damned rigour and everything all out again? Still, I'm pretty strong. I must be. Otherwise, I couldn't take it. That is, if I *can* take it. I can't I'm sorry, I can't find my pills. I always have three or so in my ticket pocket. So sorry. [*Pause*]. If you knew me, if you knew me, you'd know I wouldn't come out without them. I'm so sorry. Just a moment. The glands or what- ever these lumps are in my neck feel as if they were trying to batter their way out. Just here, trying to force their way out. Like broken marbles, real big gob stoppers. With chipped edges. I must have left them in my overcoat pocket. Do you think the constable could get my overcoat or look in the left-hand pocket? Or the inside? It shouldn't take a moment. Only. It's a bit like a gimlet too. Right up behind the eyeballs. All that and the marbles too. [*Pause.*] I know that none of this is very interesting to you, but the fact is I could do a lot better, a lot better, that is acquit myself, acquit myself better. Yes. Well, they don't seem to be there, my pills. Or tablets or whatever you call them. What's the difference? Only: I really do need three of them at least. And nothing else will do the job prop- erly. Then, if I keep my head upright and don't move it about too much, and talk fairly slowly, if you can bear with me, with your lordship's indulgence, I can make a start. Some sort of start, anyway.

JUDGE: Do you think you can proceed now?

BILL: I have a feeling there is very little choice involved. And so,

I will do my best, your lordship. I don't want you to think that because of these minor difficulties—and—that I have come here unprepared. I have always expected this, and, consequently, I have done my best to prepare myself as well as I can.

JUDGE: Yes?

BILL: In. With. Your lordship's indulgence, I will . . . make some sort of a start.

JUDGE: Please.

BILL: And see what comes to me. In the event. Now: I wish I could open my eyes. My eyelids. They're like oysters. However, this is my concern and not yours. I'll think of something. [*He presses his eyeballs*]. My name is William Henry Maitland. I am thirty-nine years old, practising solicitor and commissioner for oaths at 34, Fleet Chambers, E.C.3. I have worked in service of the law—if you can call being a solicitor, working in the service of the law—for nearly twenty-five years. In fact, I started work in this very office, this court, since I was at least fifteen. Perhaps earlier. That—[*points to* JUDGE's *seat*]—is my old boss's chair. You see, I took his position over from him. My managing clerk, old Hudson, he was working for the old man even then. Not that he was much older than me. He just always seemed older. Anyway, he works for me now. I don't even know why I took up the law. I don't think there was any reason at all much. I can't think of any now, and I couldn't think of any then. Perhaps I did think I might land up on the bench even. Or with learned counsel. Mr. Jones. No, but I never seriously thought of myself being brilliant enough to sit in that company, with those men, among any of them with their fresh complexions from their playing fields and all that, with their ringing, effortless voice production and their quiet chambers, and tailors and mess bills and Oxford Colleges and going to the opera God knows where and the 400, whatever I used to think that was. I can't remember at the time. I have always been tolerably bright.

JUDGE: Always been?

BILL: Bright. *Only* tolerably bright, my lord. But, to start with, and potentially and finally, that is to say, irredeemably mediocre. Even at fifteen, when I started out in my profession. Oh no, before that. Before that. Mark. I have never had any but fugitive reasons—recurrent for all that—that this simple, un-complicated, well, simple, assumption was correct. I knew that in order to become even a small marketplace solicitor, as distinct even from a first-rate managing clerk with a big, sub-stantial firm, I should have to study very hard indeed for my, oh for my Law Society examinations all the while I was picking up probate and conveyancing, running out for jugs of tea, packets of fags for the other clerks or calling in the chemist for the telephonist.

JUDGE: Telephonist.

BILL: I'm afraid there's always one like that, my lord. Mine is called Joy. The one who works for me now, that is. This one was called Jill.

JUDGE: Is anything the matter?

BILL: I seem to have lost my drift, my lord. What's my wife doing here? Well, she should be here, of course. No, it's Sheila, my ex-wife. I didn't even know where she was. How did she know? They all seem to *find out* about these things. They find out. I'm sure my old man's there, but I can't see him. I hope not. He'll hate this. I seem to have lost my drift, my lord.

JUDGE [*Kindly*]: Mediocrity?

BILL: Well: it might perhaps be misleading to you and every-one to dwell on it too much. I merely wanted to draw your attention.

JUDGE: There is time enough, Mr. Maitland.

BILL: I have always had a certain facility, it's true. But little else. A fairly quick mind, not profound, a bit flashy I should say, indeed, *you* would say, not even that, a little more than perky. They said I had a quick mind, for getting fags and remember-ing things for a while, long enough to get my exams, for in-stance. A quick mind they said was useful, not that I had it, but helpful, as your lordship will know, in a profession where time doesn't mean a thing to anyone except some poor bloody agonized client who wants to know whether he's going to get the house he wants, an overdraft, or a divorce, eighteen months or a fine. However, however, my lord. I seem to retain very little. Very little indeed, hardly anything at all, in fact. Which is disturbing. Because I don't see how I can carry on my work even, well I am carrying on with it, but I must be getting less

and less any good at it. *Even* my work, that's almost the least
of it, which is probably, no doubt, one of the reasons I find
myself here, in the dark dock arraigned before you. But both
my clients and my colleagues seem to think, at least they used
to think, I had a sort of dashing flair for making decisions,
which might have been true to some extent. This can't hide
the fact from me, and never has done, that I am by nature
indecisive. Nor will it escape you, my lord. I am almost forty
years old, and I know I have never made a decision which
I didn't either regret, or suspect was just plain commonplace
or shifty or scamped and indulgent or mildly stupid or undistinguished. As you must see. As for why I am here, I have to
confess this: I have to confess that: that I have depended
almost entirely on other people's efforts. Anything else would
have been impossible for me, and I always knew in my own
heart that only that it was that kept me alive and functioning
at all, let alone making decisions or being quick minded and
all that nonsense about me. . . . That I have never really been
able to tell the difference between a friend and an enemy, and
I have always made what seemed to me at the time to make
the most exhausting efforts to find out. The difference. But it
has never been clear to me, and there it is, the distinction, and
as I have got older, and as I have worked my way up—up—
to my present position. I find it even more, quite impossible.
And out of the question. And then, then I have always been
afraid of being found out.

JUDGE: Found out?
BILL: Yes.
JUDGE: Found out about what?
BILL: I'm sorry, my lord. I don't understand. I have always been
quite certain that this is where I should end up, here, I've seen
it too many times, with you there and counsel over there. There.
And there. Down to the cells. Off to the Scrubs, hand over
your watch and your money, take all your clothes off, have a
bath, get examined, take all your clothes off in the cold, and
the door shut behind you. I should like to stand down if I
may. I am not feeling very well. I never hoped or wished for
anything more than to have the good fortune of friendship
and the excitement and comfort of love and the love of women

in particular. I made a set at both of them in my own way.
With the first with friendship, I hardly succeeded at all. Not
really. No. Not at all. With the second, with love, I succeeded,
I succeeded in inflicting, quite certainly inflicting, more pain
than pleasure. I am not equal to any of it. But I can't escape
it, I can't forget it. And I can't begin again. You see?

[*A torpid moan escapes him. Fade. The light remains on* BILL.
The JUDGE *and the* CLERK *leisurely take off their wigs and
robes, coming into the office area, hanging them on the upstage end of the coat stand. The* JUDGE *who is* HUDSON, *the*
MANAGING CLERK, *speaks to the* CLERK *who is called* JONES.
During this, BILL *remains still. The actor has to indicate the
painful struggle into consciousness, without, at the same time,
making the physical metaphor too explicit: the difficulty of
breathing, the violent inner effort to throw off the burden,
the fishy, palpitating struggle of the heart being landed into
wakefulness. The gasping will takes over. The dream, the prison
of embryonic helplessness for the moment, recedes, but not
altogether. The focus fades on* BILL, *who emerges slowly out
of it. Presently, he makes his way out of it, into the outer office,
then through into the office itself.*]

HUDSON [*To* JONES]: Parky this morning.
JONES: Yes.
HUDSON: What's the matter then? Late night?
JONES: No, not specially.
HUDSON: How's that girl of yours?
JONES: O.K.
HUDSON: Still getting married?
JONES: Suppose so. Got to get these finals out of the way first.
   Hardly see her except on Sundays.

[SHIRLEY, *the secretary, comes in with post and hands it to*
HUDSON.]

SHIRLEY: There's yours.
HUDSON: Thank you, Shirley. And how are you today?
SHIRLEY: Looking forward to Friday night, thank you.

JONES: Is mine there?

SHIRLEY: Why don't you try looking for it? [*Goes out.*]

HUDSON: What's up with her?

JONES: Dunno. Packing it in, she says.

HUDSON: What, again?

JONES: I think she means it this time.

[BILL *comes into* OUTER OFFICE *fairly briskly.*]

BILL: Morning all!

JONES: Better start getting it sorted out myself then.

BILL [*Coming in.*]: Sorry I'm late.

HUDSON: You're the boss.

BILL: I couldn't get a taxi. That's the first time I've never got
   one. All got their bloody lights on and all going home. I don't
   know what they're doing. [*Goes to desk. He has a plaster by
   his ear.*]

HUDSON: Cut yourself?

BILL: Yes.

HUDSON: I don't know why—

BILL: Why I don't use an electric razor. There's quite enough
   almighty racket going on in the world without tuning it into
   my chin the minute I wake up.

HUDSON: But it's so simple.

BILL: Not for me it isn't. Two bathrooms in my house and my
   wife has to use mine while I'm having a quiet little shave to
   myself. She has to talk.

HUDSON: Not your morning.

BILL: Can't be worse than the evening.

HUDSON: What, have a skinful, did you?

BILL: More than that, one way and another.

[SHIRLEY *brings in* BILL's *post and puts it in front of him.*]

BILL: Hullo, sexy. Is that all?

HUDSON: Don't worry—there's enough here.

BILL: What—no make-up this morning?

SHIRLEY: You *do* remember Mrs. Garnsey's coming at 9:30?

BILL: Of course, I forgot you girls don't really wear make-up nowadays, do you? All leaking eyeshadow and red noses. Go and put on some lipstick, dear. What's the matter? Isn't he giving it to you?

SHIRLEY: Finished?

BILL: Don't tell me you're getting too much. I don't believe it.

SHIRLEY: Oh, knock it off.

BILL: Well, something's made you bad-tempered this morning, and I don't believe that languid pipe cleaner of an accountant you're engaged to has got *that* much lead in his pencil.

SHIRLEY: Do you ever think of anything else?

BILL: Not so much. Probably less than you do though.

SHIRLEY: Me?

BILL: I just talk about it at great boring length mostly to boring, bad-tempered, and silly girls. Without make-up.

SHIRLEY: You know what you can do! And quick.

BILL [*To* HUDSON]: Do you hear that, Wally? Do you think I should let her talk to me like that?

HUDSON: I think she'd better get back to her work. I'll see you in a minute, Shirley. [*She nods and goes out.*]

BILL: And put some lipstick on!

HUDSON: Thought she was going to let you have it there for a minute.

BILL: What's the matter with her?

HUDSON: Jones here says she's giving in her notice.

BILL: But she does that every other month.

JONES: I think she means it this time.

BILL: Oh, why?

[BILL's *manner to* JONES *is slightly hostile, more polite than he is to most people.*]

JONES: Oh—Just says she's fed up with the place.

BILL: And?

JONES: Oh, well just that really.

BILL: What else?

HUDSON: Well, out with it.

JONES: Well, this is just what she said to me—

BILL: He'd make a great witness wouldn't he? I wouldn't like to see you in the box up against someone like old Winters.

JONES [*Dimly nettled.*]: She just said last night while we were
locking up that she was sick of the sight of Mr. Maitland and
couldn't even bear to be in the same room with him.

BILL: She said what!

HUDSON [*To* JONES.]: It's all right, you needn't repeat it.

JONES: Well, you asked me what she said.

HUDSON: You know what these girls are. They get a bit, you
know. And Shirley's an independent sort of a—

BILL: What a funny thing to say. Do you think she meant it?

JONES: Dunno. Wasn't listening properly.

BILL [*Irritated.*]: I'll talk to her later. When she's calmed down
a bit. [*To* HUDSON.] Remind me. [HUDSON *looks amused.*]
What are you smirking about? Oh? Keep it outside of the
office and all that? Look, I haven't touched that girl for
months, not for about six or seven months at least. *I've* done
no harm to her. If she's unhappy it's not my fault. Besides,
she's engaged.

HUDSON: That wouldn't stop you.

BILL: No, it wouldn't, but I didn't. It's probably that droopy
young book-keeper making her miserable. Giving her dinner-
dances on the Kingston By-Pass. The morning she came back
from that she had red eyes for a week.

HUDSON: He seemed a nice, quiet, serious . . . fellow, I thought.

BILL: Nice, quiet, serious fellow, I thought. That just about
sounds like every supine, cautious, young husband all about
six degrees under proper consciousness in the land. The whole
bloody island's blocked with those flatulent, purblind, mating
weasels. You know who they are? Her fiancé? They're the
ones who go out on Bank Holidays in the car! And have mas-
cots in the rear window.

HUDSON: Well, it's their lives.

BILL: Yes, and if we only had enough Bank Holidays they'd
kill each other on every coast road from Blackpool to Brighton.

HUDSON: You're not suggesting they should all be killed off just
because they don't please you?

BILL: I'm just suggesting we might hope they'll do it themselves for us.

HUDSON: You'll be getting one of your headaches in a minute.

BILL: Don't worry. I have. Do you know who they are?

HUDSON: No. Only don't forget Mrs. Garnsey.

BILL: Damn Mrs. Garnsey. She's probably one too. They: are the people who go up every year like it was holy communion to have a look at the Christmas decorations in Regent Street. They're the ones who drive the family fifty miles into the countryside and then park their cars beside the main road with a few dozen others, get out their thermos flasks, camp stools and primuses and do you know what they do? They sit and watch the long-distance lorry drivers rattling past, and old people's coaches and all the other idiots like themselves about to do the same thing.

HUDSON: Sometimes I'd like to see you and old Winters have a go at each other—in court. I think you'd enjoy that.

BILL: Don't think I couldn't either. He's not all that good. Just because he wears a wig and I don't.

HUDSON: Well, then—

BILL: This place'd be a lot different if you were running it, wouldn't it, Wally?

HUDSON: Everyone has their own methods. You've got yours.

BILL: Yes, but mine just aren't different. They're not respectable for a solicitor. But then I don't feel like you do about the Law. I don't think the law is respectable at all. It's there to be exploited. Just as *it* exploits us.

HUDSON: You'll be putting young Jones here off the job.

BILL: I don't think there's much danger of that.

HUDSON: Well, we all have our different methods, as I say. Different ways of looking at things.

BILL: Wally, do me a favour, will you? You'll be saying 'with all due respect,' or 'be that as it may' in a minute. I'd thought I'd broken you of that stinking habit. No, I don't think young Jones here is the type to end up goosing telephonists and knocking off secretaries, to say nothing of cooking up evidence on occasion or risking collusive agreements. Do you have it off with that girl of yours? [JONES *is discomfited.*] I'm sorry. That's an impertinent question. Isn't it? Forget it.

JONES: Well—

BILL: No, don't bother. But I was right about what I said?

JONES: Yes. Yes. I think so.

BILL: Why?

JONES: I just don't think it—

BILL: What?

JONES: Any of those things are really worth the candle.

BILL: Not really worth the candle. No you're quite right. It's not. Well, now we've disposed of the candle, you'd better take it with you into Shirley. She's probably in need of it. Have you got plenty to do? [JONES *nods*.] Got to keep you busy. Busy, busy, busy. That's what you want isn't it? That's why you came to me isn't it, for no other reason. See what's in, what business there is, any money in, any problems, anything else. Right?

JONES: Yes, Mr. Maitland. [*Goes*].

HUDSON: What's the matter then?

BILL: What do you mean what's the matter then? [*Calls*.] Shirley!

HUDSON: You seem to have it in a bit for him.

BILL: He's a tent peg. Made in England. To be knocked into the ground.

[SHIRLEY *appears*.]

SHIRLEY: Yes?

BILL: What? Oh, get me a glass of water, Shirley.

SHIRLEY [*Pause*]: Helpless? [*Goes out*. HUDSON *and* BILL *look at each other. More satisfaction for* HUDSON.]

HUDSON: I think you're wrong there. He's got quite a good brain. Bit slow for your taste, but you shouldn't underestimate him.

BILL: I don't. He's got all the makings of a good, happy, democratic underdog like that bitch's boyfriend who won't even get me a glass of water when I ask her. He irritates me. He doesn't like me any more than I like him. Why does he work for me?

HUDSON: Why don't you sack him?

BILL: What for? He does his work well enough. Doesn't he?

HUDSON: Fine.

BILL: Well then. Joy! He even laughs at my rotten jokes. Or anyway, his little filleted spine rattles about a bit. Otherwise —no sound. . . . [JOY *appears*.] Joy, get me a glass of water, will you?

JOY: O.K.

BILL: And ask Shirley—no, you'd better get it. See if you can bring in Mrs. Garnsey's file. [*She goes out.*] One thing I'll say for you, Wally, you've never pretended to laugh. Not even at my good ones.

HUDSON: We don't all have your sense of humour.

BILL: Well, don't sound so pleased about it. Anyway, I haven't got a sense of humour. I haven't had a good laugh for years. Not only that, Mr. Jones may find his finals and working for me won't do him a damn bit of good in the long run. Or you, for that matter.

HUDSON: What's that?

BILL: I say: soon we'll all be out of a job. If anyone's riddled with the idea that being busy is the same thing as being alive it's our young Jones.

HUDSON: What are you talking about?

BILL: Jones.

HUDSON: You're sure you're all right?

BILL: Sure, fine. Now what about Mrs. Garnsey, why are you shoving her on to me? No. I don't, I don't think I do. Things seem a bit odd. I still can't understand why I couldn't get a taxi. They all had their lights on: for hire.

HUDSON: Well, you know what they are.

BILL: Yes, but I've never known it to happen to me before. Not in the morning.

HUDSON: You look all right. But if you'd like to . . .

BILL: And the caretaker turned his back on me. I was walking up the stairs and I was going to ask him—you know, quite politely—why the lift wasn't working. And he turned his back on me.

HUDSON: Didn't notice you, I expect.

BILL: No, he looked straight at me. And turned his back on me.

HUDSON: Well, he's a contrary old devil.

BILL: Not with me, he hasn't been.

HUDSON: I gave him a quid at Christmas, and he didn't even give me a thank you.

BILL: I gave him five. [*Self-conscious.*] Well, I know it's too much, but had a drink together over at the 'Feathers.'

HUDSON: Too much is right. [*Slight pause.*]

BILL: They won't need us much longer. They'll need no more

lawyers. Have you seen the papers this morning? Some mathematical clerk will feed all our petitions and depositions and statements and evidence into some clattering brute of a computer and the answer will come out guilty or not guilty in as much time as it takes to say it. There'll be no more laws' delays, just the insolence of somebody's office. They'll need no more lawyers. I don't understand who will be needed.

HUDSON: I shouldn't think it'll quite come to that.

BILL: How do you know what we'll come to? Or when? Sometimes I wish I were older so I had less chance of finding out. [*Bangs newspaper.*] Look at this dozy bastard: Britain's position in the world. Screw that. What about my position? Vote wheedling catchfart, just waiting to get us into his bag and turn us out into a lot of little technological dogs turning his wheel spit of endless bloody consumption and production. Why doesn't he stick his scientific rod—into the Red Sea or where he likes and take everyone he likes with him—including Jones. The sooner the sea closes up behind them the better. With Jones entering the Promised Land in his mini.

HUDSON: Oh, leave the boy alone. What's he done to you. Anyway, he's got a motor bike.

BILL: Even better. I can't think of a better way to emerge—in an emergent country. Why don't they all go and emerge? Emerge.

HUDSON: Why don't *you* do a bit of emerging yourself?

BILL: I'm never likely to do that. [*Pause.*]

HUDSON: Well, we should make a start. [*Joke.*] Before they move in the computers. [BILL *doesn't respond.*]

BILL: Joy! What are you doing?

JOY [*Off.*]: Coming.

HUDSON: Seen that Betty lately?

BILL: Where's my glass of water? Which Betty?

HUDSON: Oh, were there more?

BILL: I know three girls called Betty. No. Four.

HUDSON: What a life. I don't know.

BILL: She married some corpulent financier.

HUDSON: Who?

BILL: Betty. [JOY *comes in with glass of water and a file.*] I'm always seeing his name on building sites. Spends his time pulling down Regency squares—you know—and putting up

slabs of concrete technological nougat. Like old, pumped up
air-raid shelters. Or municipal lavatories. She's a nice kid. Don't
see much of her now. Seen her at some of those theatre first
nights he's so fond of. Hemmed in by all his thrusting syco-
phants—I think she can hardly see him through her mink.
Jones now.

JOY: Sorry. Shirley wouldn't tell me where to find it.

BILL: Jones should work for him. Britain's future. Betty's old
man is certainly one of the architects. What's that, my love?

JOY: Your glass of water.

BILL: Oh, thank you. At last, a friend.

JOY: Mrs. Garnsey's file. Shirley—

BILL: Yes, I'm sure. And how are you?

JOY: I'm all right thank you. Is that all?

BILL: Not enough for me. She looks pretty today, don't you
think, Wally.

HUDSON: Yes. She does.

BILL: When are we going to have an orgy together?

JOY: You can't have an orgy with two.

BILL: No, but you can make a start. [*She smiles and goes out.*]
Look at that beautiful bottom. Don't go much on her face.
But the way her skirt stretches over that little bum. You could
stick a bus ticket in there. Joy. What do you think, Wally?

HUDSON: Yes, it's quite nice, I suppose.

BILL: It's a beauty. Wonder what's she like?

HUDSON: No doubt you'll find out.

BILL: Don't know. Maybe not. Like who was it. You know,
Dr. Johnson said whatsit, 'Paradise Lost': more of a beauty
than a pleasure. Still she looks as though she could do with
a bit. She's got the galloping cutes all right. Joy. *She's* had
more joy sticks than hot dinners.

HUDSON: I was only waiting for that. What about Mrs. Garnsey?

BILL: I have an extraordinary thing about blondes. They're like
plague carriers for me. Even dyed blondes. My first wife was
blonde. *Really* blonde. Blonde, blonde, *blonde!* It was *beautiful.*
I've never known hair nicer. Right: Mrs. Garnsey.

HUDSON: Well, try and let her settle down a bit, will you? Joy,
I mean. She's only just mastered that simple little switchboard.
If *you* get started on her, we'll get nowhere.

BILL: Right. No Joy. For the moment, anyway. Goes against
the Rules. Which is the best thing. Right: work, work. Mrs.
Garnsey. Where are my pills? There should be some in here.
Anyway, I always keep three in reserve in my ticket pocket.
Where the hell are they? Joy! Wish I didn't drink so much.
And I keep wanting to sleep. I finally took a pill at four this
morning, went off at five, then I couldn't get up. I couldn't
even move at first. [JOY *appears*.] I was all trussed up. My
darling, have you seen my pills, my headache pills?

JOY: No, sorry.

BILL: Never mind, here they are. I might just do a bit better
with Mrs. Garnsey when she comes. Ask her to wait five
minutes when she comes. Give her a cup of that stinking tea
you and young Jones brew up together.

JOY: O.K. [*Goes out.*]

BILL: I don't know whether I really like that blonde bat or not.
She's rather a tuneful little thing, if you know what I mean.
Wally, try not to let me have anything to drink at lunch-time.
O.K.?

HUDSON: I'll do my best.

BILL: 'And if I drink oblivion of a day, so shorten I the stature
of my soul.' Who said that now? Some poor crazy bastard—
Blake I think. Just bitter lemon, all right?

HUDSON: Right.

[JOY *reappears*.]

JOY: Oh, and your wife rang just before you got in. I said you'd
ring back.

BILL: Right, thanks.

JOY: Shall I get her for you?

BILL: No, not just for the moment. But remind me. [*She goes
out.*] She knows how long it takes me to get here.

HUDSON: But you couldn't get a taxi. Remember?

BILL: I've always managed to keep everything in place, in place
enough to get on with it, do my work, enjoy things, enjoy
other people, take an interest in all kinds of things. I've tried
to read, not just my own subject. I keep trying and the circle
just seems to get smaller. If Anna rings will you speak to her,

say I'm with Mrs. Garnsey? [HUDSON *nods*.] It's only about next weekend.

HUDSON: I thought you were going to Blackpool. On a business trip.

BILL: Yes, with Liz. We'd planned it before Christmas. We haven't really had a long weekend together since last summer when Anna took the kids with her down to North Devon.

HUDSON: So what's happening?

BILL: I don't know. Anna's fixed some crazy do for the entire weekend for the girl's birthday.

HUDSON: How old is she?

BILL: I don't know. Seventeen. Eighteen. Anyway, too old and too sophisticated and too unhampered by anything in particular to need my presence at her birthday for two whole days.

HUDSON: Does your wife know about Blackpool?

BILL: Cancel it, she says. Business doesn't mean all that to *you*. Give your daughter a good time.

HUDSON: She knows you were going with Liz?

BILL: Why else should she arrange this daft junket? She doesn't like the kids' chums any more than I do. It'll be all jazz and noise and black leather and sour teenage squalor and necking, and oh—

HUDSON: You've always been pretty fond of necking and—

BILL: Squalor! I may have helped to knock it together often enough but I haven't enjoyed it, and I haven't ever been made to feel sharp or with it or representative of any damned thing. I was never, at any time, like that bunch of kids my daughter runs around with, so don't compare me to them.

HUDSON: Sorry.

BILL: And as for necking, I never went in for it, never would, and pray God I am never so old, servile or fumbling that I ever have to wriggle through that dingy assault course. Do you like it, do you want it, those are the only questions I have ever thought worth while going into. You think I'm not telling the truth? Well, it's as near the truth as I can find at this moment; for one thing I have never had very strong fingers which is why I had to give up learning the piano.

HUDSON: What are you going to do then?

BILL: Do?

HUDSON: About the weekend?

BILL: I've no idea. I don't know which is worse, which prospect frightens me more. I keep seeing their faces. Anna's. Liz. And some of the others. It's even worse when they ring up. Not that Liz rings very often She has an immaculate idea of a mistress's rights. I want to feel tender, I want to be comforting and encouraging and full of fun and future things and things like that. But all I feel is as if my head were bigger and bigger, spiked and falling off, like a mace, it gets in my way, or keeps getting too close. It's not worth the candle is it?

HUDSON: Certainly doesn't seem like it, does it?

BILL: No. But then I've never discovered what is. That blessed candle of yours and Jones, the Holy Grail of the people who hold back.

HUDSON: No, it's just that some people seem to use things like sex, for instance, as a, a place of, of escape, instead of objects, well—in themselves.

BILL: Yes, I know what you mean. I've thought of that. But what about work? I know we're not doing any at the moment, but we're going to, we both work pretty hard, Wally. You certainly do, and you don't get a great deal for it. And I think even you'll admit I work harder than most when I'm actually at it.

HUDSON: Oh, sure.

BILL: But what sort of object is that? Is it an enjoyment, a duty, an obligation, a necessity or just the effort of fighting, of fighting off the end, whatever is to come to you.

HUDSON: I don't know. I don't think it matters all that much. So long as you're reasonably interested in what you do. You mustn't ask for too much.

BILL: Then you don't get disappointed. Mrs. Garnsey'll be disappointed if we don't get her her divorce all right. You're quite right, Wally, as usual. Anyway, why have you foisted Mrs. Garnsey on to me? I thought you and Jones had been dealing with her up till now. There's nothing specially difficult is there?

HUDSON: No, nothing special.

BILL: Well?

HUDSON: We've both got rather a lot on at the moment.

BILL: Well, so have I. I'm supposed to be at the Scrubs by 11:30 to see that Bennet kid.

HUDSON: What that? The indecent assault?

BILL: Yes. We didn't get very far. He was too upset. Clothes off, possessions signed for, bath, medical inspection in the whistling cold, keys jangling. He wasn't in any state for anything. I don't know why we do any criminal work.

HUDSON: I couldn't agree more.

BILL: I thought if I did Mrs. Garnsey, you'd go down to see Bennet. I suppose it's not your line?

HUDSON: Not really.

BILL: But does it depress you?

HUDSON: No. I just don't go for it, you might say.

BILL: You'd rather not do divorce either.

HUDSON: I don't feel that strongly. I get a bit fed up listening to it, trying to find out what really did happen all the time. But I don't actually mind it. I just wouldn't go out of my way to choose it, that's all.

BILL: What would you choose? Straight-forward bit of complicated conveyancing.

HUDSON: I'd say divorce was *your* line. Living other people's lives.

BILL: What do you mean by that?

HUDSON: I thought you enjoyed it.

BILL: Enjoyed what?

HUDSON: Oh, you know. Probing, taking a part.

BILL: You mean I'm not detached enough.

HUDSON: No, I didn't say that.

BILL: I don't want to live anyone's life, not anyone's. I dread those clients, clients like Mrs. Garnsey. I've got all the lumber I can carry. Are you sure you can't get along to see Bennet?

HUDSON: Don't see how I can.

BILL: Does he disgust you that much?

HUDSON: Nothing disgusts me. Any longer. I am simply not very interested or aroused by contemplating such people or such things. Apart from that, I've got to take Mrs. Rose down to counsel at eleven. That'll take till lunch time for certain. I've tried to piece it all together, but she never says the same thing twice in the same breath.

BILL: What is it? She lying about her husband?

HUDSON: Oh yes, I think so.

BILL: What's he supposed to have done?

HUDSON: Kicked her up the bottom with his heavy gardening boots on, locked her out of the house all night, and she had to sleep in the car in her nightdress.

BILL: What else?

HUDSON: Not much. Something about hot tablespoons. But nothing really admissible.

BILL: Was it a cold night?

HUDSON: What? Oh, in the car. Right in the middle of the big freeze-up. She says she got 'flu as a result and nearly got pneumonia.

BILL: Nearly?

HUDSON: And pleurisy.

BILL: Nearly. Why didn't she go for a drive with the heater on?

HUDSON: What, in her nightie at two o'clock in the morning?

BILL: Sounds a very romantic thing to do to me. She could have taken a turn up the Great West Road in her old man's car and ended up at some pull-in with a bacon sandwich and a cup of tea. I should think she'd have been made very welcome.

HUDSON: Well, her husband had the keys of the car. [Pause.] I can see you don't like her.

BILL: Me? Haven't met her have I? I'm just listening to you.

HUDSON: No. But I don't think you'd go much on her. That's why I've done it.

BILL: Good old Wally. She'll get a good run out of you. And you'll get your revenge watching her withering in front of Winters. I—as you'd expect—feel sorry for her husband. Old heavy garden boots. What's he sound like?

HUDSON: Difficult to say. Excessive sexual demands. All that.

BILL: Oh yes. King Kong, according to her, I suppose.

HUDSON: Perversions.

BILL: Spectacular?

HUDSON: Oh, usual sort of thing.

BILL: And what's she got? A wall eye and varicose veins, I'll bet. He sounds fairly ordinary.

HUDSON: No, I don't think he's such a bad chap. Still—

BILL: Any adultery?

HUDSON: She says so, but there doesn't seem to be much evidence.

Winters has seen the papers. He didn't seem to think much of it. I'm afraid he won't touch it under 300. Still, if he can get her to stick to her story, we should get him on cruelty.

BILL: You've applied for alimony and maintenance?

HUDSON: You bet.

BILL: Poor bastard. Well, what about Jones?

HUDSON: What about him?

BILL: Well, couldn't he go along to the Scrubs for me?

HUDSON: I suppose he could. If you really want him to.

BILL: No. You're right. I'd best do that myself. I don't think Jones would exactly inspire poor old Bennet with the confidence to go through with his appeal at all.

HUDSON: Anyway, I think he's pretty busy this morning.

BILL: Perhaps I should ring Anna now—and get it over before Mrs. Garnsey. Get it *over*—what am I thinking of?

HUDSON: He's got that Pole in again this morning. Third time in a week.

BILL: Pole?

HUDSON: You know—Zubuski, or whatever his name is.

BILL: Joy, get me Mrs. Maitland will you? What's up with him?

HUDSON: Well, he wants a divorce.

BILL: Grounds?

HUDSON: Adultery.

BILL: Well?

HUDSON: Well, the thing is this, sufficient evidence all right, I don't think there's any doubt of that, but he wants it on his own terms.

BILL: What do you mean: his own terms?

HUDSON: Quite simple. He insists on having sexual relations with his wife three times a week until the case comes up.

BILL: And the wife?

HUDSON: Oh, she agrees.

BILL: Well—good for them. [*Laughs.*]

HUDSON: Extraordinary, isn't it?

BILL: Yes.

HUDSON: We've both tried speaking to him. He just gets furious and won't listen.

BILL: What's he going to do? Report us to the Law Society? What's really extraordinary is you and Jones.

HUDSON: Well, I suppose it's funny.

BILL: Yes. I think it is. [*His laugh is interrupted by buzz and* JOY's *voice from his desk.*]

JOY: Mrs. Eaves is on the line.

BILL [*Pause*]: I'll—no, tell her I'll ring her back as soon as I can.

HUDSON [*Pleased*]: Well, there's number two bringing up the rear already. Busy morning.

BILL: Come on. Be fair. It isn't often Liz rings up. Not like Anna now.

HUDSON: Well, there is—

BILL: I know: Anna's my wife. There's never any doubt which side you're on.

HUDSON: I'm not on any side.

BILL: Yes you are. Wives and angels. Me: mistresses and devils. No. I'm not the one who's on any side. I don't have any idea of where I am. I have tried not to cause pain, I really have, you think I haven't, but I do try, I ought to be able to give a better account of myself. But I don't seem to be functioning properly. I don't seem to retain anything, at least not for very long. I wish I could go back to the beginning, except I wouldn't do any better. They used to say I had a quick brain.

HUDSON: Well, you have that.

BILL: No, I haven't. I have a very small, sluggish, slow moving brain. I just run it through quickly, at the wrong speed like a piece of film, and it darts and flickers, but it perceives little, and it retains nothing. What do you think I should do, Wally?

HUDSON: About the weekend? Tell Liz the truth. [*Pause.*]

BILL: I'm always trying to do that. I'd like to cheer her up for once, to go in free and uncluttered and tell her we'd got three whole days together.

HUDSON: Well, do that then.

BILL: Thanks for the advice. I can see what put you in this business. What's your problem, Mrs. Garnsey? Well, legally you can do this. Or that. I would advise this. However, you may prefer to do that. Morally—or emotionally—do as you like.

HUDSON: I don't know.

BILL: What? How she puts up with me. [HUDSON *nods.*] Which? Anna or Liz?

HUDSON: Either of them.

BILL: But especially Anna.

HUDSON: There must be some compensations. You've got two nice kids.

BILL: They're all right. I don't think they think we're as nice as we assume *they* are. Do you know that boy actually *wanted* to go away to boarding school. I told him he was crazy. But he couldn't wait. Couldn't *wait*. And he writes dull beady little letters about house matches and photographic societies and getting up at God knows what hour every morning to go *swimming*—in February. It's like having a priest in the family.

HUDSON: How old is he?

BILL: Eleven! At his age I was thinking about girls. Madeleine Caroll.

HUDSON [*Doing his irony*]: Perhaps he's just a late developer.

BILL: Seems to me he's in the right place to stay that way.

HUDSON: Still, he's happy.

BILL: Blissful. I don't understand. I think I'd rather be in the Scrubs. Same thing really. Chaplains, lousy food, hard work, lights out, no birds.

HUDSON: Well, he's growing up.

BILL: Yes. That's what Anna says. Perhaps she should have married *you*. You have so many points of agreement.

HUDSON: I'm all right, thank you.

BILL: Yes. You are. But I don't think Anna is quite as absorbed in her children as yours. I mean, she hasn't turned their growing up into some protracted act of holy communion that'll end up with an empty chalice and hot flushes when she's fifty. [HUDSON *looks uncomfortable. Pause.*] I've asked you this before: do you think I should leave her?

HUDSON: I've told you before. I don't think it makes any difference. To you.

[JOY's *voice from desk*.]

JOY: Your wife, Mr. Maitland.

BILL: Right. [*Motions to* HUDSON *to stay*.] Shan't be a minute. [*On phone*.] Hullo. Hullo, love. Sorry, I was late. I couldn't get a cab. It was strange. Yes. First time I've never managed it. Even the old famous whistle didn't work. . . . Do I? . . . No,

I don't think so. . . . Only old Wally. Trying to get sorted out.
. . . Well, my darling, I'm sorry if I do happen to sound like
that. I didn't sleep as you know, or not much, and . . . well,
perhaps I am feeling a bit odd and you can just hear it that's
all. I've got a client coming in any minute. . . . [WALLY *goes out
in spite of* BILL's *signals*.] No, of course, it's all right. That's why
I rang you back. I just haven't got started, and nothing seems
to be working very well. . . . What's that? Yes. . . . Well, I
know. Well. I'm sorry. . . . I wish I could. What's that? . . . I
don't seem to be able to hear. . . . I said I'm sorry. It's a rotten
line. . . . I can't *hear* you very well. . . . Yes, that's a bit better.
. . . Look, why don't I ring you back . . . what about lunch
time? . . . No, I can't have lunch. . . . Well, I've got to go down
to the Scrubs. . . . Well, I can't get anyone else to go, then I'm
seeing counsel, and I'm in court the rest of the day, then I'm
. . . Yes, Bennet. . . . Well, I think I'm the best judge of that.
. . . Well, a lot of people would agree with you, especially on
the bench. . . . I'll probably be late. . . . I'm not sure yet. . . .
You know it's no good asking me at this time of day. . . . Eight
or nine I don't know. It might even be later. . . . If that's what
you think . . . well, if that's what you know, why bother to ask
me the question. . . . Look, please don't, why don't I ring you?
I may get away, we'll see. . . . You know I haven't decided. . . .
That's how I cut myself—at half past eight, remember. . . . I've
told you: I don't know yet. . . . I simply don't know. . . . I don't
know now, all I know is I probably am. . . . Well, it won't be
the greatest disappointment of her life as you well know and I
know, and *she* knows. Look, love, I've got Wally waiting to go
down to Winters. . . . Why don't you go out and . . . all right
. . . well, I'm sorry you're feeling like that . . . oh, headache . . .
yes, the usual only a bit worse . . . and just odd things . . . well
. . . all right . . . look after yourself. . . . I'm sorry love.
. . . I promised not to say that any more. . . . [*He puts the
'phone down. Stares. Looks at the file in front of him. Drinks
some more water. Presses eyeballs.*]

JOY [V*oice*]: When do you want me to get Mrs. Eaves?
BILL: When I ask you to. No. Er, remind me will you, love? Per-
haps after Mrs. Garnsey. . . .
JOY: She's not turned up yet.

BILL: Well, ask Mr. Hudson if he'll come back in will you? And
—get me another glass of water.

JOY: O.K. Oh. And I think Shirley wants to see you when you've
a minute.

BILL: All right, when I've time. How's your sex life out there?

JOY: Thrilling. How's yours?

BILL: Oh—fairly quiet. Come in and see me.

JOY: When?

BILL: Oh—before you leave work.

JOY: O.K.

BILL: And—oh, I've asked you, haven't I?

JOY: Have you?

BILL: I don't know.

[HUDSON *appears.* JOY *switches out.*]

HUDSON: D'you want me?

BILL: Yes. Yes, was there anything else?

HUDSON: No, no I don't think so.

BILL: Nothing to sign?

HUDSON: No.

BILL: Right.

HUDSON: Well, I'd—

BILL: You'd better get on. [HUDSON *turns to go.*] Wally, Wally,
there's just one thing I'd like to bring up.

HUDSON: Will it take long?

BILL: No, but I'd like to have a chat about it. Why? Aren't you
interested or something?

HUDSON: I've just got rather—

BILL: O.K. O.K.

HUDSON: And I think Shirley's a bit keen to see you.

BILL: Shirley? Yes, I just thought this seemed like a good time
to bring it up. [*Pause.*]

HUDSON: Well, I'll drop in later then.

[SHIRLEY *comes in with glass of water.*]

BILL: Wally! Wally, try and pop in before you go down to Winters. I'll try and get through Mrs. Garnsey quickly. After all,
Jones can take a lot of the stuff down from her. . . .

[BILL *looks more than deserted. He looks at* SHIRLEY *gratefully. She hands him the water.*]

BILL: Thank you love, that's very kind of you. [*He drinks. She watches.*] Anything the matter?

SHIRLEY: Not with me there isn't.

BILL: Sure? You all right?

SHIRLEY: Fine, thank you.

BILL: Then what is it? We're friends aren't we? Why are you like this?

SHIRLEY: I'm not like anything.

BILL: Then?

SHIRLEY: I just want you to know I'm giving in my notice, that's all. You owe me a week's holiday but I'll give you a week, anyway.

BILL: But what for?

SHIRLEY: I've just made up my mind I'm going, that's all. Do you mind?

BILL: Of course I mind—

SHIRLEY: Well, that's bad luck for you, isn't it?

BILL: I don't know, love. Perhaps it's bad luck for both of us.

SHIRLEY: Not for me it isn't. I don't know why I didn't clear out before.

BILL: You've always gone on about it—

SHIRLEY: And who talked me out of it?

BILL: What have I done?

SHIRLEY: Nothing. I'm just giving you notice. O.K.?

BILL: But—you must have a reason.

SHIRLEY: Sure, I've got reasons. Do I have to tell them to you?

BILL: No.

SHIRLEY: I've had enough.

BILL: What of?

SHIRLEY: Do you think I mean you?

BILL: I don't know. I don't know. I honestly don't know. If you wouldn't be in such a rush, perhaps I could—

SHIRLEY: Oh, well if you must know what for, for one thing I'm pregnant.

BILL: You're what?

SHIRLEY: Mit child, dear. You'd had two haven't you? At least.

BILL: I'm sorry. [*Trying to focus.*] I thought you were on the pills.

SHIRLEY: I was. I got fed up with them.

BILL: But you've only just got engaged.

SHIRLEY: So?

BILL: You mean you're going to get married?

SHIRLEY: That had always been the idea.

BILL: And you still want to?

SHIRLEY: Do I have to ask for your blessing or something?

BILL: I'm just a bit taken aback.

SHIRLEY: These things do happen, you know.

BILL: Are you really in love with him?

SHIRLEY: I thought you didn't go much on being in love.

BILL: Does he know?

SHIRLEY: I told him last night.

BILL [*Irritated.*]: Well?

SHIRLEY: He said he'd rather have waited a bit, he's quite pleased. What's the matter? Seen something?

BILL: Naturally, I see you a little differently. . . . I mean physically. . . . I feel. . . .

SHIRLEY: Poor you! You should feel like I do.

BILL: Is this the right thing?

SHIRLEY: Why? Should I ask advice from you? Father?

BILL: No, Shirley, no, don't do all that, I'm concerned—

SHIRLEY: Look—you can stick your long farewell. I just want you to know now: I'm pregnant. [*Even* SHIRLEY's *flush of relish is abated by* BILL's *dismay. Pause. Quieter.*] I'm getting married. And I'm giving in my notice. A week Friday. O.K.?

BILL: O.K., love. [*She waits.*] When is it?

SHIRLEY: Fortnight.

BILL: No. The baby.

SHIRLEY: Oh. September.

BILL: September! But that's, that's about nine months away.

SHIRLEY: Seven.

BILL: You could go on working for ages yet. Everybody does.

SHIRLEY: Well, *I've* decided not to.

BILL: What about the money? You'll need that more than ever now.

SHIRLEY: We'll manage.

BILL: But think how useful it'd be. What'll you do all day, sitting round the house, waiting like some silly bomb to go off?

SHIRLEY: Ted's doing all right.

BILL: But with two of you working—you'll need all sorts of things—

SHIRLEY: He doesn't want me to go on.

BILL: He doesn't want me to go on! Who is he? Godfrey Winn? He'll do what you *want*. Do you want more money? You know you can have it. Of course you can. You're worth it. You're worth it to anybody.

SHIRLEY: Perhaps I might go to anybody.

BILL: No, stay here. You're wanted here.

SHIRLEY: What's all this, are you bribing everyone now?

BILL: Shirley, I'm very fond of you. What you've told me—

SHIRLEY: Don't tell me you're short of it

BILL: No, I'm *not*!

SHIRLEY: Anyway, that's out.

BILL: I haven't touched you—

SHIRLEY: Oh. [*Pause.*] Forget it.

BILL: I haven't touched you. You're accusing me. But I haven't touched you. Not for three months. At least.

SHIRLEY: Thanks so much.

BILL: Oh, for God's sake, throw off that half-baked, cheap, showgirl act and listen to me.

SHIRLEY: Why? What have you ever done for me?

BILL: Nothing. I suppose. But I do know we had some affection for one another, beneath all the arguing and banter and waste of breath. I know I liked you. And when we were in bed together you dropped all your pretences and deceits, after a while anyway. Perhaps I did even. I don't think I let you think it was an enduring love affair—in the sense of well of endless, wheedling obligations and summonses and things. But, if you think back on it, detail by detail, I don't think you can say it was fraudulent. Can you?

SHIRLEY: No.

BILL: You can't *disown* it. If you do that, you are helping, you are conspiring to kill me. [*Pause.*]

SHIRLEY: One weekend in Leicester on client's business. Two weekends in Southend on client's business. Moss Mansions—

remember them? Four days in Hamburg on client's business. One crummy client's crummy flat in Chiswick. And three times on *this* floor. [*She moves to go.*] And another thing, just don't push any more of Joy's work on to me. I don't intend doing it. Any more than I like you, any more than I like your promising me for your clients when you're too busy with your wife or that Mrs. Eaves or—I think you'd better forget about my notice. I'm going now. [*She goes out.*]

[*Presently* JOY *buzzes.*]

JOY [*Voice.*]: Mrs. Garnsey is downstairs. [*Pause.*] I said Mrs. Garnsey is downstairs.

BILL [*Croaks.*]: Would you? Ask her to wait! Could you, could you send in Mr. Hudson?

JOY: He's just on his way out.

BILL: Well, stop him.

JOY: I think he's gone.

BILL: I need him. Get him.

JOY: Well, I'll do my best.

BILL: And then I want to speak to Mrs. Eaves. [*Silence.* BILL *tries to look through Mrs. Garnsey's file.* HUDSON *enters, wearing his overcoat.*]

HUDSON: You want me?

BILL: Oh, yes. Wally.

HUDSON: Only I'm just off. You know what old Winters is like. Can't keep him waiting two minutes.

BILL: Won't take a minute. [HUDSON *looks at his watch.*] What would you say to becoming a partner? [*Pause.*] Eh? [HUDSON *seems to react rather pleasurably.*]

HUDSON: I don't know. Really.

BILL: Well?

HUDSON: Are you asking me?

BILL: Yes. Yes. I am.

HUDSON: I see. Well . . .

BILL: I realise it's a bit . . .

HUDSON: Yes. Well. Needs a bit of thinking about, doesn't it?

BILL: Sure. Sure. Why don't we talk about it later? Chew it over.

HUDSON: Yes. Right. O.K. I will. Well thanks then. I'd . . .

BILL: You're not thinking of leaving?

HUDSON: No. Not exactly.

BILL: You mean you *are* thinking of leaving?

HUDSON: I wouldn't say that exactly.

BILL: What would you say exactly?

HUDSON: I have had an offer, as a matter of fact.

BILL: Who from?

HUDSON: Several actually.

BILL: Who?

HUDSON: Well . . .

BILL: Oh come on Wally, for God's sake.

HUDSON: Well, Piffards—

BILL: Piffards! Those crooks!

HUDSON: Very high-class crooks. *If* that's what you think they are.

BILL: Well, as you know, I think they're crooks, so do you really.
Still, if you want to wear striped trousers and work for Cabinet
Ministers' wives. [*Pause.*] As you would say, we all have our
ways of looking at these things. O.K., then. Well, perhaps you'll
have a think about it?

HUDSON [*Smiles, then slowly.*]: Yes. I will. Better get Mrs. Rose
down to the inquisition then. Cheerio. [*Goes out.*]

BILL: Joy. Did you get my call to Mrs. Eaves!

JOY: She's engaged.

BILL: Well, keep trying. Tell the exchange to break in. Where's
Shirley?

JOY: She's gone.

BILL: Gone where?

JOY: I don't know.

BILL: I mean do you think she's coming back?

JOY: No idea. Shouldn't think so somehow.

BILL: Really?

JOY: She took her soap and towel.

BILL: What'd she say?

JOY: She was just crying. Shall I send in Mrs. Garnsey?

BILL: No. I must speak to Mrs. Eaves.

JOY: Oh, wait a minute, I think they've got it. Hold on. . . .
You're through.

BILL [*On phone.*]: Liz? My darling, I've been trying to get hold
of you. . . . Are you all right? . . . Well, no. . . . Everything's

. . . I said everything's. . . . What? Oh, I couldn't get a taxi for a start, well, not a start. . . . Well, you know, if I keep my head upright and don't move it about too much, and talk fairly slowly. . . . Look, try and bear with me a minute. . . . What was what like? Oh, last night. . . . Well, yes there was an Anna situation . . . oh, before we went out and afterwards. . . . Yes, that was bad enough, but the whole thing was very strange. . . . It's difficult to explain. . . . No, I can't quite. . . . I'm sorry. I just don't seem to retain very much of anything, of anything that happened. . . . I just felt everyone was cutting me . . . cutting me. . . . I know, I should care! I like them as much as they like me. . . . I don't know whether they're more afraid than I am. . . . I think they really *want* to be liked . . . in that sort of way. . . . I don't exactly do my best, do I. No, well then. . . . No, Anna quite enjoyed herself while she was there. . . . Oh, the usual shower. . . . They all seem to adore her. . . . I know, but more than ever . . . it's only all right when I'm with her. . . . Yes. . . . But it seemed at my expense this time, it seemed to be out of me . . . as if they were disowning me. . . . It's wonderful to hear your voice. . . . Well, I don't know yet . . . sometime this evening. . . . Look, please don't *you* press me . . . Yes. It'll be all right. . . . I may not sound like it, but it will be. . . . You don't think I want to go to her silly birthday junket, do you? . . . Do you think I don't know that? Of course it's Anna. . . . Well, I'll probably talk to the kid myself. . . . Look, love, I've got to go. . . . Can I ring you back? I've got this client and she's been waiting about. . . . Let me ring you. . . . You *will* be in, won't you? . . . Yes, but you will *be* there. . . . Promise? Don't go out till I ring you back. . . . I need to talk to you. . . . It'll be all right. Don't worry. [*to* JOY.] I'll see Mrs. Garnsey now. [JOY *shows* MRS. GARNSEY *in*. BILL *rises to greet her*.] Mrs. Garnsey, I'm so sorry I've kept you waiting. [MRS. GARNSEY *nods*.] Have you had a cup of tea? Joy? [JOY *nods. Goes out*.] Right. I had a client on. I'm afraid I couldn't get her off. Now: you've already had several little sessions with Mr. Hudson haven't you?

MRS. GARNSEY: That's right.

BILL: Yes. Well, I haven't been into it in great detail. As you know, Mr. Hudson has had to pass it on to me . . . for the moment. . . . [MRS. GARNSEY *look slightly alarmed*.] Well, he

had to see counsel this morning and he also thought it might
be a good idea if you were to see me sometime.

MRS. GARNSEY: I see.

BILL: The adultery seems quite clearly established. There are
these three women, apart from all the others, there seems
to be more than enough there. You *have* made a claim for
maintenance and alimony. Two children, that's right isn't it?

MRS. GARNSEY: Do you think I should?

BILL: Mr. Hudson's already advised you, hasn't he?

MRS. GARNSEY: Yes. [*Pause.*]

BILL: Mrs. Garnsey. I can tell you what the law is, and on the
basis of what you tell me, and on the assumption that what you
tell me—is the truth—as best you know it, I can advise you
what the legal possibilities are. The rest is up to you.

MRS. GARNSEY: Yes. That's what Mr. Hudson said to me. It's the
law. And—[*Pause.*]

BILLS Perhaps Mr. Hudson hasn't. . . . Would you like to tell me
how you feel? About the whole question. I mean—[*She nods
dumbly.*]—the first question is always: Why doesn't the marriage work? [*Silence.*] Is it: the women? Only? When I say
only, as far as the law is concerned, that's quite enough.

MRS. GARNSEY: I don't know. I still don't know what to do. You
see, he's a good man really. He's kind, he's very sensitive indeed, he seems to be one step ahead of me all the time in
everything, everything. He always has been. He loves me. I know
that. . . . I think we. . . . Well, I . . . disappoint him. But no
more than he disappoints himself. . . . You've got all that stuff
that Mr. Hudson took down? [BILL *nods.*] He *is* clever, he does
his job well. He works hard. He's good looking. He has a lot of
charm, in his own way, he really has, he can make you laugh
like almost no one else. But what, what kills me is that he is
being hurt so much.

BILL: How do you mean?

MRS. GARNSEY: By everyone. He comes home to me, and I know
that nothing really works for him. Not at the office, not his
friends, not even his girls. I wish they would. God knows, he
tries hard enough. I wish I could help him. But I can't, and
everyone, everyone, wherever, we go together, whether it's a
night out, or an evening at our club, or an outing with the chil-

dren, everyone's, I know, everyone's drawing away from him.
And the more people have been good and kind and thoughtful
to me, the worse it's been for him. I know. And now. Now: *I'm*
doing the same thing. The children hardly notice him. And now
it's *me*. I can't bear to see him rejected and laughed at and
scorned behind his back and ignored—[*All this last is scarcely
audible.*] And now it's *me*. I've got to leave him. [*Nothing
more meaningful comes from her.* BILL *gets up to comfort her
but is paralysed.*]

BILL: Joy! [*Silence but for* MRS GARNSEY.] Joy! Joy! [JOY *appears,
surprised.*] Mrs. Garnsey isn't feeling very well. Would you take
her and give her a brandy? There's some in Mr. Hudson's
cabinet. [JOY *supports* MRS. GARNSEY *and takes her out.*] And
get me Mrs. Eaves.

JOY: O.K.

BILL: The minute you can. [*They go out.* BILL *takes three more
pills.*] Joy!

JOY [*Voice.*]: Yes?

BILL: Where's that call?

JOY: No reply.

BILL: What, engaged or no reply?

JOY: No reply.

BILL: Try again. Now! [*He waits.*]

JOY [*Presently.*]: Still no reply.

BILL: Oh. How's Mrs. Garnsey?

JOY: I gave her a whiskey. There wasn't any brandy. She's getting
a taxi home.

BILL: Well, get it for her.

JOY: O.K.

BILL: And Joy—

JOY: Well?

BILL: Come in a minute, will you? Now. [*She comes in.*] Close
the door a minute. [*She does so.*] How are you?

JOY: I'm all right. You don't look so hot.

BILL: Joy.

JOY: Yes?

BILL: Will you stay on a bit tonight?

JOY: Is it important?

BILL: Yes.

Joy: If you like.
BILL: Thank you. [JOY *turns to go.*]
Joy: What shall I do about Mrs. Eaves?
BILL: Keep trying her.
Joy: Will you speak to her?
BILL: No. But. Say I'll be round this evening.
Joy: What time?
BILL: Tell her: to expect me when she sees me.

Curtain

Act Two

*The same scene. A little grey light. An early morning taxi
can be heard.* BILL *is lying asleep on the sofa, his collar open,
an overcoat over him. He seems to be making an effort to
wake as he did in Act I, and the struggle becomes gradually
more frantic as he tries to escape. He is rescued by the telephone ringing. His eyes open and relief and fatigue mingle as
he sits up. Then apprehension, more than apprehension. He
goes to the telephone on his desk, looks at it. Peers at his
watch. Can't see. Draws the curtains and some light comes
in. He looks out, switches on his desk light and examines his
watch. Cautiously he picks up the telephone. It has not been
put through from the switchboard. He goes into the outer
office and picks up the one on* HUDSON'S *desk. The ringing
stops. Quiet.*

BILL [*Presently.*]: Yes? [*Pause.*] Hello? [*Pause.*] Who is it? Who's
there? [*The line is dead and he replaces the receiver. He fumbles
with the switchboard, muttering . . .*] . . . How do you put this
. . . thing through! [*He walks back into his room, picks up the
receiver. Obviously nothing. Goes back to the switchboard. Returns with a glass of water, picks up the receiver again. All right
this time. He gets his pills out of his desk drawer, and starts to
dial a number. Then loses courage or strength and puts the receiver down. He takes one pill which makes him 'gag,' as if he*

*were in a dentist's chair. He goes out for some soda water, fills a
glass, looks at the two pills to come and re-dials.*]

NOTE: *This telephone conversation and the ones that follow
it, and some of the duologues should progressively resemble
the feeling of dream and unreality of* BILL's *giving 'evidence'
at the Beginning of Act.* 1. *Some of the time it should all
seem actually taking place at the particular moment, naturally, casual, lucid, unclouded. At others the grip of the dream
grows tighter; for example, in the call that follows now, the
presence of the person on the other end should be made very
real indeed, but, sometimes it should trail off into a feeling of
doubt as to whether there is anyone to speak to at all.*

BILL [*On phone.*]: Liz? Darling? Did I wake you? . . . I'm sorry
. . . it wasn't you ringing then . . . a few minutes ago. . . . I
wasn't sure who it was. . . . Oh—I guess it must have been
Anna. Yes, I'm at the office. . . . Well, it's not like your own
bed, as they say. . . . Yes . . . like a gimlet, the old thing, right
up there behind the eyeballs. . . . How are *you*? Did you take a
sleeping pill? . . . Three? You're crazy! . . . I know, my darling,
I'm sorry. . . . Yes, I should have phoned, I should have phoned.
. . . [*He starts to take his pill with soda water.*] Just a minute.
. . . That's two. . . . That's three. . . . Sorry . . . I know I said
I'd come round. . . . Oh, come off it, anyway, Shirley walked
out yesterday. . . . Well, I not surprised either. . . . I know.
. . . Yes, well it worried me too. . . . What do you mean Joy can
do the job just as well? Look, it's too early for jokes and sus-
picion. . . . Look, hang on just one minute. [*He claps a hand
to his mouth.*] Just one minute. Hang on. [*He disappears into
the outer office. Sound of lavatory cistern. He comes back, wiping his face.*]Sorry. What? No, I just lost my pills that's all. . . .
Yes, now I'll have to take three more. . . . I made a mistake, I
just had plain water with the first one. . . . Look, I know I
should have phoned but I didn't and I couldn't. But I love you
dearly and I wanted to be with you and talk to you more than
anything. . . . Well, I'll tell you what happened . . . only no
more jolly, barbed jokes about Joy. Please . . . I know, but *I'm*
allowed to make them. . . . All right, I won't make them any
more. . . . It was a bad day, Liz, a bad day right from the begin-

ning. . . . I was just about to ring you because I reckoned on having a good three quarters of an hour before meeting Anna. . . . Well, there was a lot of work in. . . . Anyhow, she turned up here suddenly at seven-thirty. . . . No, the downstairs door was locked. . . . Well the caretaker always does that. . . . No, she didn't. . . . Darling, I said please no more Joy jokes. . . . Well, what could I do? I couldn't ring you with her here in the room. . . . Well, I know it doesn't make any difference at this stage, but I couldn't bring myself to do it. . . . I don't think you'd have cared much for the experience either. . . . She'd arranged for us to go out to these dreary friends of hers, the Watsons. . . . That's right, they're the ones, they write books together. . . . Sociology and Sex. I don't know—Natural Childbirth and C.N.D.: An Analysis. . . . All tables and diagrams and unreadable. . . . Yes. All it adds up to in the end is either do it or don't. We do. . . . You've got it. Every time she drops one he's in there in the room with a surgical mask on and popping away with his camera. . . . Yes . . . being encouraging. . . . Well, it's pretty discouraging to look at them together. . . . Oh, sure, *rotten* dinner. . . . Oh, wooden bowls, yes, sort of *Sunday Times* Supplement Primitive . . . *very* badly cooked. . . . Hullo. . . . Hullo. . . . Are you there? . . . Oh. . . . I keep thinking you're not there. . . . Well, you weren't saying anything and I suddenly . . . Hullo. . . . Hullo. . . . Oh, hell's bloody bells. . . . Well, as I say she turned up here. . . . I know, well it's not something you'd do. . . . You're too clever for that. . . . Well I didn't just mean. . . . She pitched into the weekend thing the minute I answered the door. . . . Yes—Joy answered the door. . . . No, I think that quite pleased her. She felt if anything had been going on you'd have been the loser and not her. . . . Which is kind of true. . . . I had a drink, and told her the truth . . . just that: that you and I hadn't had any time together for weeks and we were determined to have at least three whole, clear, uncluttered days together—and Jane, well just bad luck. She's a nice girl but she's a strapping nevertheless seventeen, less than half our age and looked after and cosseted and God knows what. Besides, she's young, she's got all that youth everyone's so mad about and admires. Even if she's not very clever or pretty, she's got good old youth. I'd never use anything else if I could help it. . . .

Sure, she'll not get into any mess like us. . . . Hullo. . . . Hullo.
. . . I say, like *us*. *Or*, if she does, it won't matter, it won't over-
whelm her or get the better of her. . . . I promise you that's
what I said. . . . Yes. . . . I said we just had to go. . . . I love you
very dearly. . . . Yes, I did say it. . . . Oh, what's the matter?
I don't seem to hear properly. . . . Yes, we went to the party,
don't ask me why, I think I'd even have rather gone home. . . .
Of course I had too much booze, what do you think. . . . It
was strange, as if I were there on tolerance. . . . Sure, they're
sorry for Anna and think I'm a boorish old ram but it was
more, there was no more to it than that. . . . I don't know. . . .
Liz. . . . Liz. . . . Hullo, Liz. . . . I'm frightened. . . . It was
as if I only existed because of her, because she allowed me to,
but if she turned off the switch . . . turned off the switch . . .
who knows? But if she'd turned it off I'd have been dead. . . .
They would have passed me by like a blank hoarding or a
tombstone, or waste ground by the railway line or something.
. . . And then there was Mrs. Garnsey. . . . Mrs. Garnsey, you
remember her. . . . I don't know what to do about her. . . . No,
quite straightforward really. . . . Of course we will. What did
I have the row about then? She knows all about it. Not that
she didn't anyway. . . . Believe me. . . . Oh, there was a sort
of row at the table and we left early. . . . Sure, she wanted to
stay. . . . I took her home and, oh, it went on and I came
back here. The car was in the garage, I couldn't get a taxi, so
I came back and slept here. . . . I wanted to, but I didn't want
to break in on you somehow. . . . I know I should have but
I couldn't! Well. . . . Look, I'll come over the minute I can.
I'm longing to see you and I can't wait and I'm dreading
today. . . . Well, I'll make a hole in the day. . . . Hullo. . . .
Hullo. . . . Stay in won't you? Stay in, I'll ring you. 'Bye.
[*He puts the phone down. Picks it up again several times to
see if it is alive. Gets out a razor, brush and mirror and looks
at them dully. Dials phone again.*]

[*More than ever the ambiguity of reality is marked, of whether
the phone is dead, of whether the person at the other end
exists. He trails back and forth between lucidity and near
off-handedness and fumbling and fear and addressing himself.*

Some jokes are addressed to himself, some bravado is deflated to himself, some is dialogue between real people. The telephone is stalked, abused, taken for granted, feared. Most of all the fear of being cut off, of no sound from either end.]

BILL [*On phone.*]: Anna? How are you? . . . I'm sorry. . . . Didn't you take a pill? . . . Well, it's hardly surprising then, is it? . . . You rang me . . . oh, my dear, come off it, of course I know it was you. You've got your own click. . . . No, I spent the night here, believe it or not. . . . I couldn't get a taxi so I walked here. . . . You obviously rang up to find out *where* I am not *how* I am. . . . Oh, great, especially after your little visit and then your friends. . . . Well, it wasn't exactly a load of old fun was it? . . . Well, *you* were a success, but then you always are. . . . I didn't mean it unkindly, you deserve to be. It's just that the more they despise me the more admirable and courageous and decent-spirited you become. . . . Sometimes I think you're my only grip left, if you let me go, I'll disappear, I'll be made to disappear, nothing will work, I'll be like something in a capsule in space, weightless, unable to touch anything or do anything, like a groping baby in a removed, putrefying womb. . . . No, I'll not leave you. . . . I've told you. I'll not leave you . . . *you* are leaving me. . . . I told you the weekend is out, it's out, the weekend is out. . . . Yes, I am. . . . I don't know about Liz. She may be the last to pack it in, but pack it in she will. . . . Of course she's coming with me . . . because I haven't seen her probably for six bloody weeks and I have to be with her. . . . I know I am, have I ever denied it. . . . I see Jane every day of the week and no one could be more relieved to be rid of me when her friends are around . . . because I'm only an inquisitive, hostile, undistinguished square I suppose, and I bore the jeans off her. . . . Must you always say 'mistress'? It's a very melodramatic word for a very commonplace archetype. . . . You make it sound like a pterodactyl who gives you lung cancer . . . or something. . . . Yes, well she said something almost identical about you—with a little more wit, I may say. . . . Well, she's quite a humorous girl. . . . Oh, something about your gold lamé hairstyle . . . and, oh yes, your dress: what did she call it: chintz and sequin collage.

... I don't know, someone must have described it to her—no
—not me. . . . Well, you're neither of you the greatest dressers
in the world. . . . I know, but mistresses, as you call them, are
usually less tolerant than wives. Mind you, they're also less
patronizing but totally without generosity. . . . No, I malign
her about that. . . . Yes, and you too. Look, has Jane left yet?
Could you put her on? . . . I want to speak to her, that's why.
. . . Listen, I'm a fairly rotten father but better than some,
at least I can ask my daughter a question on the telephone.
After all, she can refuse to speak to me if she wants to. But
try not to prompt her? [*Pause.*] Jane? Hullo, darling, how
are you? . . . I should say I'm more or less the same as usual.
Or, rather less than usual. How's the Drama then? I don't
mean your personal drama, if you have one, I mean speech
training and improvisation or whatever it is? . . . Good, well
I'm glad. You deserve it. You see, you'll you'll be a dame before I die. No, well by the time you're thirty. . . . What I
wanted to ask is could you pop in and see me today? . . . This
morning, any time? . . . No, it's not all that important, but
I'm just asking you if you would do me a favour and give me
ten minutes of your time. . . . We could have lunch if you'd . . .
well, can't you cut voice production or something? You speak
quite beautifully enough as it is. . . . I'm not flattering you—
or bribing you. Frankly that folk song and Poetry Recital
voice gives me the flaming pip, I'm just asking you to see
me for a few minutes at least before. . . . That's better! I'll
buy you an air cushion for the next Aldermaston. Save you
getting felt up in Trafalgar Square. . . . Sorry, well, it *is* nine
o'clock in the morning and my sofa isn't very comfortable.
. . . Thank you, darling, very much. It won't take. . . . What?
All right, put her on. [*Pause.*] Hullo. . . . I honestly don't
know. . . . No, I really don't. It's a bit of a tough day. Hudson
seems to be in court all the time nowadays. Jones is useless
. . . well, the truth is I don't like him then; it's all right him
working for me, but I'd feel differently if he wanted to marry
my daughter. I just hope to God she wouldn't want to. . . .
Of course I'm not drunk, a little of last night's fire is coursing
through the gates and natural alleys of the body with my
three pills, that's all. Anyway, Jane's sure to marry an emergent

African. Perhaps I am a bit, I don't know. That is, if she hasn't already sent her virginity to OXFAM. . . . I tell you I don't know. I've got to see Mrs. Garnsey again. I'm going to fail there, I've done it already, but she's coming in again to lose her grip or whatever it is, and then there's Tonks and Tonks and an indecent assault or criminal assault I don't remember which, and some bank manager who's a flasher and . . . Yes, I am seeing her, you must know that, you *do* know that, now. . . . I'll let you know and I'll come back . . . as soon as I can. . . . I know you do. . . . I love you. . . . It just doesn't do much good does it? . . . Look, try and take a pill and go back to bed. . . . O.K., please yourself. Oh, don't talk Jane out of coming to see me. No, forget it. If you can and you want to, well . . . 'Bye. [*He puts the phone down. There is a noise from the outer office. He calls out.*] Joy. [*No reply. He gets up, looks through the door. There is no one there. He comes back, looks at his watch. Picks up phone, dials. Waits. No reply. He waits, then looks carefully at his thumb. Puts down the phone. Not knowing what to precipitate next. Again, a noise from the outer office. Someone has certainly come in this time. He waits. No one appears and he can't bear it any longer.*] Joy? Joy? [HUDSON *appears, taking off his raincoat. He takes in the sofa-bed and situation.*]

HUDSON [*Ponderously, of course.*]: Hullo—early bird.

BILL: Oh.

HUDSON: Where's the woman, then?

BILL: Flown.

HUDSON: How was she?

BILL: Fine.

HUDSON: Well, that's good.

BILL: Sure. Let me tell you, she could lose you in five minutes.

HUDSON: Delighted to hear it.

BILL: Tell me, what about Shirley?

HUDSON: What about her?

BILL: Do you think she'll come back?

HUDSON: No. You've seen the last of her.

BILL: Really? The last?

HUDSON: She rang Joy and asked her to send her cards off last night.

84   **John Osborne**

[*Another noise from outer office.*]

BILL: If that's Jones, keep him out of my way, I don't want to
see him.
HUDSON: Well—sounds as if you've met your match this time.
BILL: What do you mean?
HUDSON: Perhaps you'd better take the day off.
BILL: I've too much to do.
HUDSON: What have you done to your thumb?
BILL: I keep looking at it, that's all. It's rather painful. But they're
rather interesting to look at, anyway. I never did look at it
properly before. Have you? I wonder if it's cancer.

[JONES *looks in.*]

JONES: Hullo.
HUDSON: Hullo. Come on your scooter?
JONES: Yes.
HUDSON: Well, you'd better go and thaw out I should think.
JONES: No Shirley then?
HUDSON: No. Not any more.
JONES: Where's Joy?
HUDSON: Overslept we believe.
JONES: Well, I'll do the post then.
HUDSON: Yes, I should if I were you.
JONES: What's that?
HUDSON: The boss has got cancer this morning.
JONES: Oh?
HUDSON: In his thumb.

[JONES *goes out.*]

BILL: Thank God for that. I suppose you're in court all day again.
HUDSON: 'Fraid so.
BILL: Why do you leave it all to me?
HUDSON: What would you like me to do?
BILL: I don't know.
HUDSON: You've got Jones.
BILL: Thanks. You can take him with you.

HUDSON: Well, I'd better leave you then. Oh, how did you get on with Mrs. Garnsey?

BILL: Didn't work out at all.

HUDSON: I didn't think it would.

BILL: Eh?

HUDSON: We got the husband's reply in after she'd left.

BILL: Well?

HUDSON: Oh. I don't think she's got anything to worry about.

[BILL *stares at him and starts to laugh. Another noise in the outer office.*]

HUDSON: That'll be Joy.

BILL: Send her in.

HUDSON: Right.

BILL: Wally—have you thought any more about my offer? [*Pause.*] The offer, Wally. The Partnership.

HUDSON: Yes. As a matter of fact I have given it a bit of thought.

BILL: And?

HUDSON: I'd like to take a bit more time over it. If you don't mind.

BILL: And Piffards?

HUDSON: They don't seem to be in any hurry for a decision.

BILL: No? Well, they're a big firm. Right, well then.
[*Pause.*] Joy!

[*She appears.*]

HUDSON: Ah, there she is.

JOY: D'you want me?

HUDSON: Bright as a button.

BILL: Bring in the post, will you?

JOY: Mr. Jones is sorting it.

BILL: Well, bring in what he's done.

JOY: O.K.

BILL: And ring Mrs. Garnsey.

JOY: Which?

BILL: Which what?

JOY: Which first?

BILL: Oh—Mrs. Garnsey. I want to catch her.

[*She nods and goes out.*]

HUDSON: You sound as though you think you'd lost her. Well, see you later. [*He goes out.* BILL *reaches for the intercom.*]
BILL: Joy! Get me Mrs. Eaves.
JOY: Which?
BILL: What? Oh, you speak to Mrs. Garnsey. Make another appointment for her as soon as she can.
JOY: O.K.
BILL: And what about Shirley?
JOY: What about her?
BILL: Well, isn't she coming in?
JOY: Why should she?
BILL: You mean she's really left?
JOY: Yes. Really.

[BILL *stares at his thumb. The phone rings.*]

BILL [*On phone.*]: Liz? Look, I'm sorry. It's just that it's going to be a day. I can see it only too well. . . . Yes, I'm all right. My thumb's a bit painful, that's all. . . . Yes, of course it's cancer. But, look, you will stay in, won't you? Whatever happens, wait for me, don't leave will you? O.K. Thank you. . . . But you won't leave. . . . 'Bye.

[JOY *reappears with some letters.*]

JOY: This is all for the moment. You know how slow he is.
BILL: O.K. Give them here. Did you get Mrs. Garnsey?
JOY: Well, I spoke to someone. Her sister or someone.
BILL: Close the door. [*She does so.*]
JOY: She said she'd changed her mind.
BILL: Changed her mind?
JOY: That's what she said.
BILL: But did you make it clear it was important I see her again?
JOY: Sure. She just said would you send in the account.
BILL: But I wanted to see her again. [*Pause.*]
JOY: Shall I send it in then?
BILL: What? Oh, yes, I suppose so. No. No, don't.

Joy: But that's crazy.

Bill: How are you this morning?

Joy: I'm fine.

Bill: Well, you look it, I must say.

Joy: Thank you, Mr. Maitland.

Bill: Did you get home all right?

Joy: Well, it was only half past seven in the evening, you know, I didn't exactly have a night out.

Bill: I'm sorry.

Joy: For what? We enjoyed ourselves. Didn't we?

Bill: Yes, I think we did.

Joy: The draught under that door's a bit much, though. And it was a bit of a shock opening the door to your old woman.

Bill: But you don't regret it?

Joy: Maybe there'll be other times, other places. And if not, well . . . She's very attractive, isn't she?

Bill: Do you think so?

Joy: Well, don't you?

Bill: Yes. Yes. I do. So many of you are.

Joy: I've only one regret, but that's more or less the usual one.

Bill: What's that then?

Joy: Bill.

Bill: Yes, Joy?

Joy: I have one flaw in my character. Well, not just one, but one that crops up all the time. You see I want to have sex constantly, I mean I'm always wanting it, I always have.

Bill: Joy, for a woman to make that admission is no shame, believe you me.

Joy: Ah, but everyone tells you differently. Right? You lose a man's respect, you lose your own sense of respect and all that old load of rubbish. Right?

Bill: Right.

Joy: So. So I've always felt guilty. There it is, daft, but I am. So I have to get them to say 'I love you.' And then, then I say 'I love you.'

Bill: And then?

Joy: And then. Then: I feel better. [Pause.] You see.

Bill: I'm sorry.

Joy: Don't be. You don't love me. And I don't love you. But

it's all right. Isn't it? [*She kisses him lightly.*] You're a funny old thing. You're scared, aren't you?

BILL: Yes.

JOY: Well, Joy won't leave you. Not yet a while. What do you want doing?

BILL: I don't know. Just cope, will you?

JOY: Sure.

BILL: There's this Tonks thing. And that boy. The indecent assault. Or was it criminal?

JOY: Shall I ask Mr. Jones?

BILL: No. Just hang on to that switchboard.

JOY: All right, love.

BILL: Oh, my daughter's coming in.

JOY: When?

BILL: Sometime this morning. Just send her right in.

JOY: O.K. See you later. [*She goes out.*]

BILL [*Calls out.*]: Oh, try and see if you can get Mrs. Garnsey personally, and I'll talk to her. If not, if not remind me to send a letter. [*Presently* JONES *looks in.*] Well?

JONES: Joy told me to bring in the rest.

BILL: Great.

JONES: There's not a great deal.

BILL: Not a great deal. Any money in? Any business? Any problems?

[JONES *looks dull.*]

JONES: Only what you see there. Mr. Hudson told me to sort it out for you.

BILL: Sort it out? Yes, I'll bet. Do you think old Wally's going to leave us?

JONES: No idea. Except he's had an offer from Piffards.

BILL: What do you think about that?

JONES: Well, they're a very respected firm. Aren't they?

BILL: Very.

JONES: Not much criminal stuff.

BILL: No.

JONES: Libel, isn't it?

BILL: Quite a lot. Would you like that?

JONES: What—libel? Not specially.

BILL: What would you like specially?

JONES: Oh, I don't know. It's all much the same when you come down to it, isn't it?

BILL: But if they—Piffards—offered you a job, you'd take it, wouldn't you?

JONES: Well, I, I'm not likely to be asked, at this stage, anyway, am I?

BILL: No. [*Pause.*]

JONES: Have I done something wrong?

BILL: No, nothing. I admit I've tried to catch you out. But usually, you come round. Even if it takes a little time. You're pretty solid, I'd say. Solid but forward-looking, you know a child of the jet age, a new age of fulfilment with streamlined institutions, a sense of purpose and looking forward to the new frontiers of knowledge. If Mr. Hudson leaves, do you think you could take his place?

JONES: I don't know. I might.

BILL: But you might not. You might go elsewhere?

JONES: Well, I haven't had a lot of experience yet, and it doesn't do any harm to strike out a bit—

BILL: That's right. I think you should. What's this?

JONES: Tonks *v.* Tonks. Anderson *v.* Anderson and Maples. Oh, and that's the supplemental petition.

BILL: What's Maples?

JONES: Indecent assault.

BILL: Well, what are you giving him to me for?

JONES: Well, Mr. Hudson thought you'd be better to deal with this one.

BILL: Yes, I see. Has this been sent to counsel?

JONES: Mr. Hudson said you might like to have a word with Mr. Winters about it, but he said he didn't think he'd touch it.

BILL: He'll touch it if I ask him. [*Disbelief between them.*]

JONES: Well, if you like, I can give them to Mr. Winters this morning.

BILL: No, I'll do it. But I'll see Maples first. Otherwise, if you send him straight down to Winters, he'll carve him up. What do you make of him?

JONES: Maples? Not much.

BILL: Oh?

JONES: Well, he hums and hahs. And stammers.

BILL: Perhaps he's nervous. At being prosecuted by the police.

JONES: But he's a bit affected at the same time.

BILL: Does he seem like a pouf?

JONES [*Casually.*]: Yes. I should say so.

BILL: Do you believe him?

JONES: Well, it's a bit fishy, isn't it?

BILL: Yes.

JONES: I mean, put him up before old Glover, and I wouldn't give him much chance. First offender and all, six months.

BILL: We'll just hope the old bastard breaks a leg. I don't think he's ever missed a day yet though. Sir Watkin Glover, V.C. For Vicious Character.

JONES: And then there's Mr. Simley.

BILL: Who's that? Oh, yes, the bank manager who's a flasher. Perhaps I can do something for Maples. What time's he due?

JONES: Eleven.

BILL: Try not to let me keep him waiting.

JONES: I'm going out.

BILL: Oh, yes. Well, tell Joy. All we want is one good reliable person.

JONES: What?

BILL: A witness?

JONES: Oh.

BILL: There isn't one is there?

JONES: No.

BILL: Well, we'll see. I like the sound of Maples. Better than I like Piffards. Ask Joy to get me a glass of water.

JONES: O.K.

BILL: Most of these police jobs are decided by someone quite outside the event. They're not the only ones who can 'lean' on the evidence. You think someone's going to shop me to the Law Society one day, don't you? Someone will send an anonymous little note, and I'll get a summons to defend my professional conduct. I wonder who it'll be. Someone's sure to do it. It's surprising it's not happened before. I've been threatened with it, you see. Someone at Piffards actually. He never did. I don't know why. Milson it was, not the old man, he wouldn't have bothered with me. The young one. I wonder who it will be though. Someone—[*Pause.*]

JONES: I hear you've lost Mrs. Garnsey.

BILL: What do you mean *I've* lost Mrs. Garnsey?

JONES: Well, *we've* lost Mrs. Garnsey. The firm has.

BILL: The *firm* has? I'm writing her a letter. Something went wrong. I scared her off. In some way. I could feel her withdrawing from me. I'm the wrong man for these things. You and Hudson should do them. *You're* the right people. You can handle them—I can't. They turn away from me, and they're probably right. [*He looks at the papers on his desk.*] And you really can't either of you, do these?

JONES: You know what we've got in. Well, I'll get on. You wanted a glass of water. O.K.?

BILL: When are you getting married?

JONES: Don't know yet. I haven't really make up my mind. Still, there's no hurry. About these things. Is there?

BILL: No. Not if you don't feel it. [*JONES goes out. BILL picks up a divorce petition and starts reading in a low voice.*] In the High Court of Justice, Probate Divorce and Admiralty Division. Divorce. To the High Court of Justice the 27th day of January 1964. The humble petition of Maureen Sheila Tonks. Maureen. I remember Maureen. She always, well not always, but most times I went out with her, wore hand-knitted suits, knitted by her mother. They'd always shrink and they were in horrible colours and her skirts would be too short because of it, which worried her. It worried me, but she always seemed to be in some pain, some funny pain, *physical* pain I mean. It was never any good. Which was a pity because she has the most strange blue eyes with dark hair, very dark. English beauty her mother called it. English beauty. And Sheila. Well I remember two of them. One was Scots with white, flaky skin. She rode a bicycle with a crossbar and didn't give a damn. She'd punch and go at you like a boy, but she'd cry too when it came to it.

JOY [*Entering.*]: Mrs. Tonks to see you.

BILL [*Rises.*]: Ah, Good Morning. [*MRS. TONKS enters. It is the same woman as MRS. GARNSEY. Played by the same actress.*] Please sit down. Would you like some tea or coffee?

Mrs. Tonks: No, thank you very much.

Bill: Right. Thank you, Joy. [JOY *goes out*.] Right. Now. I'll just give this to you, if you'd care to look at it. I want you to go over it very carefully. It's your petition, the smaller one is the supplemental petition. Mr. Hudson's just prepared it so there may be one or two things—[*Pause.*] All right?

Mrs. T. [*She nods presently. She begins.*]: The humble petition of Maureen Sheila Tonks. That. On the twenty-first day of April 1958, your petitioner Maureen Sheila Tonks, then Maureen Sheila Williams, Spinster, was lawfully married to Richard George Tonks, hereinafter called the respondent, at the Parish Church of St. Hilda's in the County Borough of Leicester. That. After the said marriage, your petitioner and the respondent lived and cohabited at divers addresses and from October 1960 to August 1963 or thereabouts at 42 Macwilliam Street.

Bill: Lived and cohabited.

Mrs. T.: Save and except that in the application of the petitioner by reason of the respondent's cruelty, the Justices of the Petty Sessional Division of Kingston did on the 12th day of August 1963 make an order that the petitioner be no longer bound to cohabit, to live with and cohabit, with the respondent and that he should pay her a weekly sum of two pounds seventeen shillings.

Bill: Skip on to paragraph nine. [*She fumbles.*] There.

Mrs. T: That. That the respondent is a man of excessive sexual appetite who has habitually and constantly made sexual demands on the petitioner which he knew she regarded as inordinate or revolting.

Bill: Habitually and constantly. I'm sorry. . . . In your husband's answers, which, admittedly aren't very coherent, he says. Now. Paras one to seven correct. Para eight I deny that I have been cruel to my wife. Here we are, paragraph nine: I deny being a man of excessive sexual appetite. There were never sexual relations between us except by mutual agreement [*Pause.*] Are you all right? [*She nods.*] Right, let's get on then.

Mrs. T: That. On many occasions, occasions insisted on having intercourse three times and even four times a day. He adopted a practice he termed . . .

BILL: Paragraph twelve, your husband says the allegations contained are a gross exaggeration of the true facts.

MRS. T: That the respondent refused to cease from having intercourse during the time of the petitioner's menstrual periods at 42 Macwilliam Street and number 11 Wicker Street, notwithstanding the petitioner's entreaties. . . .

BILL: There were difficulties between us. Such that my wife failed to reach satisfaction.

MRS. T: That. On frequent occasions at the said addresses whilst he was having intercourse with petitioner he did . . .

BILL: My wife visited the Marriage Guidance Council on at least three occasions who told her they believed the difficulty was due to my wife's reluctance. . . .

MRS. T: Notwithstanding the fact that he knew the petitioner found this conduct revolting and upsetting.

BILL: We've none of us been reluctant much, have we? Well, there were girls like Maureen, and even with you there were difficulties but not revolting or upsetting. At least, not much, I don't think so. You weren't reluctant, you should be happy, you didn't cling on to it like it was the crown jewels. You were generous, loving, bright, you should have been able to cope. *I* should have been able to cope.

MRS. T: He told the petitioner he liked to hear the noise made by . . .

BILL: To have another child. Another child. In spite of the advice given to her by the Counsel she refused to use this.

MRS. T: That. It was his desire to have sexual intercourse with a woman in this street to whom he referred. . . .

BILL: Because she said it was nasty. Nasty and messy.

MRS. T: He constantly referred to as 'that great big beautiful blonde bat.'

BILL: I wonder if it was real or dyed. Not that it matters.

MRS. T: On at least eleven occasions during the marriage he attempted to commit . . .

BILL: I deny that I persisted.

MRS. T: And did in fact.

BILL: There is no truth at all in this.

MRS. T: Upon the person of the petitioner, compelling the petitioner with force to submit.

BILL: I respected my wife's feelings at all times and especially . . .

MRS. T: To these malpractices. That. In March 1961 when the petitioner was seven months pregnant with the child Laura, the respondent violently chastised the child Edward with a heavy brush of a type . . .

BILL: No truth at all in these allegations. . . .

MRS. T: After the said occurrence on the 19th July 1961 . . .

BILL: As described, bears no relation to what actually happened. I do admit there were many times when I failed. Many times.

MRS. T: The petitioner left the respondent.

BILL: I failed in giving her complete satisfaction. My wife left me on the 12th day of September 1963.

MRS. T: Wherefore your petitioner humbly prays that the court will exercise its discretion in her favour and decree (1) That. The said marriage may be dissolved. (2) That. She may be granted the custody of the children of the said marriage. (3) That. The respondent be condemned in the costs of the proceedings.

BILL:All the time we have lived together she has been a very highly strung person. She has been constantly depressed and been to the doctor, but it all seems to have come to no good. I have done all I can. Signed. Richard George Tonks. [*Pause.*]

[JOY *enters.*]

JOY: I'm sorry, but Mrs. Anderson is downstairs. What do you want me to do?

BILL: Has Mr. Jones gone yet?

JOY: He's just leaving.

BILL: Well, stop him. He can't leave yet. Not yet. We need . . . Mrs. Tonks, would you mind going into the other room? I think you've met Mr. Jones. There are one or two things to be sorted out here, and, we really ought to get on with them. All right? [*She smiles.*] I've just got someone else to see. You'll be looked after. You'll be looked after. It's *not* a question of passing you on. All right? Joy will look after you. I'm sure you wouldn't mind a cup of coffee or something now? [JOY *takes* MRS. TONKS *out*. BILL *picks up another petition.*] Audrey Jane Anderson. Audrey, I remember Audrey. Even an Audrey Jane. I thought she was a bit posh. Except she wasn't. She just took elocution and dancing and wore patent shoes. I think. I'm not sure, I though I could remember. And I've no idea of what's to come. I can't even call to mind little details like that. If only it could be fixed. And improved. Improved. But it doesn't, nothing does. I can't even reassemble it. Why do I do it? Well, not because it's good. I suppose: I suppose: because it still has a little withered ball of interest. Somewhere. Audrey Jane Anderson. The returns are coming in and they aren't good. [JOY *enters with* MRS. ANDERSON. *Again it is the same woman as* MRS. GARNSEY, *as* MRS. TONKS.] Ah. Please sit down. Would you like some tea or coffee?

MRS. ANDERSON: No thank you.

BILL: All right. Thank you, Joy. [JOY *goes out.*] Right. Now. I'll just give this to you. Mrs. Anderson. If you'd like to take a look at it. It's just a rough, rough summary of the statement Mr. Jones, Mr. Hudson took down for you. So I'm sure there'll be one or two things to clear up. All right? [*She nods.*] Good. Carry on then.

MRS. A: Audrey Jane Anderson will prove as follows:

BILL: What goes wrong? Nothing happens for you, I fail you, and you're frightened and full of dislike.

MRS. A: I was married at Kidderminster Registry Office. I was a spinster. My maiden name was Wall. My husband was then a clerk in the local post office. Our marriage—

BILL: Our marriage. What a phrase.

MRS. A: Our marriage seemed normal for a time and reasonably happy. There were difficulties owing to the fact that we were living at my mother's house, 148 Chadacre Road, for two years. [BILL *makes a massive effort to assemble the facts in his mind. It is very difficult.*]

BILL: Two years. You know, you mustn't expect people to behave well towards you, Audrey. You mustn't. I know you have and I know you will.

MRS. ANDERSON: There was discord when I was pregnant with the little boy Patrick John.

BILL: Patrick John.

MRS. A: My parents persuaded me to return to him.

BILL: You must always ask yourself. Is it dangerous or is it safe? And then make your choice. If you can, if you can.

MRS. A: Things became increasingly unhappy and difficult when
my husband gave up his job and became a traveller for a
firm in electrical fittings. He was able to be at home most
of the time, but when he was away, never more than for the
odd day or two, he would accuse me of going out with men.

BILL: Well. She thinks I've got mistresses all over London. They
both do. And it's not even true. Worst luck. No, thank God.

MRS. A: He said I ought to go on the streets.

BILL: You might have met me then. You might have been
worse off.

MRS. A: I have never been with anyone apart from my husband.

BILL: That's what's wrong with all of you, you dim deluded
little loving things. You listen to promiscuous lady journalists
and bishops and your mother. And hang on to it.

MRS. A: But he's always saying these things.

BILL: He listens.

MRS. A: It's as if he can't help it. When he wanted to, he would
have intercourse two or three times a day. He would, he would
go as far as he could but that was all. But it's not only that,
it's not even that. If it were only that I could put up with
all kinds of things. Because I know he is a good man, really,
and a kind man. He can be, and he has been kind to me.

BILL: I love you. He never said, he hardly ever said, he stopped
saying, he found it difficult to say I love you. It has to be
heaved and dropped into the pool after you, a great rock of
I love you, and then you have to duck down below the surface and bring it up, like some gasping, grateful, stupid dog.

MRS. A: He loves the children, and is always making a fuss of
them, and giving them things. My sister used to come in to
watch T. V., but I hardly ever went out while she was there.
We went to the doctor and he made me go to Weymouth
for two weeks for a complete rest.

BILL: I often think of my dying. And her, I mean. Of her being
a widow. As opposed to a wife. A blackened wife. Of the
kind of suit she would wear and wear and where she would
get it from. She hasn't got a useful black suit. Liz has, but I
don't think she'd get there. Which worries me. Because the
idea of her not being there is disturbing. I've asked her to be
there, and she's promised me, which is damned silly and a

lot to ask, especially if you think of her having to face Anna in her black suit. I wonder if they'd notice what the other was wearing. In the crematorium with all that G-Plan light oak and electrical department brass fittings and spanking new magenta hassocks. And the pink curate sending me off at thirty bob a head as I go rattling on little rails behind him and disappear like a truck on the ghost train at Dreamland, in the Amusement Park, behind the black curtains, and all the noise.

MRS. A: I am on National Assistance. Three pounds twelve shilling a week. I am not working now, not since early May.

BILL: But did you really enjoy work? Did you? You didn't enjoy sex. Wasn't it just another effort, um? I mean an effort on your part, some way of helping, of fighting off what's going to happen to you?

MRS. A: I'm still under the doctor. The defendant has given me housekeeping all the time—barring a short period of about a fortnight. He has not touched me sexually since August Bank Holiday. He slept in another room for a few weeks, but he used to cry quite often and it kept me awake. We would both cry sometimes. He offered to leave me alone. I told him I would leave him if that's what he wanted. I still wanted some happiness for him. We are buying the house and the T.V. has been paid for. He said he would save for the down payment on a car and take us all out—a mini—and take us all out at the weekends to the sea. I am quite sure he meant it. I think he wanted to, I think he really did.

BILL: There was a time when I used to speculate about *her* death. Oh, but not only Anna's. I'd be crunching back up that new path with the planks and the wet clay and the flowers. Perhaps I'd have walked out of that place on my own, there'd have been no one else, I could have done as I liked. I could have sat in Lyons and got myself a cup of coffee and a roll and butter all on my own. I might have looked around me, and my throat would have been tight and I'd have trouble with my coffee, and I'd smile sentimentally at the coloured girl who was clearing away the plates just because she was coloured, and my throat seemed to be closed up with the business of dying, and I'd kid myself we were friendly to one

another. I might have gone mad and bought myself a new
suit. Something a bit too sharp for someone my age and
size, but I'd have stalked into some popular camp store and
got something off the peg. And some shirts. I'd make up my
mind to throw out all my old shirts and buy new ones, clean
cotton shirts with that new smell, and lots of large handker-
chiefs. All new. I'd have walked around, trying to remember
London, trying to put it together, looking for street musicians
with my pockets full of change.

MRS. A: I have often contributed to finance. Often by simply
going without new things or buying things cheap from my
sister.

BILL: I think I'd have gone on a bus. An eleven or a thirty-eight.
All the way. Say, from Putney to Hackney.

MRS. A: When he gets in at night after work and early in the
morning. Before I get up to get his breakfast.

BILL: I'd have had dinner alone, very, very slowly. I'd have
had a cigar and a Calvados or Marc de Bourgogne. Or—and
—or I'd have gone to the pictures or a theatre with no one
beside me except my new overcoat and a new book to read
at home in bed, a new novel perhaps, by some woman perhaps. Something which might surprise me, take me by surprise a bit. Something I hadn't quite thought of, or not in
that way, or so well, or, but not something that necessarily,
no, something that didn't disturb me. Perhaps something
easier. Something new but old. Something. A fat biography,
perhaps something scandalous, about Marshall Hall. Or Rufus
Isaacs. Something new.

MRS. A: He says I'm not natural. He says I'm not like a woman
should be.

BILL: My death and hers. Theirs? Yours: and mine. Who
first? Um?

MRS. A: He says I've no intelligence and no brains and no
education. And I'm not fit to run anything, not even a brothel.
I have not imagined, imagined any of these things because
I may be unhappy or unwell. [*Her voice is disappearing, but
she rallies for her last speech.*]

BILL: Good. Now. Joy!

[JOY *appears*.]

MRS. A: I know I'm no good at all to him. He humiliates me. I know he hates me. I wish I could have done better. That I could go back. [JOY *touches her shoulder and she follows her out. Pause.*]

BILL: Joy!

JOY: Yes.

BILL: Get me Mr. Winters, will you?

JOY: O.K.

BILL: Tell him it's urgent.

JOY: Mr. Maples is downstairs. Shall I send him in?

BILL: No. I want to speak to Winters first. Then afterwards. Did you look after Mrs. Tonks?

JOY: She went.

BILL: Went?

JOY: That's right. Well, I'll get Winters. [*She goes out. Presently her voice comes from his desk.*]

JOY: Mr. Winters is engaged at present.

BILL: Well, of course he is. Hudson's with him isn't he?

JOY: I'll see. [*Pause.*] They say Mr. Hudson's gone.

BILL: What's the matter with them all? Well, put me on to Roberts. [*Pause.*] His managing clerk. Come on. Don't *you* start. [*Pause.*]

JOY [*Off.*] He's not available.

BILL: Not available! But that's his job: to be available. He doesn't ever have to be anything else.

JOY: Well, that's what they say.

BILL: Here: put me on to them.

JOY: What?

BILL: Put me through! Hullo. Charley! Hullo! What's going on? Can I speak to Mr. Roberts, please? What do you mean? Out? He can't be out. I can hear his voice. . . . I tell you: I can hear his voice. . . . I see. . . . All right. . . . Well, please ask him . . . to ring me . . . when he can. [*He puts down the phone.*]

JOY [*Off.*] Shall I send in Mr. Maples?

BILL: No. Get me Mrs. Eaves. Tell him I'm, tell him I'll be a

couple of minutes. Now, get her quickly in case she's popped
out. [*He waits. Very disturbed indeed. Buzz.*]

JOY [*Off.*] Mrs. Eaves.

BILL: Liz! Thank God: I thought you'd gone out. What? Do I?
Well, I'll tell you, I'm sorry, but I just rung up old Winters.
You know. . . . Well, he wouldn't speak to me. Which is all
right, but he always speaks to me, even if it's only for half a
minute, especially if I say it's urgent, which I did. And the
funny thing is I *know* Hudson was with him. They swore he
wasn't but he must have been. He couldn't have finished in
the time. But old Winters and I have been quite pals. I must
have put more work in his way over the past. . . . Exactly. . . .
And he's a nice straightforward . . . a bit brusque, but forthright. He even laughs at . . . And then there was his clerk,
Roberts. Charley Roberts. . . . I picked up the phone and I
heard him say, I heard him say quite clearly 'Oh tell him
I'm out or something. Anything'. He didn't even bother to
lower his voice. It was like talking to you now. . . . But,
Charley. He's not like that. Bit dull, like Hudson. But—he's
just a posh office boy. He's known me fifteen years. . . . But why
should he do that? . . . Well, sorry to bother you. It was a just
funny experience. . . . As soon as we can—I'll ring you. Now,
don't go out, will you? Eh? Well, I'm seeing some kid for impor-
tuning. That could take up a bit . . . Well, Jones has been doing it but he's obviously muffed it, and I'll have to start more or
less . . . I *must* try and help. . . . Yes, perhaps too hard, perhaps.
. . . Well, I'm hoping Jane will come in. . . . I'm just going to
tell her that I shan't be at her birthday weekend. That she
knows quite well it's because I'll be with you, and that to please
be honest with both of us, and own up that she doesn't care
whether I'm there or not and that she's just letting herself be
used, or rather lending herself, as a blunt instrument by her
mother. . . . All right. . . . Don't forget. . . . [*He rings off.*]

JOY [*Off.*]: Shall I—

BILL: Yes. And keep trying Winters. And tell them I know Charley Roberts is there. . . . No, just keep ringing. And when Mr.
Hudson gets in, tell him to come and see me right away.

JOY: O.K.

BILL: And say right away. Even if I have a client with me.

Joy: Yes, Sir. [*Presently she appears at the door and announces—*]
Mr. Maples.

[JONES *comes in.* JONES-MAPLES *has some of* JONES's *unattrac-
tiveness but with other elements. In place of his puny arrogance
and closed mind, there is a quick-witted, improvising nature, not
without courage. His flashes of fear are like bursts of creative
energy, in contrast to* JONES's *whining fixity and confidence.*]

Bill: Mr. Maples. Sorry about all this waiting about for you. I'm
afraid it's . . . Do sit down. No calls, Joy. Right?
Joy: What about Mr. Winters?
Bill: Oh. Yes. Him.
Joy: And.
Bill: I don't know, do I? Use your judgement. Well, try me if
you're not sure. But I must see to Mr. Maples, I must see he's
looked after. We *must* get on with it. [*Slight pause as he falters
into another distraction. They watch him. He wrenches himself
out and dismisses her.*] All right. [JOY *goes out.*] Now, at last.
So sorry. You've [*He looks for* MAPLES' *file. Flips through
papers.*] You've, yes, you've been seeing—Mr. Jones. [MAPLES
nods.] Yes, there's a fairly longish statement. And, of course, a
copy of your statement to the police. And these other things.
. . . It doesn't make a very clear. . . . at the moment, does it?
Shall we start more or less. . . .

[JOY *buzzes.*]

Joy *Off.*]: Your daughter's here.
Bill: Ask her to wait.
Joy: Only thing is she says she's not got very long. Shall I—
Bill: Who has? Tell her to wait. Give her a cup of tea and discuss
your teenage interests together.
Joy: I'm no teenager, thank you!
Bill: No one would know it. And look—don't let her go. She's
got to stay and see me. After I'm through with Mr. Maples. Tell
her that. [*Switches off.*] Fresh start was right. Yes, let me say
to you— [*He is thrown by the image of his daughter waiting
outside. She is just visible to the audience.*] As your lawyer, you

have no, no obligations to me. Whatsoever. However, if you wish me to act in your interests, you should regard me like, the, the Queen, with the right to, to be consulted, to encourage and to warn I don't even ask for the truth. You may not be capable of it, it's difficult to retain for most of us, some of us at least, and when you're in a spot of trouble, as well, you are, let's be quite honest about it, and you feel you are gradually being deserted and isolated, it becomes elusive, more than ever, one can grasp so little, trust nothing, it's inhuman to be expected to be capable of giving a decent account of oneself. . . . Could you just shift your chair a little nearer to the desk. There, then I can see you properly. I hate to have my clients halfway across the room, having to talk to themselves. Instead of to me. Shall we see if we can't find anything that's been left out. [*Pause.*] Who are you?

[*When* MAPLES *replies, his delivery adopts roughly the same style as in the* MRS. GARNSEY-ANDERSON-TONKS *dialogue.*]

MAPLES: How can I describe myself to you? I do seem to be very ordinary, don't I?

BILL: I don't know. I wish I could see you more clearly. This statement . . .

MAPLES: Isn't true.

BILL: Well, I knew that before you came in.

[*Presently, he gives his evidence, like* BILL *himself. Mostly at speed, more polemic than reflection.*]

MAPLES: All right then. My name is John Montague, after my uncle Monty, Maples. I am married, I am quite young though I don't feel as if being young ever happened to me. I've always been married or in the army or living with my parents. I have one child, aged six, a little girl, Daphne, Susan, my wife's choice not mine. My wife's name is Hilda. That was about the only name she didn't need to be talked out of as she hated it too. I met Hilda when I was still doing my National Service, which was a bit of a difficult time for me. But it isn't very interesting to tell anyone because I don't have any proper characteristics at all, save one, and there's not even any interest in that, any more than there is in being five feet seven or prone to hay fever. Physically I'm lazy, on the whole, that is, but it doesn't stop me being restless. I can't stop at home, but most of the time I'm scared to death of putting my nose outside the front door. But sometimes I do. I'm there somehow, on the, because of some row with Hilda, or some excuse or I get back late from one of the shops, and in twenty five minutes I'm in the West End. I used to like to play tennis, which I'm rather good at—And badminton, that too, I played that at school. Hilda doesn't like anything like that, and I haven't bothered. But I used to be rather good and full of energy and I could beat quite a lot of the others. There were always a few, though, and we used to have wonderful, great long duels when we should have been doing our homework. And it might even end up in a bit of a fight. A couple of times I even burst into tears when I was playing against someone called Shipley, his name was. He thought I was a bit mad, but it was all right. We were old friends. Nothing else. We talked about girls constantly, all the time. [BILL *tries to take some of this in.* MAPLES *sees the effort and slows down the concentration for a few moments.*] I'm sorry.

BILL: No. Go on.

MAPLES: Well, I met my wife, Hilda, while I was still in the Services.

BILL: Yes, I see. Let's see, you're . . .

MAPLES: I'm in the drapery business. My father-in-law's business actually, but I've done a bit about building it up. He had this old shop in Richmond, you see, ribbons, buttons, calico, towels, oh—cheap lot of old stuff. He'd have lost the lot in another year. Then Hilda and I got engaged, while I was still in the forces. There was nothing much I could think of to do then, I wanted. I'd got a pass 'O' level in G.C.E. but I didn't have a clue what to do with it. And I'd a sort of feeling for materials and I could organize a bit. I got rid of some of the old hags in the shop. Anyone could have done it, honestly. Anyway, now there's these three shops—the old one, one in Kingston and a new one just opened up in Hounslow. I'd come back late from Hounslow on this particular night.

BILL: Tell me about the arrest.

MAPLES: All right.

BILL: So I might as well throw this away.

MAPLES: I'll have to tell you about Denis.

BILL: Denis who? Oh, all right, tell me later.

MAPLES: Well, a year ago I nearly left Hilda. I fell in love. I still think it was the first time. But I couldn't bear the thought that I couldn't get over it, that it was bigger than me, however ordinary I might be. I never liked girls except my sister but she wasn't always easy to talk to. She could be suspicious and sort of unwelcoming. We all talked about girls all the time and we'd play games like seeing how we could look up their skirts when they were playing games or going upstairs on the bus.

BILL: I'll bet Shipley was good at that.

MAPLES: Yes. He was.

BILL: So was I, I'm afraid.

MAPLES: The only thing that excited me was playing tennis, and especially the badminton with him. I'd sweat for hours, before, during and afterwards, and I couldn't get my homework done in time for bed which scared me because I was terrified of getting into trouble or being found out in even little things, like not dubbing my football boots or never understanding what 'parsing' was. I never wanted to marry Hilda or anyone else but I was scared stupid, I was stupid anyway, not to. My mother was always going on about the rottenest thing men did was to get girls pregnant, which is what I did, of course. So did my brother. But it didn't matter for him. He's got three more now, and he's happy enough, and so's mother. No, I was never very fixed on her. My father's *much* nicer. Yes, I know you're thinking he was ineffectual and all that, but so was she, what was she so good at, at least he didn't scare anyone, or lean on anyone. He's all right. He maybe should have belted her across the chops a few times, but I doubt if anything or any of us could have changed. No, I never liked girls, but I didn't like men who didn't seem like men either. I think I believe in God. Still, I seem to let things happen to me. I have always let the others make the first advances, usually if it's possible in the dark, or with the lights turned down or something of that sort.

BILL: What about Hilda?

MAPLES: Oh, Hilda. We're getting on better.

BILL: And—she knows about this charge?

MAPLES: Oh yes. One of the detectives made a big point, coming round. We even had a drink together, the three of us by the end of it. I was offering him a drink. And he took it. But he knew what he was doing—I couldn't bribe anyone, not anywhere. I suppose you'll have to get up and say 'his wife is standing by him.'

BILL: Well it often makes a better impression in Court to say you're undergoing medical treatment.

MAPLES: Shall I tell you what the doctor said to me?

BILL: No. I've heard it. Did you get another doctor?

MAPLESS Yes. He agrees with *me*. But then he's the same. Just keep out of the law, keep out of the law and not to invite trouble. I don't want to change. I want to be who I am. But I stayed with Hilda, I'd even given up Denis four months ago, I hadn't spoken to him even for four months and this happened. On the way back from the new Hounslow shop. Hilda's mother tries to call it a boutique, but I think I've talked her out of that now. I used to have to get drunk, first, like I did when I forced myself into bed with Hilda and got married for it. But I haven't had to do that for a long time. Do you think I should plead guilty?

BILL: Not yet.

MAPLES: What's the advantage?

BILL: Of pleading guilty? It has the advantage of certainty, that's all.

MAPLES: That sounds very attractive at the moment.

BILL: Well, I can't even guarantee that yet.

[JOY *buzzes.*]

JOY: I'm sorry, but your daughter wants to know how much longer, because she can come back.

BILL: Tell her she's got to wait. I don't care. She's got to wait. Now tell her. [*Switches off.*] Can I offer you anything? [MAPLES *shakes his head.*]

MAPLES: Sometimes I would think I was unique, of course. You know, years ago. I hoped I was. But I'm not. I'm ordinary. But I wish I wasn't. I didn't have a clue. Nothing happened until after I was married, after Daphne was born. For some reason

I got on the wrong train, but it was the right direction more or less and I just stayed on it, standing up, all those bodies pressed together and suddenly I felt two, maybe three, fingers touch me, very lightly. Every time the train stopped more people got out and there was more room. I was scared to look up from my paper and there wasn't any longer any excuse to be so close to anyone. A great draught of air came in from the platform and I felt cold, and it was Gunnersbury Station which is not too far from me, so I looked up and got out. I didn't dare look back but I heard the footsteps behind me. That was the first time and I'd had a few drinks first and I was very cold, at the back of some row of shops called something Parade, by the Midland Bank. About half past seven at night. That's about all I remember of it. When I got in, my dinner was all overcooked and simmering on a plate over the gas stove with the gravy gone hard round the edge of the plate, which is a bit like the way Hilda does things, spills them or upsets them or does them too much and she wasn't feeling well and couldn't get the baby to sleep. I went out into the garden, put my fingers down my throat and then buried it all with a trowel. If I wasn't married I'd have done it all the time, one to another, I suppose, but I don't think so. That's never been what I wanted. Oh, not that I haven't behaved. . . . They're right to get me, people like me. There was a young fellow, a sales manager at a store in Kingston. Do you know what I did? He was married. Nice girl. Rather attractive, not long married. Well, I set my sights and one night the three of us went out, got drunk, and while, all the time, while his wife was in the front—

BILL: Driving?—

MAPLES: Driving—

BILL: Actually in the back?

MAPLES: And she never knew. We were so damned sharp, she never knew from beginning to end. Still doesn't know. Like Hilda, she never knew about Denis, about giving him up. I gave him up, you see. He wanted me to leave Hilda and take on a new life altogether. He begged me. He threatened to phone up or write to me. But he hasn't. He kept his promise. I longed to break the whole thing, and I think I would have done this particular night.

BILL: Do you still want to give him up?

MAPLES: No.

BILL: Do you think he's given you up? [*Pause.*]

MAPLES: Yes. Probably. What's going to happen to me?

BILL: I don't know enough yet. I need to know more than that. I should think Sir Watkin Glover Q.C. is sure to apply the full rigour of the law and send the both of us down. What about the police?

MAPLES: I've only had one brush with the police before. Late one night by Turnham Green. He flashed his torch on us. He let the other one go, but he took my name and address and made me meet him the next night. Only about three times. I know you think I haven't tried. I can't make any more effort, any more, I want to plead guilty.

BILL: Well, you can't, now go on!

MAPLES: He asked me for a light, this policeman.

BILL: In plain clothes?

MAPLES: Naturally.

BILL: Look, try to help me, will you. Where?

MAPLES: Piccadilly Tube Station.

BILL: You're crazy.

MAPLES: I know. But I knew it was going to happen. Sounds camp, but then the truth so often is. He was quite young, younger than I am, with lots of fair, wavy hair, like mine used to be, when I just went in the Army, before I met Hilda, before it started to go; he looked up. In the usual way. His eyes were pale and his cheekbones looked sharp and frail as if you could have smashed them with a knock from your finger, but when he walked away, you could see how really strong he must be. He walked straight into the cottage at number one entrance, you know, by the Regent Palace. And that was it. There was another one in there and they both of them grabbed me. Savile Row Station. Oh, quite gently, And no surprise to any of us. Denis and I had often talked about it happening. They seemed nice enough at first. I began to feel better and relaxed, as if I was being loved openly and attended on, and then, then the pressure turned on. What I ought to do. What the magistrate would say. What they knew. The one who had asked for the light had seen me with Denis. He said they knew all about him.

About both of us. I had to keep him out of it. I knew nothing could be worse. So I, I signed this statement. And there it is. In front of you. So. Are you all right?

BILL [*Just audible.*]: Yes.

MAPLES: You haven't taken anything down. Was it . . .

BILL: Don't worry, we'll go through it all again with Hudson.

MAPLES: No. I don't think so.

BILL: You haven't seen me, my friend, you haven't seen me, cross-examining coppers is my speciality. But we'll get Winters in on this. Was there anybody else there? It's a pity nobody saw you. [MAPLES *rises.*] Joy! What's happening about Winters?

JOY [*Off.*]: I tell you: I keep trying.

BILL: Well, Hudson'll be in soon. Tell him to come straight in. [*Switches off.*] Don't move. It's only my daughter outside. It's a pity about nobody seeing you. Oh, well—perhaps there was. [*Pause.*] Don't worry—we'll get someone. [*They look at each other.*]

MAPLES: Thank you. [*Pause.*] In the meantime, maybe you'd better see your daughter. [*He goes out. Presently* JANE *comes in.* BILL, *barely seeing her, waves her to the chair* MAPLES *has been sitting in. Slowly he takes her in. He buzzes* JOY.]

BILL: Joy!

JOY [*Off.*]: Well?

BILL: Joy.

JOY [*Off.*]: Yes?

BILL: Don't let Mr. Maples go.

JOY [*Off.*]: Well, I'm sorry—

BILL: All right. No. Wait.

JOY [*Sympathetically. Off.*]: Yes?

BILL: Get me another glass of water. [*He looks across at his daughter. She fidgets. Slowly.*] You can wait just: one more minute—

[FADE.]

[FADE UP *on* JANE *and* BILL *together.* BILL's *speech must be started at the full flood. When he fails it is with his longing. His daughter is cool, distressed, scared.*]

BILL: They're all pretending to ignore me. No they're not pretending, they are! And that'll be the going of you except that it's happened already. Of course, it has, ages ago. Look at me. Why you can't have looked at me and seen anything, what, not for years, not since you were a little tiny girl and I used to take you out and hold your hand in the street. I always used to think then that when you're the age you are now, I'd take you out to restaurants for dinner, big restaurants like I used to think posh restaurants were like, with marble columns and glass and orchestras. Like Lyons used to be before you knew it. And I thought we'd behave like a rather grand married couple, a bit casual but with lots and lots of signals for one another. And waves of waiters would pass in front of us and admire us and envy us and we'd dance together. [*Holds her to him.*] Very slowly. [*Pause.*] And when we got back to our table, and when it was all over, we'd lean forward and look at each other with such, such oh, pleasure—we'd hardly be able to eat our dinner. [*Releases her.*] So that when we got up, after a bit too much champagne, we'd have to hang on to each other very tightly indeed. And then: go home. . . . I always wish I'd been brought up in the country you know. Won't be possible much longer. There isn't any place for me, not like you. In the law, in the country, or, indeed, in any place in this city. My old father lives in the country, as you know, but he doesn't want to see me these days. Can't say I blame him. When I went to see him the other day—whenever it was, do you know, I tried to remind him of all sorts of things we'd done together, but he simply wouldn't, he wouldn't remember. And then the old devil got mad and told me I was imagining it. I had to go in the end. He was tired and he wanted me to go. When I bent down and kissed him, he didn't look up. . . . Your other grandparents can hardly bring themselves to acknowledge me. The old woman crossed to the other side of the street once when I was pushing you in the pram so as to avoid speaking to me. Which surprised me. With you, I mean. They have you over there and your mother goes, I know, and they still give you generous presents Christmas and birthday, but do you know when they write to your mother, they never even mention me by name, love to Bill, how's Bill, nothing, not for ten years, and they only did it in the early years after you were born because they thought they had to if they were going to be able to see you! And then they discovered

that they didn't even have to mime that genteel little courtesy.
How much do you think your safety depends on the goodwill
of others? Well? Tell me. Or your safety? How safe do you
think you are? How? Safe? [*She turns away increasingly frightened.*] Do you want to get rid of me? Do *you*? Um? Because
I want to get rid of you. [*She moves to the door. Toweringly
cool for a while.*] Just a moment, Jane. You can't go yet. Till I
tell you. About this famous weekend. [*She shrugs impatiently.*]
Oh, I know it's none of your fault. But you should know I
shan't be with you, or, at least, your mother then, just because
I shall be with Liz—a subject that bores you, I know, as much
as it's beginning to her, if you see—I'll be with her for three
whole days or something, if she'll have me, I don't know that
she will, but I'll be with her instead of you on your seventeenth
—is it seventeen?—anyway, birthday and the reason for that is
because I know: that when I see you, I cause you little else but
distaste or distress, or, at the least, your own vintage, swinging,
indifference. But nothing, certainly not your swinging distaste
can match what I feel for you. [*Small pause as he changes
tack.*] Or any of those who are more and more like you. Oh, I
read about you, I see you in the streets. I hear what you say,
the sounds you make, the few jokes you make, the wounds you
inflict without even longing to hurt, there is no lather or fear in
you, all cool, dreamy, young, cool and not a proper blemish,
forthright, unimpressed, contemptuous of ambition but good
and pushy all the same. You've no shame of what you are, and
very little, well, not much doubt as to what you'll become. And
quite right, at least so I used to think. They're young, I said,
and for the first time they're being allowed to roll about in it
and have clothes and money and music and sex, and you can
take or leave any of it. No one before has been able to do such
things with such charm, such ease, such frozen innocence as all
of you seem to have, to me. Only you, and girls like you,
naturally, could get on that poor old erotic carthorse, the well-
known plastic mac and manage to make it look pretty. Pretty,
mark you! Chic. Lively. You've stopped its lumbering, indecent,
slobbering ancient longing and banged it into the middle of the
Daily Express—where they're only allowed to say the word
'rape' if a black African's involved. Or perhaps a nun. *You* don't

even, not moved, to wear make-up any longer. Your hair looks like a Yorkshire terrier's come in from out of the monsoon. And, yet, somehow, perversely, you are more beautiful and certainly more dashing than any of the girls I used to know and lust after from morning to night, with their sweety tacky lipsticks and silk stockings on coupons and permanent waves and thick-hipped heavy skirts. I don't know what you have to do with me at all, and soon you won't, you'll go out of that door and I'll not see you again. I am quite sure of *that* by this time if nothing else. You hardly drink except for some wine and pintfuls of murky coffee. You'll go anywhere and more or less seem to do anything, you've already permanent sunless, bleached stains beneath your breasts and two, likewise, crescents, on your buttocks. You'll read any menu without bothering, order what you want, and, what's more, get it. Then maybe leave it. You'll hitchhike and make your young noises from one end of Europe to the other without a thought of having the correct currency or the necessary language. And you're right. And you dance with each other, in such a way I would never have been able to master. [*He gazes longingly across.*] But, and this is the but, I still don't think what you're doing will ever, even, even, even approach the fibbing, mumping, pinched little worm of energy eating away in this me, of mine, I mean. That is: which is that of being slowly munched and then diminished altogether. That worm, thank heaven, is not in your little cherry rose. You are unselfconscious, which I am not. You are without guilt, which I am not. Quite rightly. Of course, you are stuffed full of paltry relief for emergent countries, and marches and boycotts and rallies, you, you kink your innocent way along tirelessly to all that poetry and endless jazz and folk worship, *and* looking gay and touching and stylish all at the same time. But there isn't much loving in any of your kindnesses, Jane, not much kindness, not even cruelty, really, in any of you, not much craving for the harm of others, perhaps just a very easy, controlled sharp, I mean 'sharp' pleasure in discomfiture. You're flip and offhand and if you are the unfeeling things you appear to be, no one can really accuse you of being cruel in the proper sense. If you should ever, and I hope you shan't, my dear, I truly do for I've leapt at the very idea of you, before you were ever born, let

alone the sight and smell of you; if you should one day start
to shrink slowly into an unremarkable, gummy little hole into a
world outside the care or consciousness of anyone, you'll have
no rattlings of shame or death, there'll be no little sweating,
eruptions of blood, no fevers or clots or flesh splitting anywhere
or haemorrhage. You'll have done everything well and sensibly
and stylishly. You'll know it wasn't worth any candle that ever
burned. You will have to be blown out, snuffed, decently, and
not be watched spluttering and spilling and hardening. You
know what God is supposed to have said, well in Sunday School,
anyway? God said, He said: Be fruitful and multiply and re-
plenish the earth. And *subdue* it. It seems to me Jane, little
Jane, you don't look little any longer, you are on your way at
last, all, to doing all four of them. For the first time. Go on
now. [*She waits. They elude each other. She goes out.*]

[FADE.]
[FADE UP *on* BILL.]

BILL: Joy! Joy! What's going on out there? What? Joy! Where are
you? What is it then? Joy!

[JOY *enters in her overcoat.*]

JOY: So he's gone?
BILL: Oh, there you are. Who?
JOY: Hudson.
BILL: Yes.
JOY: Oh? Is he going to Piffards then?
BILL: Apparently.
JOY: I always thought he would.
BILL: So did I.
JOY: Well . . .
BILL: Are you going home?
JOY: There's not much to stay for, is there?
BILL: I don't think so. Did you try Winters again before—
JOY: They've all gone home now. Which is where I should be. Is
the Law Society really on to you?
BILL: Did Jones say so?

Joy: Yes.

Bill: Then I'm sure he's right.

Joy: Aren't you going to see Mrs. Eaves?

Bill: Do you know what a client said to me today?

Joy: No, who?

Bill: Oh, I don't know. One of them. She said when I go out to the shops, I go to the ones furthest away so that I can be out of the house and away from him longer. Then I get angry when the shopping is so heavy, and I can't carry it on my own.

Joy: Crazy.

Bill: Stay a little longer.

Joy: What for?

Bill: Have a drink.

Joy: No thanks.

Bill: Well, stay and talk.

Joy: No.

Bill: I promised not to say 'please.'

Joy: What do you want me to do? Press myself in a book for you? You know what? I think they're all right. I don't like you either.

Bill: I know.

Joy: Well, I'm off. Like I should have done. . . .

Bill: I'm still surprised to hear you say it though. I always am. And I shouldn't be. . . . Why does it shock me? Why? I myself am more packed with spite and twitching with revenge than anyone I know of. I actually often, frequently, daily want to see people die for their errors. I wish to kill them myself, to throw the switch with my own fist. Fortunately, I've had no more opportunities than most men. Still, I've made more than the best of them. Will you come in tomorrow?

Joy: I'll see.

Bill: Try to.

Joy: I have to take the day off.

Bill: Oh?

Joy: I've not been feeling so good lately. I think maybe I need a bit of a rest.

Bill: I see.

[LIZ *enters.*]

LIZ: Hullo.

JOY: Hullo, Mrs. Eaves.

LIZ [*Nods to* BILL.]: How's your thumb?

BILL: Painful. A fat little tumour. On the end of another.

LIZ: In his usual state of catatonic immobility, are we?

BILL: Yes. [*To* JOY.] That's her way of saying I don't seem to be
  able to hold on, on to, to anything. She talks in that funny way
  because her father is a don and is what is called a conceptual
  thinker, which, it's all too clear, I am not. No, darling, it's not
  something in a rubber goods shop, it's what her father is. One
  of those little intellectual monkeys who chatter on the telly
  about Copernicus at two hundred words a minute. And don't
  ask me who Copernicus is. I don't know the name of the Prime
  Minister, at this moment. He's a very cold fish, Joy. Her father
  I mean. He's probably the only man living whose unconscious
  desires are entirely impersonal.

JOY: Well. I'll be off. Goodnight, Mrs. Eaves.

LIZ: Goodnight, Joy.

BILL: Goodnight.

JOY: 'Bye.

BILL: Joy.

[*She goes out.* LIZ *goes over to him.*]

LIZ: My darling: are you all right?

BILL: Splendid.

LIZ: Why don't you come home?

BILL: Yes.

LIZ: I'm sorry, I had to come. You didn't answer the telephone.

BILL: Didn't I?

LIZ: I wasn't interrupting anything was I?

BILL: No.

LIZ: Oh, come along. I don't know why you don't admit you
  knock off that girl—

BILL: Because I don't need to.

LIZ: I keep giving you opportunities.

BILL: Well, I don't want them. I don't want to be cued in by
  you—

LIZ: It's a lot to ask, you know.

BILL: Yes. I see that too. [*Pause.*]

LIZ: You do ask a great deal of both of us, you know. It's unnecessary and it diminishes you.

BILL: True.

LIZ: I do love you.

BILL: Your assessment's impeccable. As usual.

LIZ: You're a dishonest little creep.

BILL: Why the 'little'? Because you seem to have more authority
than I have. [*Pause.*] You're not *bigger*. You're cleverer. More
accomplished, more generous. And more loving

LIZ: I've always managed to avoid guilt. It's a real peasant's pleasure, you know. For people without a sliver of self-knowledge or
courage.

BILL: There *are* other qualities besides courage.

LIZ: Well?

BILL: Cowardice for instance. For example.

LIZ: I've not seen you since Thursday. I thought somehow we'd
managed to resolve the pain of that particular evening. Even on
the telephone.

BILL: So did I. So we did. Till the next time.

LIZ: I love you so dearly. I can't think what to say to you.

BILL: I think you will.

LIZ: Why can't you trust me? Please?

BILL: It isn't easy.

LIZ: I know.

BILL: It isn't easy to trust someone: you're busily betraying. Sit
down. I can't see you over there. I don't like my clients sitting
halfway across the room talking to themselves.

[*She sits. Pause.*]

LIZ: What do you want to do?

BILL: Do?

LIZ: Yes, my darling . . . do.

BILL: I don't know. I haven't given it much thought.

LIZ: Did you see Jane?

BILL: Yes.

LIZ: How was that? [*He looks at her.*] I see. So. What's going to
happen?

BILL: Liz!

LIZ: What!

BILL: I'm tired of being watched. I'm tired of being watched by you, and observed and scrutinized and assessed and guessed about.

LIZ: Who gives a damn!

BILL: You do, you did. But you won't.

LIZ: What are you saying? Do you want me to go—? Really?

BILL: Well, you're the one who insisted on what you called an ethic of frankness.

LIZ: Believe me, the last thing I would insist on is an ethic like that. I can't think of anything more destructive.

[*Phone rings.*]

BILL: Hullo. . . . No, everyone's gone.

LIZ: Well, we know who that is.

BILL: I'm just clearing up. . . . I told you, everyone's gone. . . . Just me. . . . Yes, she *is* here. . . . Because I couldn't be bothered to tell the truth. . . . Listen, now's not a very good time, is it? Look, I'll ring you back. [*Pause.* LIZ *looks slightly mocking, but doesn't exploit it. She is too concerned for him.*] When I leave you sometimes and I get in, deliberately, of course, about three or four A.M. and Anna's lying there in bed, pretending to be asleep. After making love to you and the drive back, I'm so tired and there's the following morning a couple of hours away only, but I pretend to sleep because I can't to begin with. We both just lie there. And if I'm lucky or drunk enough and I do go to sleep, she lies there choking in silence unable to sleep again till she wakes me in the morning. Do you know I can't remember one detail of what she looks like, not since I left this morning and we'd had the row about the weekend. I sat down to read *The Charterhouse of Parma* while you were away at Christmas. You said I'd like it. So I started. It took ten days and I gave up round about the middle somewhere. I can't tell you what it's about. I can't grasp anything. I used to be good at my job because I had what they called an instinct and a quick brain. Quick! I can't get through the Law reports. I leave everything to Hudson and now he's gone, and I wouldn't leave a camel's breakfast to Jones even if he *were* still here.

Liz: Bill. What are we going to do?

Bill: Go away. I suppose.

Liz: But where?

Bill: Far away, as far away as possible from this place. There's no place for me here.

Liz [*Half humouring.*]: I never think of you as a traveler.

Bill: Meaning?

Liz: Well, you never seem to enjoy it much, do you? [*Pause.*] Well, do you?

Bill: Damn it, I've, travelled thousands of miles in the past few years for various clients in the last—

Liz: Oh yes, flights to New York and Amsterdam and Geneva. They're just businessmen's bus rides.

Bill: What do you want then? What should I be? Lady Hester Stanhope with a briefcase of legal documents perched on a camel?

Liz: I just don't think of your business trips as travel—

Bill: Oh, travel—

Liz: They're just for getting from one place to another for a particular purpose.

Bill [*Bitterly.*]: Well, what do *you* call travelling?

Liz: Well, like, like going in a boat round the Isles of Greece.

Bill: Yes. With a lot of tight-lipped, fast-shooting dons on the lookout for someone else's wife or crumpet.

Liz: When you're anywhere, you're always desperately miserable. You want to get back.

Bill: Yes?

Liz: Oh, to your clients. Or something. I was thinking, on my way here, and now . . .

Bill: Well?

Liz: I was thinking: perhaps you'd rather I didn't come away for the weekend. [*Silence. He faces her.*] I just thought you seemed . . . as if . . . you might . . . want to be alone. [*Pause.*]

Bill: I was only waiting, from the moment you came in, for you to say that.

Liz: I'm sorry to be so predictable. One often is, you know, when someone knows you well and loves you.

Bill: As I do. As I certainly do.

Liz: I was trying my hardest to be honest. It's a failing—

BILL: Well, why don't you take something for it.

LIZ: I don't care what you are or what you do—

BILL: Or who I am.

LIZ: I need you.

BILL: Not that word, please.

LIZ: You pretend to be ill and ignorant just so you can escape reproach. You beggar and belittle yourself just to get out of the game.

BILL: Whenever I do it, I enjoy, I think you do know, being some, some sort of, sort of good and comfort and pleasure to you because I love you. I don't love you for the sake of that pleasure. I can get it anywhere. [*She touches his shoulder and kisses the back of his head. He won't look up.*]

LIZ: You can always ring me.

BILL: But you won't be there. [*She can't reply.*] You do know that I love you?

LIZ: Yes.

BILL: And I shall never forget your face or anything about you. It won't be possible. I think, I'm quite certain, not that it matters, I loved you more than anyone.

LIZ: More than Jane?

BILL: Yes.

LIZ: Goodbye. [*She goes out.* BILL *takes a pill with a glass of water. He dials a number on the telephone.*]

BILL: Anna? Anna, what time is it? I can't see very clearly. . . . Do you think I should come home? . . . I don't think there's much point, do you? . . . Please don't cry, love. . . . I, I think it must be better if you don't see me . . . don't see me . . . yes . . . don't. Please don't don't . . . I'll have to put the receiver down. . . . I think I'll stay here. . . . Well the Law Society or someone will, sometime. . . . I think I'll just stay here. . . . Goodbye. [*He replaces the receiver and sits back waiting.*]

Curtain

THE SUNDAY PROMENADE

A Play in Three Acts and an Epilogue

Lars Forssell

Translated by Harry G. Carlson

CHARACTERS

JUSTUS CORIANDER, a grocery owner
ELSA, his wife
SULEIMA, his mother
ANGELICA, his deaf-mute daughter
CARL MICHAEL, his elder son
WILLY, his younger son
RAGNAR RURIKSSON, a rector
ABRAHAM, a clerk in the Coriander grocery
MISS ATTIE, later Mrs. Ambergriss
MR. AMBERGRISS, a game-preserve supervisor
MR. PLOUGHMAN, the sheriff

SCENE: *The dining room of* MR. CORIANDER's *home in a small city in Sweden.*

TIME: *The turn of the century. Early July.*

ACT ONE: *Saturday afternoon.*

ACT TWO: *Sunday midday.*

ACT THREE: *Sunday evening.*

EPILOGUE: *A Sunday afternoon seven years later.*

Act One

An elaborate Victorian-style dining room encumbered with tabourets, palms and other potted plants, leather-top tables, and assorted bric-a-brac.

A door upstage leads to the kitchen and several other rooms.

In the middle of the room is a giant mahogany dining-room table, surrounded by high-backed, richly ornamented chairs.

Suspended over the table, a pretentious crystal chandelier shimmers in several colors.

At stage right, quite close to the audience, is an ugly furniture cluster of chairs, table and sofa. Also at stage right, extending almost the full length from floor to ceiling, is a large window opening out on the main street of the small city.

As the curtain rises, the sun is shining brightly through the window. It is early July, but the strong summer sunlight is unable to dissipate the pall of dusty, stuffy, tasteless Victorian chaos.

RECTOR RURIKSSON, in clerical garb, stands looking out the window, greeting passersby with benevolent nods and ceremonious gestures. Seated in a repulsive armchair, which dominates the furniture cluster, is MRS. SULEIMA CORIANDER, playing solitaire. She reacts to each card she plays—now swear-

*ing to herself, now shaking her head, now smiling exul-
tantly. She is dressed in a black silk dress. A violet wool
shawl hangs about her shoulders.*

*A stairway upstage leads to a balcony which yields access
to the second floor. Seated on one of the top steps is
ANGELICA, lost in her thoughts. Dressed in a white blouse
and a long black skirt, she appears to be about sixteen or
seventeen years old. She is a deaf-mute.*

*At stage left is a piano covered with tattered sheet music
and a number of pictures. Everything is true to the period.
Nevertheless, there is a touch—perhaps in the color of the
setting— of unreality.*

*Street noises stream in through the window: the clatter of
wagon wheels; voices shouting—"Look up there" "Good afternoon, Mrs. Anderson!"; the barking of dogs; footsteps and
hoofbeats.*

MRS. CORIANDER: Bosh!

RURIKSSON [*At the window*]: What's that?

MRS. CORIANDER: Bosh!, I said. Bosh!

RURIKSSON: I don't understand . . .

MRS. CORIANDER: So you don't understand? You're pretty pleased
when Justus isn't here.

RURIKSSON: How you talk, Mrs. Coriander. . . .

MRS. CORIANDER [*Mockingly*]: "How you talk, Mrs. Coriander
. . ." Ha! You're beaming all over, Ruriksson.

RURIKSSON: I am pleased—with the peace and quiet of a Saturday afternoon. [*Waving out the window.*] Well, good afternoon . . .

MRS. CORIANDER: Bosh, I say! Bosh!

RURIKSSON [*Talking through the window*]: Good afternoon, Miss
Netz . . . good afternoon. Oh no, Miss Netz! Thanks anyway
for those *kind* words, Miss Netz! Why, hello there! [*To* MRS.
CORIANDER.] It's that big wholesaler. [*Back at the window.*]
Still in town? That's true, it isn't bad in town, for July. I didn't
see you in church on Sunday. Oh . . . I understand. Of course,
I understand, I understand. Regards to your wife . . . [*He
waves, then turns back to* MRS. CORIANDER.] . . . that hypocrite!
Here comes Miss Blomstroem . . . we'll see you in church to-

morrow, won't we? Oh thank you . . . we try to express things as best we can. Thank you for those *kind* words, Miss Blomstroem! Oh . . . Miss Nicander . . .

MRS. CORIANDER [*Anticipating the conversation as she continues playing*]: We'll see you in church tomorrow . . .

RURIKSSON: We'll see you in church tomorrow, won't we, Miss Nicander?

MRS. CORIANDER: Oh thank you for those *kind* words . . .

RURIKSSON: Thank you for those *kind* words. No, is that right, Miss Nicander? [MRS. CORIANDER *looks up and listens carefully.*] That'll be nice! That'll *really* be nice!

MRS. CORIANDER: What'll be nice?

RURIKSSON [*To* MRS. CORIANDER]: Miss Nicander is going away to visit her sisters in Surte.

MRS. CORIANDER [*Half-audibly*]: Hurray!

RURIKSSON: What?

MRS. CORIANDER: Hurray!, I said. One less gossipy hag in town!

RURIKSSON [*Toward the street*]: The elder Mrs. Coriander sends her best. Have a nice trip, Miss Nicander. God be with you. We'll see you in church again soon. Well, there's Mrs. Rong! Oh, just an old parson, Mrs. Rong, doing the best he can . . .

MRS. CORIANDER: Say what you will about old parsons, they sure are tiresome. [*Curtly.*] He makes me sick.

RURIKSSON [*Pricking up his ears*]:What did you say, Mrs. Coriander?

MRS. CORIANDER: The king goes on the ace, and how's little Peter?

RURIKSSON [*Toward the street*]: How is little Peter?

MRS. CORIANDER [*Quickly*]: I hope he dies. Funerals mean extra cash.

RURIKSSON [*Absentmindedly.*]: I hope he dies. Funerals mean . . . No! *Forgive* me, Mrs. Rong. I didn't mean . . .

MRS. CORIANDER [*Shaking with laughter.*]: And the jack goes on the queen . . .

RURIKSSON [*Beside himself with shame.*]: No, my *dear* Mrs. Rong!

MRS. CORIANDER [*Passionately*]: Oh, he makes me so sick!

RURIKSSON: Mrs. Rong . . . Mrs. Rong . . . I just wasn't thinking! You see . . . a minister is always thinking about death. . . . I knew you'd understand . . . yes, yes . . . Now I hope little Peter'll *soon* be fit as a fiddle. Goodbye, goodbye . . . [*He slams the window shut and crosses to* MRS. CORIANDER.] Why did you do that? [*Bitterly.*] You always have to make me a laughingstock! You and Justus. You're always making a fool out of me . . . a fool.

MRS. CORIANDER: That's because you *are* a fool, Ruriksson.

RURIKSSON [*Behind her, he cannot resist following her game while he speaks.*]: Can't I have some peace . . . the three of spades on the four of hearts . . . at least on Saturday afternoon. That's the only quiet time an old minister has.

MRS. CORIANDER: You'll have peace in the grave, Ruriksson.

RURIKSSON: Peace in God this Saturday afternoon and peace for the short time Mr. Coriander is in Marstrand. Doesn't it feel calm and wonderful . . . the five of spades on the six of diamonds . . . Yes, even if he is your son, you'll have to agree it's good to have him out of the house for awhile. Admit it, Mrs. Coriander!

MRS. CORIANDER: No. I miss him. I always do. But I can understand how *you* find it wonderful, Ruriksson—you and Elsa! I have eyes, you know. Don't you think I've noticed . . .

RURIKSSON [*Quickly, to cut her off.*]: The seven on the eight . . .

MRS. CORIANDER [*She hurls the cards from her and they fly about.*]: *There!* Play your own game!

RURIKSSON: Calm down, calm down. You were nearly out.

MRS. CORIANDER: . . . noticed you and Elsa running around whispering and sniggering in every corner since Justus left? Do you think I'm *blind?* Oh no, sniggerer . . . oh no, sneak. . . . No, you don't fool me. "Come for coffee on Saturday, Ragnar dear!" . . . "Sit in the comfortable chair, Ragnar dear!" "How sensibly you talk, Ragnar—if only Justus talked like that." It's disgusting, Ruriksson, it's shameful! Ha! What else lures you to this house when Justus isn't here? Is it *me!*

RURIKSSON: No . . .

MRS. CORIANDER: I hardly thought so, Ruriksson!!

RURIKSSON: Shhhhhhh, please! [*Looking upstairs at* ANGELICA.] Angelica is . . .

MRS. CORIANDER: She can't hear, you damned fool. You know that.

RURIKSSON: Of course . . . I'm sorry. [*Still staring at the girl.*] But sometimes she almost seems to be listening.

Mrs. Coriander: She's lucky. She's out of it. But *I'm not* deaf and dumb, or blind either. And I tell you, Ruriksson, if this *sniggering* doesn't stop, I'm writing to Justus in the morning.

Ruriksson: But my dear Mrs. Coriander, you're mistaken.

Mrs. Coriander: Just remember.

Ruriksson: But I assure you . . . that you . . . [ELSA, *Coriander's wife, comes into view through the upstage door carrying a heavily laden coffee tray. She is middle-aged, but not past her prime. Her face shines like a bland sun.*] . . . have it all wrong, Suleima. All wrong. [*Pause.*] May I help you, Elsa dear? [*Smiling broadly, and with an air of self-importance, he rushes over to help.* MRS. CORIANDER *snorts.*]

Elsa: Thank you, Ragnar dear. Put the tray there on the table. [*As* RURIKSSON *takes the tray, something on his coat catches her attention.*] Never mind, just put the tray down. What sort of spot have you got on your collar? It looks like butter. I'll have to fix it with a little hot water. . . . So . . . here you are talking and relaxing. [MRS. CORIANDER *snorts again.*] Saturday afternoon is such a blessing!

Mrs. Coriander: When Justus is away, yes!

Elsa: Why do you say that, Mother Coriander?

Mrs. Coriander: When Justus is away, the mice will . . . ah! You don't even do that. You just sit. You even avoid taking a Sunday promenade.

Elsa: I don't understand . . .

Rurikksson: Well now, I like promenades . . . ha ha . . . [*His spirits have improved since* ELSA's *entrance. He is cocky and self-assured.*] . . . but *outside*—in God's free, beautiful, open air! That's where one should promenade! It's really not the same thing . . . ha ha . . . around the dining-room table! No, say what you will about Justus, he is original.

Mrs. Coriander: Justus is a poet.

Elsa: Please, no quarreling!

Ruriksson [*Ironically.*]: Have you ever heard of Count Snoilsky taking his Sunday promenade around . . . [*Giggling at the thought.*] . . . a dining-room table! And Count Snoilsky *is a real poet!*

Elsa: Now, now, drink your coffee and don't argue.

RURIKSSON: If you're going to daydream, daydream about something that could come true. At least that's the way I feel!

MRS. CORIANDER [*Ironically.*]: Like a missionary journey? To Outer Mongolia?

RURIKSSON: Exactly Mrs. Coriander. A missionary journey . . . My missionary journey . . . [*Dreamily.*] . . . to save lost souls . . . to inspire the needy. . . . Would you believe it, Elsa—there was an article last night in the newspaper about . . . Outer Mongolia. . . . [*Smiling, he loses himself in the dream.*] Outer Mongolia . . . such spiritual need . . . such spiritual poverty . . .

MRS. CORIANDER [*Provocatively.*]: Ask me no questions and I'll tell you no lies.

RURIKSSON [*Awakening.*]: Elsa . . . would you ask your mother-in-law to . . .

ELSA: Tch, tch, tch. The Lord would say, "What do I care about your worldly bickering?"

MRS. CORIANDER [*Authoritatively, her voice ringing.*]: And I'd say, "Lord, this is no prayer, just advice—punish Rector Ruriksson!"

RURIKSSON [*Jumping up.*]: Mrs. Coriander . . . ! Mrs. Coriander . . . [*Choking with anger, his hands flap about forlornly as he tries to regain his power of speech.* MRS. CORIANDER *glowers.*]

MRS. CORIANDER [*Hoarsely.*]: Two lumps, Elsa, thank you . . .

[ELSA, *glancing uneasily toward* RURIKSSON, *pours a cup of coffee, and puts in two lumps of sugar. During the last four or five speeches,* ANGELICA, *unnoticed by the others, has casually made her way down the stairs. Although she is somewhat untidily dressed, she has great dignity. She manages to reach the table just as* RURIKSSON *launches into his angry outburst. She seems not to notice—or in any case is completely unmoved by—what is going on. Her hand darts out with snake-like speed to snatch a cookie from the tray. Crunching it greedily, she settles into an armchair, her legs tucked agilely beneath her.*]

ELSA: Quiet now! Quiet! Angelica is here!

MRS. CORIANDER [*Muttering.*]: So what? She doesn't know what's going on . . . she's lucky!

ELSA [*Uncomfortably.*]: We always forget that . . .

MRS. CORIANDER: Maybe it's best that way.

[*Silence. The clinking of coffee cups.* MRS. CORIANDER, *her hands quavering, drinks with difficulty.* RURIKSSON's *little finger is extended. He stuffs a cookie in his mouth, cramming in the last piece. With his handkerchief, he brushes the crumbs off his cassock. In a dignified, clerical manner, he maneuvers the conversation onto a neutral tack.*]

RURIKSSON [*His mouth full.*]: And where [*gulp, gulp*] is the rest of the family? Willy and Carl Michael and [*gulp*] . . .

ELSA: Upstairs. I guess Carl Michael is reading as usual.

MRS. CORIANDER: . . . and Willy isn't doing anything. Dear God, he has nothing up . . . [*She taps her temple. To* ELSA.] He takes after you, that way.

ELSA [*Pretending not to notice.*]: I'll call them! [*She hastens to the foot of the stairs with an air of importance.*] Carl Michaaaeell! Willlllllyyy! Coffeeeee!

RURIKSSON: How is [*gulp, gulp*] . . . Carl Michael anyway?

MRS. CORIANDER: He's fine—right now. But that doesn't mean he's well.

RURIKSSON: Oh, that's too bad! And . . . [*gulp, gulp*] . . . Abraham?

MRS. CORIANDER: In the store, of course.

RURIKSSON: He has to work too much. And even on Sunday. One should observe the sabbath.

MRS. CORIANDER: Justus doesn't observe any sabbaths. He keeps on *working*—and Abraham, too. Faith for some people is only laziness!

ELSA [*Who has returned*]: Mother Coriander, do you believe the Creator rested on the seventh day because he was *lazy?*

MRS. CORIANDER: No, because he was *finished!*

RURIKSSON: Don't blaspheme, Mrs. Coriander!

MRS. CORIANDER: Justus—he *creates*, he does!

RURIKSSON: Don't blaspheme, Mrs. Coriander!

MRS. CORIANDER: When he's not home, everything stands still! The whole town turns into a duck pond and the store into a tomb! Here we sit and nothing happens. No laughter, no one who can tell jokes. No one dances, or whistles, or sings!

RURIKSSON: And no one gets taken in, Mrs. Coriander, or over-charged, or cheated!

MRS. CORIANDER: Small towns and their ministers have one thing in common.

RURIKSSON: Their own church!

MRS. CORIANDER: No. *No sense of humor!* And that's something Justus has—he got that from me! But I guess you know that, Ruriksson . . . [*She tries to stifle a titter.*] . . . if *anyone* does!

RURIKSSON: I am not amused!

ELSA: Now mother, you mustn't pour salt in old wounds!

MRS. CORIANDER [*Paying no attention.*]: Tell us about that *vision* you had, Ruriksson!

ELSA: Mother Coriander!

MRS. CORIANDER: Vision—my eye! Do you remember, Elsa . . .

ELSA: No.

MRS. CORIANDER [*Indignantly.*]: No, she says! A vision, if you please, and what a *commotion!* It was nothing less than an angel, wasn't it, Pastor? [*She plays questions and answers.*] Remember that night? On the corner of Main Street and Kasken's Alley . . . ho hoooo! . . .

RURIKSSON: Mrs. Coriander . . . I beg you . . . I beg . . .

MRS. CORIANDER [*Chanting scornfully and pompously.*]: I remember what it said in the newspaper. "The pastor had spent the whole evening in his room, absorbed in theological studies . . . in Imannuel Swedenborg! Around midnight he felt tired" . . . according to the story . . . [*She pretends to read an invisible newspaper.*] . . . "put on his overcoat, took his silver-handled walking stick, and set out meditatively into the winter night . . . for a breath of fresh air. . . ."

RURIKSSON: Stop it, Mrs. Coriander!

ELSA: Stop it, Suleima . . . please . . .

MRS. CORIANDER: "The stars sparkled and glittered. And then suddenly—as the pastor tells it to our special correspondent—suddenly, on the corner of Main Street and Kasken's alley . . . he meets the *angel.*" Or was it really Jesus, Pastor Ruriksson?

ELSA: Suleima . . .

MRS. CORIANDER: Was it Jesus, Angelica? [*She looks questioningly at the girl.* ANGELICA *shakes her head dubiously.*] No!

Was it Peter, Paul, John the Baptist? [ANGELICA *shakes her head.*] No! Was it the archangel Gabriel, or Moses? Was it the evangelist Luke? No! [*Whispering rhetorically.*] Was it the Almighty himself then, who stood there in gleaming white, stretching out his wide, white, welcoming arms toward Pastor Ruriksson? Was it He whom the Pastor thought he saw, and then screamed about from his pulpit the next day? Was it God who came to Ruriksson, Ruriksson?

RURIKSSON: No . . . no . . .

MRS. CORIANDER: No, it wasn't . . . because it was really . . . ha, ha! . . . Justus! [*She explodes with laughter.*] It wasn't God's son—it was *mine!* Out for an evening promenade in his powdery white grocery smock! It was Justus, hallelujah, it was Justus! Standing there in the moonlight, and mistaken by the Pastor for a vision from God!

ELSA: Quiet, Suleima! You know . . .

MRS. CORIANDER: I know what I know! That's the way it happened! But what was even worse, much worse, Pastor Ruriksson . . . [*She takes out a handkerchief, wipes her mouth, and continues in a calmer, more assertive tone.*] . . . was that when Justus went to Ruriksson after all the fuss in church and in the newspaper, and told him the truth about the heavenly apparition, the Pastor didn't dare tell it to his congregation—that was much worse!

RURIKSSON: I didn't want . . .

ELSA: Why should he destroy their faith?

MRS. CORIANDER: No, ask instead: Why won't he be made a laughingstock?

RURIKSSON: That's happened to me here, a thousand times over!

MRS. CORIANDER [*Pretending not to hear.*]: And my answer is: He was too cowardly to tell the truth, and that's a fact! A rabbit, that's what your Ruriksson is. May I have another cup of coffee. . . .

RURIKSSON: How often do I have to listen to that story?

MRS. CORIANDER: Two lumps. [*Turning to* RURIKSSON.] Every time, Ruriksson, you don't know your place. [*She looks knowingly from the minister to* ELSA, *from* ELSA *to the minister, trembling as she conveys the cup to her mouth.*] You know what I'm talking about.

ELSA [*In the same breath.*]: Mother Suleima, what do you mean? Oh, now you've spilled on your shawl . . .

MRS. CORIANDER: He knows. Ask *him*. Hah! [*Slurping her coffee.*] Thanks to that "vision," he got to be vicar. Of course, he had to bargain to get the church—promising to make Justus a warden! Hah! It would have been more appropriate to put him in charge of the collection plate. Now the whole congregation flocks to the Coriander flour bins, the dear little sheep. No business for Rackey's store, no matter how godlike that rascal tries to appear! Anything but the truth, eh Ruriksson? Bargaining for God, Ruriksson? Lies and inventions for God, Ruriksson?

RURIKSSON: Mrs. Coriander, this is something you don't understand.

MRS. CORIANDER: Don't I? I understand *one* thing, anyway! Justus Coriander has a sense of humor! [*She bursts into laughter, wiping away happy tears with her handkerchief.*] And *that's* what we were talking about in the first place . . . [*Softly.*] . . . right?

ELSA [*Absentmindedly.*]: Yes . . . yes.

RURIKSSON [*Sullenly.*]: Yes, of course!

[*At long last* CARL MICHAEL *and* WILLY *appear on their way down the stairs.* CARL MICHAEL *is short and slight, a pale, bookish man. In contrast,* WILLY'S *appearance is coarse. He has bushy red hair, prominent front teeth, and is inclined to giggle.*]

ELSA [*Relieved by the interruption.*]: Well, here you are! Why didn't you come when I called? Your coffee has gotten cold! [*She signals to* ANGELICA.] Fetch some hot coffee, Angelica. It's on the stove. [ANGELICA *takes the coffee server and exits through the upstage door.*] Carl Michael! [*Indignantly.*] What have I said about those shoes! I told you to throw them away! Boys are always . . .

[CARL MICHAEL *and* WILLY *have greeted* RURIKSSON, *rather formally. They sit.*]

CARL MICHAEL: I shaaalll!

MRS. CORIANDER: Willy dear, we were just talking about what a sense of humor your father has!

WILLY [*Who has difficulty expressing himself.*]: Oh, yeah . . . yeah . . .

MRS. CORIANDER: Yes. Don't you think so, Carl Michael?

CARL MICHAEL: It's possible. Especially to people who don't have one themselves.

WILLY: Come on, Carl Michael. You know. You remember.

CARL MICHAEL: What?

WILLY: You know. You remember. Sure. You know, that time he made Martin Andersson believe. God, was he dumb! [*He pauses, embarrassed, hunting for words.*] Don't you remember?

CARL MICHAEL [*Resignedly.*[: Who?

WILLY: Martin. Martin. The time Pa said to Martin that he'd get *invisible* if he . . . if he first rubbed a stick of sealing wax, you remember? With a hunk of wool? And then . . . stuck it . . . ha ha ha! . . . in his mouth! Ha ha ha! [*He doubles over with laughter.*] That he'd get *invisible* if he did like that! Shhh, let me tell this. Martin—he believed—you remember. [*He nearly chokes with laughter.*] Then, one day . . . when Pa came into the store . . . shhh, let me tell this. And Martin Andersson, old Martin, was sitting in a corner winking one eye, like this . . . sneaky-like! *With a long stick of sealing wax in his craw* . . . like a cigar! Shhh . . . and Pa . . . he made believe he didn't notice nothing. And Martin . . . he sits there, real pleased with himself. Real sneaky-like! And Pa starts mumbling, "I wonder where Martin is. He was going to come in and pay his bill." And then Martin he jumps up and pulls the sealing wax out of his mouth and yells, "Justus, Justus, I'm here, I'm *here!*" [*He chokes again with laughter. Everybody else joins in, more or less spontaneously, except* CARL MICHAEL.] Carl Michael, don't you remember?

CARL MICHAEL: I think it was cruel!

WILLY: "I'm here . . . " [*His laughter is delightfully contagious.*]

MRS. CORIANDER [*Blowing her nose and addressing* CARL MICHAEL *dryly.*]: You have no sense of humor, Carl Michael. You're your mother's son.

WILLY: "I'm here! I'm here!" And then there was the time the Pastor had that vision . . .

ELSA: Willy! [WILLY *puts his hand over his mouth.*]

CARL MICHAEL: Why must Father's fantasies always be at other people's expense? He says the world is beautiful, and you have to use your eyes, and you have to love . . . [*Imitating his father, he throws his arms out pompously.*] Love life, my chiillldren! And yet he does everything in his power to ridicule the world and defile the people in it!

WILLY [*Bouncing in his chair, unable to restrain his mirth, choking.*]: And he thought he was invisible . . . sealing wax . . .

RURIKSSON: All right, Willy . . .

WILLY: Sealing wax in his mouth . . . [*He tries to stifle his laughter. Suddenly, he explodes, hissing loudly.*]

CARL MICHAEL: Father is cruel! He'd sacrifice anything for a joke!

[WILLY *sits shaking in his chair.*]

RURIKSSON: Preaching is *my* business, Carl Michael!

[WILLY *is still shaking.*]

CARL MICHAEL: Yes, and that's all you preachers can do! Father preaches about the beauty of life—Seize the day! Seize the moment—but everything he does conceals its beauty from others. And you—you talk about the world's suffering, but what do you do to prevent it? [WILLY *is still shaking.*] Shut up, Willy!

ELSA: What about my sewing circle, Carl Michael? By the way, your sleeve needs mending.

CARL MICHAEL: Stockings for children in Africa—Damn it to hell!!

ELSA: Don't talk like that!

CARL MICHAEL: Damn it to hell, damn it to hell, I say! [WILLY *bounces up and down in his chair.*] Willy!

ELSA: Willy!

MRS. CORIANDER: That's enough now, Willy.

CARL MICHAEL: Stockings! Damn it to hell! Words, words, words, words instead of action! Instead of bread! Take a look through your dusty windows and you'll see the world is starting to smolder. And the day isn't far off, Pastor Ruriksson . . .

[WILLY *has finally calmed down. Gaping, he follows the conversation as if it were a tennis match.*]

RURIKSSON: Yes, the day will come . . . [*He finds himself in the pulpit. Standing stiff as a ramrod, he cautions his audience with a stern forefinger.*] . . . and I say to you and to you and to *you*, Carl Michael, in all your ungodliness . . .

ELSA: Now Ragnar!

RURIKSSON: The day will come . . . quiet Elsa! . . . when Christ will return to earth and redeem the fallen and the suffering. . . .

CARL MICHAEL [*With a youthful zest for protest.*]: The day He comes . . . *if* He comes . . .

ELSA: Carl Michael!

CARL MICHAEL: . . . humanity will have long since redeemed itself! So, on that day there'll be no more suffering, no fallen!

MRS. CORIANDER: What kind of books have you been reading boy? [*As she lifts her cup to her lips she discovers that it is empty and slams it down.*] Bosh!

CARL MICHAEL: That day . . . [*He is moved.*] . . . the red flag will fly everywhere.

MRS. CORIANDER: Does he mean the Salvation Army?

WILLY [*His mouth full of bun, he begins shaking again.*]: I'm heeerrre, Martin screamed, I'm here. [*He collapses into new paroxysms.*] Ahhh ha ha ha . . .

CARL MICHAEL: Can't you understand *anything*, Willy?

RURIKSSON: Blessed, blessed are the pure in heart for they shall see God! But you, Carl Michael—named for that blaspheming poet, Bellman—oh, I remember my anguish that day by the baptismal font. And you've earned your ungodly name!

[*The door opens.* ANGELICA *enters, followed by* ABRAHAM, *who carries the coffee server. He is a pale, pimply-faced, slight young man. He holds* ANGELICA *lightly by the arm and gazes at her lovingly.*]

MRS. CORIANDER: Here comes more coffee. Quiet now, Carl

Michael! Shake hands with the Pastor! Some day . . . [*Sinking back in her chair; there is bitterness in her voice.*] . . . you'll learn to quit your reading and your worrying about other people . . . as we have.

CARL MICHAEL [*Confused and trying to control himself, he stares at* MRS. CORIANDER. *It is as if he has gotten some support from her words.*]: All right, for the sake of a peaceful Saturday afternoon. Forgive me, Pastor.

RURIKSSON [*Reluctantly taking his hand.*]: Of course! That's what ministers are for!

ELSA [*Sighing*]: What a fuss! You can tell that Justus is away. [*Taking the coffee server out of* ABRAHAM's *hands, she scrapes something off his threadbare coat.*] You *do* wear your white coat in the store, don't you?

ABRAHAM [*Earnestly.*]: Oh sure, Mrs. Coriander. [*Explaining with embarrassment.*] When I came in through the kitchen I saw Angelica there and thought to myself, she could use a little help.

MRS. CORIANDER [*Reaching out her cup for more coffee.*]: Uh huh. Took quite a while—to help her . . .

ABRAHAM [*Reddening as he tries, haltingly, to speak.*]: Well, what happened was . . .

ELSA: All right, all right. Get yourself a cup from the cupboard and you can have some coffee with us.

[ABRAHAM *withdraws to the cupboard, watching* ANGELICA *all the while, as if to attract her attention.* ANGELICA, *in an obvious way, stares after him.*]

ELSA [*Stroking the girl's hair tenderly.*] There, there, Angelica . . . [ELSA *pours coffee for everyone, including* ABRAHAM *when he returns. The ritual of drinking continues, self-consciously: the clinking of cups, the crunching of cookies.*]

RURIKSSON: Yes . . . yes . . . yes. Elsa knows about making coffee, all right.

MRS. CORIANDER [*After an awkward pause.*]: Have you heard anything from Justus, Elsa?

[RURIKSSON, *cup in hand, rises and crosses to his former place by the window. He stands, preoccupied, staring out. It is obvious that he finds the mention of* JUSTUS's *name disagreeable.*]

ELSA: I got a letter yesterday.

MRS. CORIANDER: And how does he find Marstrand?

ELSA: Calm and beautiful, it seems.

MRS. CORIANDER: Beautiful, maybe, but calm, never—not while Justus is there. [WILLY *begins to shake again, his mouth full of coffee cake.* MRS. CORIANDER *smiles at him, indulgently.*] Shshshsh. Any nice little tidbits?

ELSA: I have the letter in the secretary. [*She rises to get it, taking time to make a turn around the Pastor. In a motherly, comforting way, she pats and caresses his coat. There is malice in* MRS. CORIANDER'S *eyes as they follow* ELSA *across the room. She snorts: "Bosh"!* ABRAHAM *wants to move closer to* ANGELICA, *but he too gets a cold eye from the old lady, so he focuses his attention on his cup. He begins drinking so eagerly that the coffee gets stuck in his throat.* WILLY *thumps him obligingly on the back.*]

MRS. CORIANDER: Bosh! [ELSA *has returned with the letter.*] Come on, let's hear it, let's hear it.

ELSA [*Putting on her glasses, she begins reading.*]: Here we are . . . "My beloved wife . . . I am sighting . . ."

MRS. CORIANDER: It must be "sitting." He never could spell.

CARL MICHAEL [*Ironically.*]: Ha!

ELSA: " . . . here in beautiful Marstrand, staring out, in a melancholy way . . ."

CARL MICHAEL [*Ironically.*]: Melancholy, hah!

ELSA [*With an angry glance at* CARL MICHAEL] ". . . in a melancholy way, on the shimmering water. Melancholy—when I think of how frightfully far I am from home—the dear confines of home—so infinitely distant from my loved ones . . . "

MRS. CORIANDER: Skip all that! No juicy tidbits?

ELSA [*Skipping over.*]: Bla bla bla . . . [*Looking up, preoccupied.*]

MRS. CORIANDER: Well?

ELSA: Oh, I do hope he took his long underwear along.

WILLY: I saw when you packed them down, Ma!

MRS. CORIANDER: Yes, yes. Go on.

ELSA [*Returning to the letter*.]: "Count Snoilsky . . ." [*To* WILLY. Are you sure you did?

MRS. CORIANDER [*Irritatedly*.]: Yes, yes, yes. What does he say about Count Snoilsky?

CARL MICHAEL [*Scornfully*.]: Count Snoilsky! If that . . . if he offered me his hand, I'd spit on it!

MRS. CORIANDER: You couldn't spit that far! [*To* ELSA.] Now. what about Count Snoilsky?

ELSA [*Reading*.]: "Count Snoilsky walks by here every day . . . and . . . " Listen to this! "King Oscar can be seen everyday about noon on the beach going to his Kneipp cure treatment . . . "

MRS. CORIANDER: Kneipp cure? What's that?

CARL MICHAEL: He washes his feet! But it's his hands—his filthy rotten, aristocratic hands that he *should* wash!

MRS. CORIANDER: Shut up!! And may God preserve the King's health!

RURIKSSON [*Motionless at the window*.]: Aaaamen!

[WILLY *starts shaking again and draws a severe frown from* MRS. CORIANDER.]

MRS. CORIANDER: Let's hear some more. Anything about the Queen?

ELSA [*Searching*.]: No, nothing.

MRS. CORIANDER: Why doesn't he write more about the *important* things?

ELSA: He writes about his room.

MRS. CORIANDER: What about it?

ELSA: "Upon arrival here at Marstrand, I soon noticed, my dearest wife, a certain noise in the room above mine. I complained immediately to the management . . . bla bla bla . . . and as soon as it was emptied, I rented it, too . . . "

MRS. CORIANDER: What does he want with two rooms?

RURIKSSON [*At the window*.]: And the congregation paying the bills!

MRS. CORIANDER: [*Toward the window*.]: And whose fault is *that*, if I may ask?

ELSA [*Reading further in the letter*.]: He's rented three rooms! No, four!

MRS. CORIANDER: *Four* rooms? Why?

ELSA: He thought he heard noises in each of the rooms around him, so he rented them all. "Creakings and commotions, but now, since I rented *all* the rooms bordering mine, I rest peacefully at night, nestled, as it were, in a cocoon of silence . . . "

CARL MICHAEL [*Counting.*]: Why, he must have rented five!

MRS. CORIANDER: What's a cocoon?

CARL MICHAEL: Five rooms in Marstrand! Ha! There he lies, snoring in his soft bed, surrounded by four empty rooms and beds, while thousands and thousands of people have to be satisfied with the hard ground for a pillow, thousands . . .

WILLY: And what about you, huh? Just sitting there gobbling up cookies . . .

MRS. CORIANDER: Bravo, Willy!

[*Willy nods knowingly, takes a cookie and starts munching proudly. Just prior to this, a loud, strident shout is heard from the street. Other voices join in.* ELSA *has to raise her voice when she continues her reading.*]

ELSA [*In a high voice.*]: "It is now quiet and peaceful here, my dear wife. I intend to stay an additional *three weeks* . . . " [*Sighing dolefully.*] Three weeks! [*Continuing to read.*] " . . . Warmest regards to you all, from your son, husband and father . . ." What's that noise out in the street? ". . . Your own . . ."

MRS. CORIANDER: What in Heaven's name is that, Ruriksson?

ELSA [*Booming.*]: " . . . Your own, Justus, J. W. Y. Coriander."

RURIKSSON [*Leaning out.*]: No, no, no . . . [*Spinsterishly.*] No, I said, my good man, we don't want any . . . [*To the others.*] It's a gypsy selling rugs! I said, *no!* [*To the others.*] It's one of those Romany beggars trying to sell . . . God! How I despise gypsies! [*Shouting out.*] I said *no!* Nix, herr gypsy! Nicht rugs, nicht rugs. Non, monsieur, nein!

[ANGELICA *has grabbed* ABRAHAM *and rushed to the window. She is delighted. Her eyes twinkle. She tries with gestures to show the others, who have risen in dismay, how the intruder looks, how he swaggers and cavorts. She pulls* ABRAHAM *by the arm. She has realized something and tries vainly to explain.*]

ELSA: Disturbing a peaceful Saturday afternoon! [*She rushes to the window, puts her arm around* RURIKSSON'S *shoulders, and shakes her fist.*] Nix! Go away, go away! [*A screaming voice can be heard from outside, but the words are not clear.*] No, no . . . go away! Don't you dare come in here, don't you dare! . . . Ohhhhh!

[CARL MICHAEL *and* WILLY *rush forward to help hold back the gypsy, but to no avail.* MRS. CORIANDER *pales, sits bolt upright, and watches the proceedings with a diabolical expression. The* GYPSY, *quacking wildly*—"Here comes Chack! Here comes Chack! Let me in! Let me in!"—*climbs in over the low windowsill. He is dressed in a conventional gypsy outfit, wild and gaudy. Over his arm variegated rugs and some of the usual oriental trinkets: silver bracelets, dolls in different colors and shapes, and canes—all in bright crimsons and violets. Despite everyone's best efforts to stop him, he forces his way to the furniture group, where—after disrespectfully shoving the coffee tray aside—he begins to spread out his wares. The whole time he gabbles:* "See! See! See! Look! Chust look! Look! Fine tings, eh? Beautiful tings, not so? Look, chust look, look! See! See! See!" *Hanging on his belt, prominently displayed, is a long, curved knife in a gaudy scabbard.* ANGELICA *has hurled herself at him, trying to embrace him. She hops up and down and succeeds in kissing his brown cheek before* ELSA *and* ABRAHAM *tear her away.*]

ELSA *and* **ABRAHAM** [*Pulling* ANGELICA.]: Angelica! Really, Angelica! Stay here!

[*After being forced to one side,* ANGELICA *stands rather shyly by herself and follows what is happening. A finger pressed against her mouth, she wears an expectant, slightly ironic expression.*]

GYPSY: See my vares, mein herr, ja? See how zey shine, eh? Like ze sun, mein herr, like ze moon, like ze *shtars*, ja? But look den, look, look . . . [*To* ELSA.] Madame, how beautiful you are. Yes, I mean *you*, Madame . . .

ELSA: Get out, I said! We don't want to buy anything!

GYPSY: *You*, who are so beautiful. Not so, herr bishop? She is beautiful . . . [*When the* GYPSY *tries to pay her on the cheek,* RURIKSSON *motions as if to step between them. But he does nothing, he is too cowardly, and the result is only an awkward gesture.*] But you vould be even more beautiful mitt zis silver bracelet around your wrist, ja? Ten crowns—but for ze sake of your intoxicating loveliness, for *zat*, I cut the price to five. Five crowns for zis bracelet, herr bishop? I see in her beautiful eyes zat she wants zis bracelet. And in yours, herr bishop, in yours I see admiration, admiration, ja, for madame's intoxicating beauty. Admiration and . . . love, herr bishop? [*He pokes* RURIKSSON *in the ribs.*] Admit it, come on, admit it!! I know zat you're a man of God, herr bishop, but love travels the strangest routes . . . maybe even the road to Calvary, ja? Zo, Zo, herr bishop, buy zis for ze madame . . . But, vat's zis? [*He pretends to have just spotted the elder* MRS. CORIANDER. *During the* GYPSY'S *harangue, everyone has tried to halt the verbiage with a:* "But . . . ", *or* "Get out of here!" *or* "Now see here, my good man!", *or* "We're sending for help!", *but finally, they give up.*] Aha, what's this? [*Pointing at* MRS. CORIANDER, *he questions each of the assembled in turn.*] Who's *dis*? . . . Who's *dis*? . . . Who's dis? Chack has always said: as for beauty, it's all right, it's fine, but wisdom, *wisdom*, that's *really* something! Ah, mein frau [*To the elder* MRS. CORIANDER] . . . in your eyes, in your deep, good, wonderful peppercorn eyes, I see the reflection, as if at the bottom of a deep, deep, deep, deep, deep, deep well, the reflection of Wisdom! And wisdom . . . wisdom, mein frau, makes you *beautiful*! [*In a business-like way.*] Your feet are cold, ja? They're cold, I know they are, I *know* . . . because wisdom, mein frau, *always* has cold feet!

MRS. CORIANDER [*Thundering*]: I'm wise enough to ask you to be on your way! There's the door, Mr. Bum! [*She extends a long, authoritative forefinger.*] There it is!

GYPSY [*Fawning.*]: But mein frau . . . bum? Drive out a poor gypsy like zis on a Saturday afternoon, ja? Just look . . . look . . . at these rugs! Your feet are cold right? Vell I have ze remedy! Genuine . . . [*Spreading out his rugs.*] . . . soft . . . warm . . .

Mrs. Coriander [*Sneaking glances at the rugs as the* gypsy *lays them out at her feet.*]: There's the door, I said! Or go out the way you came in—through the window!

Gypsy [*Whispering, cajoling*]: Rugs . . . mein frau . . . green, red, fine, Afghan, Oriental, Persian rugs, ja? To put your small, elegant, small, wise, cold little feet on . . . to keep them warm as kittens ja? Chust feel, mein frau, feel the quality!

Ruriksson [*Timidly trying to muster up some boldness*]: If you don't leave immediately, sir, I'll call the police, and *then* . . .

Gypsy [*Angrily*]: The police, eh? And that from a churchman, too! Read your Bible, herr bishop—"Whatsoever ye would that men should do to you," . . . [*His tone changes from solemn to wheedling.*] Rugs . . . ja?

Ruriksson [*To* carl michael *and* willy]: Help me get him out of here! [abraham, carl michael *and* willy, *their sleeves rolled up, rush the* gypsy. *They try to grab him, while* ruriksson *directs the troops from the background. But the* gypsy, *cat like, slips away.*] Hold him . . . hold him . . . the scum . . . hold him! [carl michael *grabs at the* gypsy *time and again, but the man eludes him skillfully. Hiding behind chairs and tables,* willy *tries awkwardly to sneak up behind him.*] He's not like . . . not like . . . other people!

Gypsy: Just try . . . come on, try . . . ha ha!

[willy *grabs him from behind and tries to pin his arms to his sides. The women gather in a trembling group and follow the action with stony, frightened stares. But the* gypsy *is as lithe as a panther, even though by this time he is puffing and slowing down his movements. He breaks away, leaps up on the dining-room table, and draws his knife. It glitters in a ray of dusty sunlight.* ruriksson, abraham, carl michael *and* willy *shrink back. The women scream.*]

Abraham: Watch out for the knife!

Elsa *and* **Mrs. Coriander**: Ohhhhhh! Watch out for the knife!

Gypsy: You just try, you just try to touch me, ja? [*He descends slowly from the table. Stealthily, in a crouched position, he advances on* ruriksson.] Now, you holier than holy . . . now, you little lamb of God . . . now, you're going to get it! Now you're

going to be slaughtered like the Lord is the Shepherd, ja? Now
you're scared, aren't you, ja? Now . . .

RURIKSSON [*Pale and trembling, on his knees*]: Mercy, have
mercy . . .

ELSA [*Breaking free of the spell, she runs to the window and
shouts out in a ringing voice.*]: Help, help! Murder!!

GYPSY [*Hissing dramatically between his teeth.*]: Shut up,
woman! Shhhhh, otherwise . . .

[ELSA *turns around near the window, standing stock-still, her
hand over her mouth, as if she were hypnotized. Voices sound
weakly fron outside.*]

VOICES OUTSIDE: What is it? Who's that. Who screamed? The
Corianders! Over here! Over here!

RURIKSSON [*Still on his knees.*]: I beg you . . . if you're going to
do it, do it *quickly!*

GYPSY: What do you say, knife? Shall we do it quickly, ja? Nein!
Not quickly. We have to let him think over his life, ja? . . .
carefully . . . slowly. . . . How many people do you think he's
betrayed, knife? How many times do you think he's lied, knife?
How many times has he desired other men's wives, knife? What
did you say, knife? [*He puts the knife to his ear and listens, nodding as if he heard an answer.*] That's right, *that's* right, knife!
We two, we understand each other, ja?

RURIKSSON: Mercy, mercy . . .

MRS. CORIANDER [*With pity in her voice.*]: Don't do it. You'll
be destroyed.

GYPSY: I am already. Not so, dear knife? That's right! [*He goes
right up to* RURIKSSON, *raises his knife, and for a moment stands
as still as a statue.*] Now . . . now . . . now . . .

VOICES OUTSIDE: Was it from this house? What's the matter?
Elsa! Suleima? And Justus not home! Hello, there . . . *hello!*

GYPSY: Now . . . now . . . now . . . now . . . [*Suddenly he changes
his tone. He throws the knife away and it lands on the dining-
room table. He begins to dance around pulling off his gypsy rags,
his false nose, and his wig as he goes. He is jubilant. He leaps
and bounds, blowing kisses on the way. He yanks a tablecloth
to him and wipes his face eagerly.*] Ha ha ha ha ha ha!

Ohooooo! *It's me, my children!* It's me, it's me! Look . . . look
. . . [*Wiping off his makeup as he dances.*] You see! It's me!
Justus Coriander!

[*At first they are all struck dumb with amazement. They cannot
believe their eyes.* CORIANDER *pauses for a moment, looking
around in silence from one face to another.*]

CORIANDER: Don't you see . . . it's me!
WILLY [*Breaking the silence, he starts jumping with laughter.*]:
Oh, Papa! Oh, Papa!
MRS. CORIANDER [*Breaking out in a high crackle.*]: Oh, Justus . . .
my dear boy . . . ahhhh! [*She nearly slaps her leg with delight.*]
Didn't I tell you, didn't I tell you about Justus! Now, there's a
sense of humor! [*She rushes to her son and begins dancing with
him, shoving aside* WILLY *and* ANGELICA, *who also want to pay
tribute. The old lady kisses* CORIANDER *several times and gives
him several playful slaps on the back.*] Ohhhh! Coming in and
scaring us like that! Aren't you ashamed, you naughty boy!
There! That's for being bad!
WILLY [*Bellowing.*]: "I'm *here!* I'm *here.*"

[ANGELICA, WILLY *and* MRS. CORIANDER *encircle* CORIANDER, *fond-
ling and caressing him. He has landed in an armchair, and sits
there, catching his breath.* ABRAHAM *stands at a distance, finger-
ing the crease in his trousers. He tries to join in the laughter,
but cannot. Mostly, he is embarrassed and does not really know
what to do with himself.* ELSA, *too, is not in the same good
humor as the group around* CORIANDER. *She has crossed to* RU-
RIKSSON, *who, still trembling, rises slowly. She helps him up,
brushes him off, and tries to comfort him, casting angry glances
over her shoulder toward* CORIANDER. CARL MICHAEL *has run
down stage right, where he stands alone, quite conspicuous, close
to the audience. Clenching and unclenching his fists, he is
deathly pale and speechless with rage. Three faces appear at the
stage right window:* MISS ATTIE, MR. AMBERGRISS, *and* SHERIFF
PLOUGHMAN. *What dominates the stage, however, is* CARL
MICHAEL's *trembling, stifled rage.*]

MRS. CORIANDER: My boy. My darling boy . . .

CORIANDER [*Warding off their affection.*]: Yeah, yeah. Thanks . . . thanks a lot. Ha! I fooled you all, didn't I? Yessir. Old "Chack" really put one over, right? Sure.

THE FACES AT THE WINDOW: What in Heaven's name! Look! Coriander is back!

RURIKSSON [*Rising with great difficulty.*] Ha! . . . Of course, I thought it was him . . . [*He is embarrassed over the way he behaved.*] I had a pretty good idea it was Justus!

ELSA [*Helping to support him.*]: You never know what to expect with Justus! Come Ragnar . . . sit down and take it easy!

RURIKSSON [*Laughing embarrassedly.*]: Ha ha. He really gave me a scare . . . [*Sinking down in the chair offered to him.*] He made me act like a . . . I . . .

ELSA: It was nothing, Ragnar. We're all afraid of dying.

RURIKSSON: He's an actor. Justus is a real . . . rascal, that's what he is . . . ha ha . . .

[*The circle around* CORIANDER *gradually dissolves.* CORIANDER *rises. He is a short, red-faced man, somewhere between fifty and sixty years of age. At times he illustrates his speech with generous, sweeping gestures.*]

CORIANDER: Hello, Elsa . . . hello, everybody. How are you, Ruriksson, my friend? Aren't you glad to see me?

ELSA: Coming home and scaring the wits out of us? You wrote you were going to stay . . . three weeks . . .

CORIANDER: Oh, Elsa, I'm a migratory bird, you know that! So when the King left Marstrand yesterday, together with the Chief Justice, I thought to myself: "Coriander! This is no longer your place. You belong with your loved ones!" Elsa, my dear, my migratory wings started to quiver . . . [*He stretches out his short arms and starts flapping them.*] . . . and homeward I flew! [*He takes a flapping turn across the stage, catching sight of the gaping faces at the window as he goes.*] What are they staring at? [*Changing his tone.*] Oh, it's Sheriff Ploughman . . . and Mr. Ambergriss, the game warden . . . [*With a flirty air which only looks comical on him.*] . . . and little Miss Attie! Well, come

on in, come on in! Come through the window! [*He embraces
them as they climb in, one after the other.* MISS ATTIE *snickers
as he chivalrously kisses her hand.*]

MISS ATTIE: Oh, Mr. Coriander!

CORIANDER: I'm sure grateful to you folks! Coming to defend my
home against a vile intruder! Now I know the kind of friends
I have!

[*There is much pounding on backs and embracing.*]

PLOUGHMAN: It's lucky it was you, Justus, otherwise . . .

AMBERGRISS: Yes, if it had been a murderer, I would have . . .
[*Demonstrating with an imaginary shotgun.*] . . . I would have
. . . bam! bam! bam!

MRS. CORIANDER: He's not the game warden for nothing!

MISS ATTIE [*Breathlessly.*]: And look . . . look what I have . . .
[*Her thin little body shakes with excitement.*] . . . look everybody! . . .

MRS. CORIANDER [*Her voice ringing.*]: A hat pin!

EVERYBODY [Laughing.]: A hat pin! Ha ha ha!

[MISS ATTIE *fences with the hat pin, making violent lunges to
the left and to the right.*]

CORIANDER [*Moved*]: Miss Attie, let me hug you once more! [*He
kisses her on both cheeks in the French manner.*] What made
you do it?

MISS ATTIE [*Idiotically pompous.*]: It was our silent answer to
your unspoken appeal.

[CARL MICHAEL, *quaking with anger, has approached the others
during the last few speeches. Now he stands stage right of the
dining-room table, leaning over it.*]

CARL MICHAEL: You disgust me!

MRS. CORIANDER: Carl Michael!

[*They all turn to look at him.*]

CARL MICHAEL [*Stumbling over his words.*]: You disgust me . . .
all of you! You . . . you come home completely unexpectedly

and scare the Pastor half to death! Look at him! And then you have the gall to call it a *joke!* And the rest of you—[*He is close to swearing.*]—damned milksops—stand there laughing . . . hahahahah . . . Bawling and bleating . . . baaa baaaa . . . like idiotic sheep! You don't dare do anything else . . . you . . . you [*He begins coughing violently.*] . . . you . . .

ELSA [*Uneasily.*]: Calm down, Carl Michael, you know you're not well.

CORIANDER: I forbid you to talk like that to your father!

CARL MICHAEL [*Choking, in a nasty tone.*]: You can't forbid me anything. Oh no, I say what I think. [*Stooping over the table, he has gotten hold of the gypsy knife.*] And I do what I do. [*He raises the knife threateningly and rushes at* CORIANDER.] You . . .

WILLY: Carl Michael!

[*Everyone stands speechless.* ANGELICA *presses herself against* ABRAHAM.]

CARL MICHAEL: One day you'll be punished for what you do . . . and what you are . . . I'll . . .

CORIANDER [*Contemptuously.*]: Do you think I'm afraid of *you!*

CARL MICHAEL: I try to understand you, but I *can't.* Why do you have to laugh at someone who's . . . who's . . . well, moral? I can't help that I'm not like you . . . As a matter of fact . . . I'm proud I'm not. . . .

CORIANDER: You talk about morality . . . with a knife in your hand!

CARL MICHAEL: A minute ago you had it!

MRS. CORIANDER: Drop the knife, Carl Michael!

ELSA: Drop the knife, Carl Michael!

RURIKSSON: For God's sake, Carl Michael, drop the knife!

WILLY: Drop the knife, Carl Michael!

CORIANDER: You heard them! Don't be a fool!

CARL MICHAEL: Maybe you're the fool!

CORIANDER: Drop the knife!

[CARL MICHAEL, *trembling, stands quietly.* CORIANDER *holds his hand out for the knife.*]

MRS. CORIANDER: Give your father the knife, Carl Michael!

[CARL MICHAEL *winces and heaves the knife through the window with all his strength. He turns around the dashes toward the stairs. Stumbling, he runs up and disappears. A door slams. No one speaks.*]

CORIANDER [*Somewhat disconcerted.*]: Whew! If I could only understand that boy!

ELSA: Well, I can!

CORIANDER: Yes, I *know* I go to extremes . . . It's just . . . when I pretend to be a gypsy, I *become* a gypsy. . . .

RURIKSSON: A devil is one thing you don't have to pretend to be, Coriander, because that's what you *are—a devil!*

WILLY: But he's a . . . *funny* devil. [*He collapses under another attack of laughter.*]

CORIANDER: Elsa, go up to the boy. He might be sick, you know . . . Ha! Here I come home thinking to cheer you up with a little joke . . . ah! Go on, Elsa. [ELSA *goes upstairs.*] Ah . . . saying he doesn't understand me! [*Becoming furious.*] But he doesn't *want* to understand me! *None* of you do! *None* of . . . [*While he talks he picks up the rugs and other trash, and carries them to the upstage door. Muttering and swearing, he stops at the door, turning to face the others. Shouting.*] You know . . . you *bore* me . . . all of you! [*He exits, slamming the door behind him.*]

MRS. CORIANDER [*Looking at* RURIKSSON, *her voice ringing*]: Lord, this is no prayer . . . just advice . . . I . . .

RURIKSSON: Well?

[*Pause.*]

WILLY: What is it, Grandma??

MRS. CORIANDER [*Looking around contemptuously at the others, she hesitates to answer.*]: Bosh! [*Leaning heavily on her cane, she moves angrily toward the stairs.*]

Curtain

Act Two

Scene One

Noon the following day.

CORIANDER is seated at the dining-room table eating a late breakfast. With a renaissance greediness he attacks a chicken. Picking up pieces with his hands, he loudly sucks out the bone marrow. The fat drips down his fingers as he breaks the wings off the bird. He drinks red wine out of a huge wine glass, which he constantly empties and refills. He has just begun his meal, and continues eating during the first part of the scene with CARL MICHAEL. Most of the time, he washes down a mouthful of food before speaking.

CORIANDER has been eating several minutes when CARL MICHAEL enters down the stairs. The memory of the explosion of the day before has made the young man timid. When he reaches the foot of the stairs, he approaches his father cautiously. Some time passes before CORIANDER notices him. When he finally does catch sight of him, he pretends indifference at first. CORIANDER continues eating, now and then looking askance at his son.

Clearly, CORIANDER is waiting for CARL MICHAEL to say the first word. Perhaps he wishes to appear a bit wronged. Actually, he is much too egocentric and preoccupied with his meal and with his grand ideas to sustain the illusion.

CORIANDER: Lucullus has lunch with Lucullus! [*He gulps out of*

the glass and refills it.] If King Oscar were to come up to me
right now and ask: "Justus Wilhelm Yngve Coriander, will you
change places with me?," I would answer . . . [*In a natural and
easy intonation.*] . . . "No thanks, Your Majesty. I'm *perfectly*
satisfied the way things are." [*Gulping wine.*] Of course, with
fowl you can also drink sherry, lots of sherry . . . as long as it's
dry, bone-dry! And in *big* glasses . . .

CARL MICHAEL [*Timidly*]: Father . . . [CORIANDER *does not look
up.*] Father . . . [CORIANDER *looks up but does not answer.* CARL
MICHAEL *blurts out his speech as if by rote.*] I'm sorry about
yesterday, it was awful. But I didn't mean anything really bad.
You know how I am. Mother said . . . [*Coughing.*] . . . you
were upset. . . . [CORIANDER *turns back to his plate, sucking
thoughtfully on a bone.*] Forgive me.

CORIANDER: How's your cough?

CARL MICHAEL: All right . . . forgive me.

CORIANDER: For what?

CARL MICHAEL: Well, for flaring up like that . . . for saying all
those things. You remember . . .

CORIANDER: No. I remember only that I had a bad dream. I've
forgotten what it was about. Sit down, Carl Michael.

CARL MICHAEL [*Sitting on the edge of one of the high-backed
chairs.*]: So you've forgotten, huh? Everything I said. That I got
so mad that . . . that . . . I grabbed the knife . . .

CORIANDER: I'm going to tell you something, Carl Michael. Listen
. . . you have to use your fingers to eat chicken. [CARL MICHAEL
sighs and shrugs his shoulders.] You see, animal needs have to
be satisfied naturally. Always drink . . . [*Another gulp.*] . . .
with your whole mouth, crap in a sitting position, and eat with
your fingers! Have a glass of wine!

CARL MICHAEL [*Getting a glass from the cupboard.*]: What good
does it do to get mad at you? You don't get bothered . . . you
don't even react. I think you're unfeeling!

CORIANDER [*Flattered.*] Ha! Like the king of the Vikings!

CARL MICHAEL: It'll take a silver bullet to kill you!

CORIANDER: Yes . . . antique silver . . . not a bad idea. [*He pours
wine for* CARL MICHAEL.] But the wine isn't antique! [CARL
MICHAEL *drinks.*] Aaaaahh! Good, eh? Say, where is everybody?

CARL MICHAEL: In church, of course!

CORIANDER: Yes, of course! in church. You don't believe in that stuff either, do you? That's one thing we have in common, anyway.

CARL MICHAEL: But I believe in *something*. You . . . you believe in nothing.

CORIANDER: In nothing! Me! I believe in dreams. I believe in imagination, in this wine here, this chicken, this salad. Is that nothing?

CARL MICHAEL: You only think you believe. [*Vehemently.*] You only dream you're dreaming! But you'll never break out of yourself. Sure . . . you think you can fly, but you're trapped. You're just a cage, and your heart, if you have one, is a bird cooped up inside!

CORIANDER: *Psychology!* Goddamned *psychology!* Ha . . . [*Gulping.*] Listen . . . I'm going to tell you something before that sanctimonious crowd gets back . . . a damned important thing! I made an experiment the other day . . .

CARL MICHAEL [*Sighing, he knows what is coming.*]: You and your experiments!

CORIANDER: Now listen! In the stock room in back of the store . . . you know . . . there's a strip of flypaper hanging! [*He talks as if the subject were vital and sensational.*] Have you ever noticed it?

CARL MICHAEL: Of course I have.

CORIANDER: But have you *studied* it?

CARL MICHAEL: Studied . . . how do you . . .?

CORIANDER: No! but you see . . . *I have!* Because I keep my eyes open! It was one o'clock in the afternoon . . . [*He takes out his pocket watch, with its wide-dangling chain, and examines it to demonstrate how he acted.*] . . . exactly one o'clock. I made a note of the time! I saw, while on an errand back there, a fly get stuck on it . . . the flypaper, that is. Not until . . . [*He stares intensively at the watch as if he were seeing the hours pass.*] . . . four o'clock, in other words *three* hours later, did I have a chance to return to the stock room. We were real busy that day. And do you know what I discovered? Can you guess?

CARL MICHAEL [*Not especially interested.*] No . . .

CORIANDER [*As if he were announcing something fascinating and unprecedented.*]: *The fly was still stuck there!* The same fly, the same flypaper, at *exactly* the same spot! Now, what does that show, Carl Michael?

CARL MICHAEL: That the flypaper was good. And that you're getting drunk.

CORIANDER: Ah! No imagination! No ability to put two and two together! No, Carl Michael, it showed that there's no better metaphor for life than flypaper! We can't shake *it* loose, and it can't shake *us* loose. But there's one more point, Carl Michael, a *damned* important point . . . I saved it till last. [*He gulps out of the glass.* CARL MICHAEL *shakes his head.*] The fly . . . [*Wiping his mouth with his hand.*] . . . the fly was still *alive!* Its little wings were beating like this. [*Fluttering his hands.*] It sucked and sucked with its little proboscis, which was stuck in the sugar paste. It was a terrible thing to see, Carl Michael, but at the same time, it was *heroic!* [*Quietly.*] I'll be damned if it didn't sit there dreaming. It was dreaming that it was flying . . . a tiny, tiny buzzing speck in the broad, yellow sunlight. Buzz, buzz, buzz. But that was only what the naked eye could see. To the inner eye, the *thinking eye* . . . get this . . . the fly's life was ended. Ended at one o'clock in the afternoon of an ordinary workday in the stock room in back of Coriander's store! And yet, when you looked at it, it was still alive! There! That's what I call a *probable*, er, a *parabola!*

CARL MICHAEL: And I call it talk!

CORIANDER [*Offended.*]: And what's wrong with talk, if I may ask? Can't you see that words have wings, just as flies do, just as this chicken . . . [*He bites into a wing.*] . . . which by the way is damned tough! Goddammit, I'll have to talk to Mrs. Eriksson! [*Rinsing his mouth and gargling.*] Bringing out a damned chicken like that! . . . Yes, words have wings and we . . . we fly with them! [*Springing up from the table, he spreads out his big red hands, flaps them as if he were flying, and swoops about the room.*] Wheeeee! We perch snugly on the back of a word, and down there the world spreads out! Hah! How tiny and trifling it looks from up here! People are just like flies! Haha! Oh! [*A spleen attack hits him suddenly. He staggers back to his chair, falling gasping into it.*] Oh! Jeez . . . [*Groaning.*] I'm getting old . . . [*Gulping wine.*] You have no imagination, Carl Michael!

CARL MICHAEL: No, but I live on that little globe you spit on from your feathery perch on the back of a word.

CORIANDER: You get the whole picture from there. Oh! [*He clutches his side.*] An overview!

CARL MICHAEL: You think everything will always be the same, Father. But it's not true. History doesn't agree with you!

CORIANDER [*Eating and gasping.*]: Ahhh! You read too much of that Max . . .

CARL MICHAEL: Marx!

CORIANDER: If I say Max, it's Max. You hear me . . . Max!

CARL MICHAEL: Max . . .

CORIANDER: Max, Max, Max, Max. You read too much of that there Max. But I . . . I read poetry!

CARL MICHAEL: Poetry! What good does it do? Abstractions!

CORIANDER: Bosh! It gives us the whole picture, that's what it does!

CARL MICHAEL: Oh no, it doesn't. Just look at you. You talk about Life. But you don't give a damn about the living. You talk about Death. But you've forgotten the dead. You talk about Love. But you can't love! [*He gulps the rest of his wine rapidly.*] The same is true of the poetry you read . . .

CORIANDER: Wait a minute! I have parabola . . .

CARL MICHAEL: . . . drawn from a reality you talk about but have never seen!

CORIANDER: And what about you, Carl Michael? What have you seen? You can only dream with your Max. And Ruriksson dreams about Outer Mongolia.

CARL MICHAEL: And you . . . you dream in general!

CORIANDER: I know what I know. Therefore I dream. Therefore I believe in the dream.

CARL MICHAEL: You don't want to hear about *reality*! That's how closed your mind is!

CORIANDER: All right, so my mind is closed! But it's in the truly closed societies that culture grows! Look at the French. For all their silly "wee we mon-sure," they have culture! The dirtier the rooms, the cleaner the culture, and the bigger and freer the *dreams*! Do you know why you believe in reality, Carl Michael?

CARL MICHAEL: I have to believe in it in order to change it.

CORIANDER: No! Just remember the probable about the fly, my

boy! You have things too *easy* . . . *that's* why you believe in reality! If you'd had it as I . . .

CARL MICHAEL: And now you're a success, I know! But you won't let others be the same. You talk out of both sides of your mouth at once.

CORIANDER [*His mouth full.*]: I do not talk out of both sides of my mouth! I can only speak for myself. I'm too . . . modest to speak for others!

CARL MICHAEL: Ha! Modest!

CORIANDER: The Erikssons are going to get it for this chicken. [*Unmotivatedly.*] Papa was a cardsharp.

CARL MICHAEL: Just like you!

CORIANDER: You should have seen him! Right here on his left hand, he had a big red scar. It was from a knife.

CARL MICHAEL [*Troubled.*]: Knife?

CORIANDER: That's right! I saw when he got the scar. It happened one night in a card game. I remember I was watching him cheat. Unfortunately, the guy he was beating noticed it, too! His name was Ekstroem, he was a shoemaker . . .

CARL MICHAEL: Well?

CORIANDER [*He pours more wine for himself and* CARL MICHAEL.]: Papa's hand was spread like a fan on the table, and under it was an ace of hearts! He used to do that often . . . with an ace of hearts. I saw it lots of times! [*Gulping out of the glass.*] But Ekstroem saw it, too! And . . . bang! . . . he put that knife right through Papa's hand! And the hand stuck to the table and the knife went right through the ace. Ha! But Papa didn't cry out, he didn't make a sound. He just pulled the knife out. You could hardly recognize that it was the ace of hearts!

CARL MICHAEL: You never told me that before.

CORIANDER [*A bit excitedly.*]: Didn't I? Well, is that so strange?

CARL MICHAEL: I don't believe you. It's just something you read some place! You're lying!

CORIANDER: Ask Grandma then . . . no, for God's sake, don't ask Grandma!

CARL MICHAEL [*Laughing uneasily, he does not know what to believe.*]: An ace of hearts . . . a scar on the hand . . . ahh, you're lying!

CORIANDER: You could hardly see it was the ace of hearts. It's around here somewhere. I saved it. [*Drinking.*] I've done some cheating, too. But that experience taught me to keep my hand under the table. It's not enough just to *believe* in the lie. You have to be able to *tell* it, too. And that's no mean trick. But you wouldn't understand . . . [*Hissing contemptuously.*] . . . because you have it too easy . . . too easy . . .

CARL MICHAEL: I believe humanity can advance honestly.

CORIANDER: Ask Grandma . . . she's honest.

CARL MICHAEL: What about you?

CORIANDER: I'm honest because I like myself. *Like* yourself, Carl Michael, and you won't have to fear God! It gets a little lonely. [*Gulping.*] But loneliness is strong. [*He extends his arms and soars fancifully. He is becoming quite drunk.*] And loneliness has wings . . . wheeee . . .

CARL MICHAEL: You really are strange, Father. [*He takes away the plate with the chicken and replaces it with an ugly plate of peaches.*] I . . .

CORIANDER: We're all strange.

CARL MICHAEL: I don't understand any part of you. And yet, the pieces seem to fit together!

CORIANDER [*Very absentmindedly.*]: In some cockeyed way, yes, in some cockeyed way. The way life and death fit together, and the seed and the fruit . . . [*Picking up a knife, he begins, grandly, to pare a peach.*] Have a peach!

CARL MICHAEL: Aren't you *aware* of anything?

CORIANDER: What did you say? [*He is fully occupied with his peach.*]

CARL MICHAEL: I said, aren't you *aware* of anything?

CORIANDER: Of what?

CARL MICHAEL: Well, for example, Mother and Ruriksson. The other day when I came into the dining room they were standing over there in the corner and . . .

CORIANDER: I'm going to tell you something. When you pare a peach, you have to be terribly awfully careful, because the fruit closest to the pit . . . is the . . . [*He has sliced out a wedge, which disappears in his mouth.*] . . . healthiest! [*En passant.*] Leave them alone. And here . . . here's the pit . . . red . . . almost crimson, eh? Just look! [*Drunkenly near-sighted, he holds the pit close to his face in order to examine it.*] Like a giant garnet, isn't it? Like the heart on an anatomical chart!

CARL MICHAEL: I guess you have one some place. God knows where.

CORIANDER: Don't ask God! He doesn't know *anything*! The pit is hard . . . do you know why? To protect the seed! Underneath this hard, beautiful crimson shell, a whole, new fragrant peach tree is growing! That's what has to be protected! At all costs!

CARL MICHAEL: All right, so don't take notice of anything, then! You're afraid of people—because you think they're all like you. And you're afraid of yourself.

CORIANDER: Ha!

CARL MICHAEL: As far as you're concerned, the world can either advance or go to hell! Well, it doesn't take notice of you, either, don't you believe it! It loves, and grows, and blooms *without* you, in *spite* of you! Everything beautiful happens behind your back!

CORIANDER: No, in here! [*He strikes his fist against his chest.*] Pour out some white wine!

[CARL MICHAEL *pours from the white-wine bottle while he talks. The operation distracts him a bit and takes half the sting out of his new attack.*]

CARL MICHAEL: I think they hate you . . .

CORIANDER: Who? [CARL MICHAEL *gestures impatiently upstage.*] Nonsense . . . aahh! . . . [*He drinks some of the white wine.*] Liebfraumilch . . . [*Singing.*] Liebfraumilch 91! Good, eh? But it has to be chilled! [*In the same breath.*] Nonsense . . . they don't have the strength to hate. Or love either. They just pretend. Pour some more. For you, too.

CARL MICHAEL [*Pouring.*]: And what about you?

CORIANDER: What's that?

CARL MICHAEL: Can you hate or love?

[CORIANDER *grows silent. Then he rises suddenly, yawns, and crosses to behind the stairs. When he returns he is carrying a can of varnish and two large brushes. He goes up to* CARL MICHAEL *and looks at him thoughtfully.*]

CORIANDER: That's a secret. Here. [*He hands a brush to the bewildered* CARL MICHAEL.]

CARL MICHAEL: What's this?

CORIANDER [*Pedagogically.*]: A brush, my friend. [*Pointing at the can.*] And this is a gallon of Retzen's new sulfur varnish. Dries in a second, says Retzen. But I never sell anything without first trying it myself! I'm like Lucretia Borgia's wine-tester . . . ready to die at my post! Let's go!

[*Together,* CORIANDER *and* CARL MICHAEL *varnish the dining-room table, the chairs, the big Bible on the cupboard, in short, everything in sight. They exchange such directions as "Put some more there!" and "Well, that's finished!" and "Make the Bible glisten!" and so forth.*]

CARL MICHAEL [*Varnishing.*]: I can hate. You, for example. Sometimes.

CORIANDER: Yes, I've noticed that. Ha ha! [*He imitates* CARL MICHAEL's *tone of the day before.*] "One day you'll be punished for what you are . . . and what you do . . ." Ha ha!

CARL MICHAEL: So you remember your bad dream after all?

CORIANDER: "One day you'll be punished . . ." It's things like that make me . . . love you. For me, opposition is not just opposition. It's also a support! [*The exertion of the painting nearly sends him careening.*] Dammit!

CARL MICHAEL: God, you're *horrible*!

CORIANDER: And I need support. I'm getting old. Even if it's only a wall erected *against* me. You need support, too . . . the support of my opposition . . . because you're . . . you're so young!

CARL MICHAEL: You're a fool, Father. A sentimental old fool. And your sentimentalities are just the tears of heartlessness . . . damn it to hell!

CORIANDER: What's that . . . Max coming out again? The opium of the people—and what's wrong with opium, anyway? I hear it gives you beautiful dreams!

CARL MICHAEL: Ah, chatter!

CORIANDER [*Straining with work.*]: Say . . . have you . . . ever heard talk about that there . . . Darvin?

CARL MICHAEL [*Timidly.*]: DarWIN.

CORIANDER: Well? Did you understand him, huh? I mean what his theory means?

CARL MICHAEL: That we're evolving toward something better . . .

CORIANDER: Is that right? And this "natural selection," what does that show?

CARL MICHAEL: That . . .

CORIANDER: Well, you see, *that* shows that you and I, we're descended from the apes and then from the people who were the most *devilish*! It's the strongest, hardest, most terrible apes who have survived, you see! The hairiest . . . the cruelest . . . there you have your forefathers! What devils they must have been, but thanks to them, you're alive! You and your damned Max!

CARL MICHAEL: His name is Marx!

CORIANDER: Ho ho! You got scared, huh? Bringing Max to bed with you when you sleep! It's like your're in love with your Max!

CARL MICHAEL [*Shouting.*]: Abraham and Angelica, Pa . . . [*He throws his brush away and wrenches the can out of his father's hand.* CORIANDER *laughs teasingly and pretends to be about to poke his son in the face with his brush.*] . . . there you have *love!* Accept it, Pa . . . let them have each other!

CORIANDER [*He takes a fencing position with the brush, as if protecting himself against a lunge.*]: Angelica and my grocery clerk . . . ho ho! Social justice! [*Abruptly, he throws his brush away and playfully grabs* CARL MICHAEL'S *arms.*] May I have this dance, Max . . . may I kiss you, Max!

CARL MICHAEL: Stop it, Pa! let them have each other, Pa . . . [*He pulls away.*] Their love is the only thing beautiful and clean in this house, Pa! [*He, too, is influenced by the wine. He takes cover behind a chair.*] Let them have each other!

CORIANDER: A candidate for the poorhouse who can hardly measure out five pounds of potatoes . . . and Angelica, my lily, my blushing rose! Oh no, . . . you'll have to talk to your Max about . . .

CARL MICHAEL: Materialist!

CORIANDER [*Playfully solemn.*]: My interpretation of history is materialistic . . . exactly like your Max's!

CARL MICHAEL [*Suddenly moved, he rushes to his father and embraces him.*]: Let them have each other, you old idiot! [*They stand embracing each other. Sensing a sudden affinity, they both begin to laugh.*] Old fool . . . old idiot . . .

[CORIANDER *bows elegantly, if also awkwardly, begins humming, and invites* CARL MICHAEL *to join in a formal eighteenth-century dance.*]

CORIANDER: Remember the fly, Max! Remember the fly! [*They both laugh. After several moments of formal dancing, they change to a polka tempo, singing, bouncing and stumbling. The upstage door opens, but they do not notice* MRS. CORIANDER *stands in the doorway, and behind her,* ELSA *and* RURIKSSON. *After a time.* CORIANDER *breaks off, groaning, laughing and clutching his side. He stumbles toward a chair in the furniture group.*] Oh . . . oh . . . [*Clutching his left side.*] My spleen . . . my liver . . . my stomach . . . my corns. Oh . . . jeez . . . oh . . . [*He is about to sink into a chair when* MRS. CORIANDER, *her eyes flashing, explodes.*]

MRS. CORIANDER: What in God's name is going on here? ! ! ?

[CORIANDER *and* CARL MICHAEL *cringe and stare at each other in horror. They begin laughing again, but quickly stifle it. The others parade in solemnly—*MRS. CORIANDER, ELSA, RURIKSSON, WILLY, ANGELICA, ABRAHAM, MISS ATTIE, MR. AMBERGRISS, *and* SHERIFF PLOUGHMAN.]

CARL MICHAEL [*Having difficulty breathing.*]: We were just . . .
CORIANDER: We were just . . . sitting here . . . talking . . .
MRS. CORIANDER: *Talking?* [*She skips a little to imitate their polka.*] Do you call that talking?
RURIKSSON: I am acquainted with your godlessness, Justus. But even if you have no faith yourself, you can at least respect it in other people!
MRS. CORIANDER [*Relenting, she crosses to the funiture group.*]: Nincompoops! [*Sinking down in a chair.*] Nincompoops, that's what you are!
ELSA [*Feeling inside* CARL MICHAEL'S *collar as the young man starts to cough again.*]: Why, you're soaking wet! You know what the doctor said: You *mustn't* exert yourself!

CARL MICHAEL [*With a parrying gesture.*]: Ahh! Leave me alone!
[*He fights a new coughing attack with his handkerchief.*] Leave
me . . . alone . . . I said!

ELSA [*Observing the two empty wine bottles.*]: And you, Justus!
Drinking and dancing—on a Sunday!

RURIKSSON [*Gravely.*]: . . . and while services were going on!

MRS. CORIANDER [*Equally gravely.*]: You boys are tipsy!

ELSA [*To* ANGELICA.]: Clear away your father's dishes, Angelica!
[*She speaks gently, almost whispering, as one speaks to a child
or a puppy. She then turns to the disconcerted trio,* PLOUGHMAN,
MISS ATTIE *and* MR. AMBERGRISS, *who have tarried at the door.*]
Come in, come in!

[*Meanwhile,* RURIKSSON *has crossed to the cupboard and grasped
the Bible. He soon discovers that he is stuck to it, and begins to
attempt to shake it loose.*
[*At the same time,* MRS. CORIANDER *discovers that she is stuck
to the back of the chair she is sitting in.*
[*At the same time,* ABRAHAM *is stuck to a lamp, which he is at-
tempting to move to the furniture group.*
[*At the same time,* MISS ATTIE, MR. AMBERGRISS *and* SHERIFF
PLOUGHMAN *find that the chairs they are leaning on have attached themselves to coat cuffs and skirts. They drag the chairs
after them as they try to shake themselves loose.*
[*At the same time,* ANGELICA *is stuck to the tray she is carrying
out.*
[*At the same time,* ELSA *is stuck to an alarm clock, which rings
loudly as she attempts to free herself from it.*]

RURIKSSON: I'm stuck to the Bible! I'm stuck to the Bible! [*He
crosses and takes the center stake among the figures struggling
with their predicament.*]

MRS. CORIANDER: What is this? What is this?

MISS ATTIE: My dress! My dress!

SHERIFF PLOUGHMAN: My uniform! My uniform!

MR. AMBERGRISS: My frock coat! My frock coat!

ABRAHAM: I'm stuck! I'm stuck!

[ANGELICA *shakes the tray loose and it falls amid a crash of
porcelain.*]

ELSA [*Shaking the ringing clock.*]: Justus! Justus!
CORIANDER: Damn that Retzen!

[*Everyone shouts simultaneously, in a total cacophony.*]

MRS. CORIANDER: Justus! What have you done?
CORIANDER [*Screeching over the din.*]: It *says* on the can, Mama!
It says on the can that . . .
RURIKSSON [*Pitiably.*]: I'm stuck to the Bible . . . stuck to the
Bible!

[WILLY, *the only one not fastened to anything, laughs until the
tears flow.*]

WILLY: Oh . . . what a sense of humor, Papa! "I'm here! I'm
here!"
RURIKSSON: Get this Bible away from me . . . for God's sake . . .
get it away!
CORIANDER: That *devil* Retzen!

[CARL MICHAEL *tries to tear the Bible away from* RURIKSSON, *but,
of course, he too becomes fastened to it.*]

CARL MICHAEL: Pull . . . pull . . . [*Laughing.*] . . . ha ha ha . . .
MRS. CORIANDER: Justus!
ELSA: This time, Justus, you've gone too far . . .
MRS. CORIANDER: You're no son of mine!
CORIANDER: But it says on the can . . .
EVERYBODY: My dress! My uniform! My frock coat! Get this Bible
away from me! Oh, oh! What a sense of humor!
CORIANDER: It says on the can . . .

Blackout

Curtain

Scene Two

Several minutes later.
Order is restored, but everyone is silent. There is a sense of dread in the air.
CORIANDER *sits with his back turned.*

Coriander [*Muttering.*]: It *said* on the can! Damned Retzen! [*Then he turns about, springs to his feet, and claps his hands.*] It's time for the Sunday Promenade!

Elsa: Oh, not today . . . we have guests!

Coriander: All the more reason! Right, Mama?

Mrs. Coriander: Oh, sure. It's just that my poor old legs . . .

Coriander: Bosh! What about my spleen? And Carl Michael's cough?

Elsa: Not Carl Michael! Surely he can stay home!

Coriander: Carl Michael comes along and that's final! Willy, Abraham . . . go out in the kitchen and help Angelica with the picnic basket. [ABRAHAM *and* WILLY *obey, but they are halted halfway to the door.*] Wait a minute! Don't forget the strawberry jam . . . for me . . . and Miss Attie! [MISS ATTIE *giggles coquettishly.* WILLY *and* ABRAHAM *nod and are about to disappear.*] Wait! Don't be in such a damned hurry! Get a bottle of port wine . . . on the far left in the big cupboard, right in back of the box of rolled oats. What do you say, men, a good port wine to speed up the marching? Oh, and Willy . . . three Havana cigars . . . lower left cupboard in back of the garbage pail. Today is a real occasion!

Miss Attie: It'll be nice to take a promenade! Where shall we go?

Coriander: Around the dining-room table.

SHERIFF PLOUGHMAN: Around the . . . dining-room table?

CORIANDER: That's right. Around the dining-room table!

MR. AMBERGRISS [*Skeptically.*]: But how . . . you mean *around* the table?

CORIANDER: Quiet, Henry! Wait and see!

RURIKSSON: Perhaps an explanation is in order.

CORIANDER: No explanation needed! Imagination will lead the way! Right . . . Elsa?

ELSA: But maybe you should tell a little about . . .

RURIKSSON [*Aware that he sounds silly.*]: It's one of Justus's inventions. One of his more pleasant ones, actually. You see, we promenade around the table and pretend that we're walking in the woods, or in a foreign city or . . . well, on the moon, or . . .

MR. AMBERGRISS [*Confusedly.*]: On the moon?

SHERIFF PLOUGHMAN: You promenade . . . on the moon?

[RURIKSSON *is embarrassed, but enthusiastic, nevertheless.*]

RURIKSSON: Yes. Heh, heh. On the moon. Or in Paris! Or . . .

MISS ATTIE: In Paris? Oh, Pastor!

RURIKSSON: Heh heh. Or in Rome, then. Perhaps that would be more appropriate . . . on a Sunday. It's an . . . he he . . . an imaginary picnic, you see, a journey in . . . well, fantasy!

CORIANDER: You'll see! Aha! [WILLY, ANGELICA *and* ABRAHAM *enter with two baskets, the contents of which are covered with white tablecloths.*] Here they come! Everything's ready! Fall in! [*Everyone assembles about him, the three newcomers with trepidation.*] Give us the key, Mama! [MRS. CORIANDER *trips over to the piano and strikes an "f". They all hum, except the newcomers.* CORIANDER *supervises the chorus with the flapping arms of a conductor.*] A *one* and a *two* and a *three!*

[*During the following song, they all pair off and march clockwise around the dining-room table. At the head of the column is* CORIANDER, *with his mother on one arm, and a somewhat intoxicated but still recalcitrant* CARL MICHAEL *on the other. They are followed by* ELSA *and* RURIKSSON, *who carries one of the baskets. Then come* MISS ATTIE *and* MR. AMBERGRISS, *at first disconcerted, but gradually becoming enthusiastic participants.*

Then come SHERIFF PLOUGHMAN *and* WILLY, *and finally the last couple*—ABRAHAM *and* ANGELICA. *At first, she is carrying the second basket, but* ABRAHAM *gallantly and lovingly relieves her of the burden.* ANGELICA *skips, hopping twice on each foot, like a little girl. After each lap around the table she raises another finger to keep track of the number. Three laps are completed during the song.*]

ALL [*Singing.*]:
    Everyone, everyone come along
    It's Sunday, let's sing our Promenade Song!
      The North Wind roars,
      The North Wind roars,
    It's strong and brisk, though we march indoors!
CORIANDER:
    Is the basket full?
ELSA:
    Yes, the basket's full,
    Of apples and cakes and nice Swiss cheese!
MRS. CORIANDER:
    And swarms of bees!
ALL:
    Ho ho ho!
SHERIFF PLOUGHMAN [*With a newly-found certainty.*]:
    And wine, if you please?
ALL:
    Ho ho ho!

[RURIKSSON *looks in his basket and discovers that the wine is missing.*]

WILLY:
    And as long as we march we'll never freeze!
ALL:
    Everyone, everyone come along
    It's Sunday, let's sing our promenade song!
      The North Wind roars,
      The North Wind roars,
    It's strong and brisk, though we march indoors!

CORIANDER:
We travel and travel as far as we're able . . .
RURIKSSON:
. . . yet all we do is circle the table!
ELSA:
See the Southern Cross shining here up north!
MISS ATTIE:
Oh! Imagination as we go forth . . .
MR. AMBERGRISS:
. . . makes us buzz along like a swarm of bees . . .
ABRAHAM:
. . . and we praise God's name while down on our knees!
ALL:
    The North Wind roars,
    The North Wind roars,
It's strong and brisk though we march indoors.
CORIANDER [*Shouting.*] Make a full circle, Miss Attie! No cheating there!
ALL:
    Everyone, everyone come along
    It's Sunday, let's sing our Promenade Song!
    Everyone, everyone come along
    It's Sunday, let's sing our Promenade Song!
RURIKSSON [*Timidly.*]: The wine!
CORIANDER [*Not listening.*]: What do you think of the song, Miss Attie?
RURIKSSON: We . . .
CORIANDER: Brilliant, hah? I wrote it myself. . . . What did you say, Ruriksson?
RURIKSSON: The wine . . .
CORIANDER: Well?
RURIKSSON: It seems to have been left behind.
CORIANDER: That's criminal! Willy, go get the wine!
WILLY: Yes sir!
CORIANDER: Angelica, how many laps?

[ANGELICA *holds up three fingers.*]

WILLY: Three!

CORIANDER: Three it was and three it'll be . . . and no cheating! [WILLY, *watched attentively by the others, begins running three laps, counterclockwise, around the table.*]

RURIKSSON [*To* MISS ATTIE *and the other newcomers*]: Perhaps this calls for a *little* explanation . . .
CORIANDER: Don't question their powers of imagination, Ruriksson!
RURIKSSON: No one is allowed to break the spell during the Sunday Promenade. Since we've come three laps, anyone who has to go back must return three laps. Those are the rules of the game. They must not be broken. Whoever breaks them is . . . dead, you might say. He he. It probably seems a little silly . . .
MRS. CORIANDER: *Silly?*
RURIKSSON: Well, I mean, to the uninitiated . . .

[WILLY *has finished his laps.*]

WILLY: Three!
RURIKSSON: Pretend not to hear! You see, we're too far away to be able to hear him. Yes . . . it does seem a little silly, I guess.
MISS ATTIE ([*Enthusiastically.*]: Certainly not!
CORIANDER: Bravo, Miss Attie!
PLOUGHMAN *and* AMBERGRISS [*Still disconcerted*]: Not at all! Not the least bit!

[WILLY *is on has way back from the kitchen with a bottle of wine under each arm. He hustles around with naive eagerness.*]

CORIANDER: There we are! Welcome back, Willy! [WILLY *packs the bottles down in* ABRAHAM'S *basket and reoccupies his place in the procession.*] That was quick work. Off we go again! Where to, my friends?
MRS. CORIANDER: Not much further, eh? My legs . . . Can't we sit down for awhile? [*She looks longingly at the furniture group.*]
CORIANDER: Oh no! We'll try a few more laps! You can lean on me, Mama. [*To the others.*] Well, have you decided?
SHERIFF PLOUGHMAN: Let's go to the riding stable!
MISS ATTIE: No thanks! I hate horses! How about Lookout Point?

MR. AMBERGRISS: Me and Miss Attie vote for Lookout Point.

CORIANDER: Hold it!

MRS. CORIANDER: What is it now?

CORIANDER: Don't you see, Mama?

MRS. CORIANDER: What?

CORIANDER: The fog . . . [*In a spooky voice.*] . . . fog!

RURIKSSON: Not fog again! We had that last Sunday! [*He crouches, groping his way forward, like all the others.*]

CORIANDER [*Gravely.*]: Fog . . . fog . . . bad luck, Ruriksson! Fog . . . wherever you look. . . . Stay close together! Elsa, Mama, Carl Michael . . . stay close to me!

MRS. CORIANDER: Ugh! Fog . . . let's go home, then!

CORIANDER: You just try, Mama! Not in this fog . . . dense . . . billowing . . . lingering . . .

WILLY: Thick as soup!

ABRAHAM [*Who has fallen a little behind.*]: Where are you? Where are you? Hello there!

ELSA: Hello! Over here!

ALL: Here we are! Yoohoo!

ABRAHAM [*Groping for* ANGELICA, *he presses her to him.*]: Here's Angelica! I found you!

CORIANDER: Good! We'll go on! Watch your step! [*He cups his hands in front of his mouth and imitates a foghorn.*] Uuuuuuuh . . . uuuuuuh.

SHERIFF PLOUGHMAN: What was that?

MISS ATTIE [*Shrilly.*]: A foghorn! Watch out! We must be near the ocean!

RURIKSSON: You can't see a hand in front of your face. I'm blind!

MRS. CORIANDER: Oh, we know that, all right! Maybe you'll have a little vision!

ELSA: Mother Coriander!

ABRAHAM: Has anyone got a shawl to lend to Angelica? She's freezing. [*He takes a chance and embraces her.*]

MRS. CORIANDER: The fog's going to have to let up! I don't like this!

CORIANDER: Yes, it should, and it is letting up! [*Singing.*] The sun's coming out!

MISS ATTIE [*Pathetically.*]: Oh, how dazzling! What dazzling loveliness!

Mrs. Coriander [*Sourly.*]: Bosh!

Coriander: No, look! [*Whispering to the others.*]Look, look! Isn't that Miss Nicander out walking? And who's that with her? . . . isn't that . . .

Mrs. Coriander: Yes, it is!

Ruriksson [*Idiotically*]: Yes, by golly! What can those two be up to out here . . . [*Giggling.*] . . . on a foggy Sunday afternoon?

Mrs. Coriander: Probably relaxing after Ruriksson's sermon.

Elsa [*Naïvely*]: Mother! It was beautiful!

Coriander: And the way she's dressed! Just look! Ho ho!

Miss Attie: How unfashionable! Ha!

Coriander: Sh . . . do you see what they're doing?

Mrs. Coriander: Oh . . . now I must say . . . !

Sheriff Ploughman: Now, see here . . .

Mrs. Ambergriss [*Contrivedly. He has the hardest time of all developing a style for the game.*]: Isn't there any sense of shame left!!

Elsa: And on a Sunday!

Ruriksson: Come, let's hurry by! [*He speeds up his marching.*] Don't look, Miss Attie, I beg you!

Coriander: How many laps?

[*ANGELICA holds up her fingers and WILLY counts them.*]

Willy: Seven!

Coriander: With the weather so beautiful, we'll have to make it a really long promenade! Watch out for snakes, my friends! [*He jumps involuntarily. Suspicious, he examines the dining-room rug.*] It's time to eat soon . . . but where?

Mrs. Coriander: Here! Justus . . . I told you that my legs . . .

Miss Attie *and* **Mr. Ambergriss**: At Lookout Point!

Sheriff Ploughman: No, at the riding stable!

Elsa: On Clover Meadow, I say! It's so pretty in July!

Mrs. Coriander: And I say Lighthouse Park! At least there are benches there to sit on!

Coriander: [*Pompously shaking his head.*]: Children, children . . . no! You have no imagination! You're earthbound creatures . . . I'm sorry . . . but that's what you are! Here I treat you to a promenade, and where do you want to go? To familiar places you've been to hundreds of times! No, let your imagination play . . . like a big brass band! Carl Michael, you're always reading so much, why don't you say something . . . whither away? To Africa, maybe, to the great plains where the lion prowls and the jackals scream in the night? Let's go far, far away! To China, maybe . . . to Outer Mongolia.

RURIKSSON [*Dreamily*]: Yes, Outer Mongolia . . . to Outer Mongolia . . . where souls cry out for comfort and consolation!

CORIANDER: I was asking Carl Michael! Where? To China, with its cruel forms of execution. Have I told you about their water-barrel punishment? Ha! All you see are the victim's feet sticking up through the lid . . . China, with its Great Wall and its bamboo? Or, to the moon, with craters like the holes in old teeth.

MRS. CORIANDER: Don't remind me!

CORIANDER: To Venus, to Saturn, to the ends of the earth! Just say where, Carl Michael! You've read Jules Verne, haven't you?

CARL MICHAEL: All right, then . . . into the future. To fifty or a hundred years from now, when people will finally live peacefully, side by side . . . when everybody has enough to eat and nobody gets eaten. . . . To the future!

CORIANDER: No! You'd be disappointed, I'm sure of that. Time is our enemy. Let's not talk about anything but the *now*. *Now* we're alive, *now* we exist!

MRS. CORIANDER: And *now* I'm sitting down.

CORIANDER: But Mama . . .

MRS. CORIANDER: . . . and *now* I sat down. My legs tell me what to do, not you. You go ahead and run, if you can. I'm staying here. [*With great determination she has occupied the most comfortable chair. Confusion. After a pause.*] Go ahead now! But leave me a sandwich!

ELSA: Well, I think . . .

MR. AMBERGRISS: I could go for a little . . .

MISS ATTIE: I think we've walked far enough!

RURIKSSON: My stomach is rumbling a bit.

CORIANDER [*Giving in to superior odds.*]: All right, lazybones! Bring out the food! I guess it will taste pretty good. [*They sit down on the rug in a circle around* MRS. CORIANDER. *The picnic baskets are examined and emptied of their rich contents amid loud, joyful shouts:* "Wonderful! Look, sausage!

I've never seen anything like it! Ham! Strawberries! It never
ends! Ahhh!" *Glasses and plates are passed out. Wine is poured
for the men and the bottles are recorked. Although the march-
ers have scattered more or less at random,* RURIKSSON *has managed to be close to* ELSA, *and* ABRAHAM *to* ANGELICA.] Guess
where we are. [*He is eating a sandwich and washing it down
with wine.*]

RURIKSSON: In the park around the Villa Borghese?

SHERIFF PLOUGHMAN: In Paris . . . he he . . .

MR. AMBERGRISS [*Snapping his fingers to imitate castonets.*]: In
Madrid! In Lisbon!

CORIANDER: No, around a campfire.

MR. AMBERGRISS: Are we soldiers?

CORIANDER: Yes, we're soldiers.

[*The women giggle, but they shrug their shoulders and do not
protest. Peace reigns. The atmosphere of a summer picnic in the
country settles over the bizarre company. It is as if there were
a warm drowsiness in the air. They hum, eat and yawn.* CORI-
ANDER *talks in a low, soft voice. As the scene progresses, the
lighting changes to an atmosphere of dreamlike unreality.*]

MRS. CORIANDER [*Snickering to herself*]: Soldiers? Us!

CORIANDER: Soldiers. It's evening. It'll be dark soon, We've lighted
a campfire. In the distance we can see other campfires blazing.
They're like beacons, like a glowing string of pearls disappearing
over the horizon. We're tired. We must get to sleep soon.
Sleep's important, because tomorrow the battle begins, the
great, decisive battle.

ABRAHAM [*in a low voice*]:
    What'll it be like?
    It looks dark to me. And yet . . . and yet
    I trust tomorrow.

WILLY [*caught up in the mood*]:
    How can you?

ABRAHAM:
    Well, if I'm brave—and still survive—
    Maybe they'll find a hero in me
    And if they promote me
    I won't have to be a private all my life.

WILLY:

>   You're better off, my friend, as a private.
>   They don't expect too much from you.
>   As a private you're a slave, but still free . . .

MR. AMBERGRISS:

>   Throw another log on the fire!

WILLY:

>   Yes sir!

ABRAHAM:

>   You're right. But I'm not free
>   To wed the one I love most of all.

WILLY:

>   For a soldier there are lots of . . .

ABRAHAM:

>   But for me there's only one. She's the one and only.
>   If you once saw her, you'd still be dazzled.
>   You never saw what I saw. The loveliest.
>   You never heard what I hear, a fountain . . .
>   Like the ringing of a bell . . .

WILLY:

>   I wish I could feel that way for someone.

SHERIFF PLOUGHMAN:

>   So do I! Once . . . [*He smiles at the memory.*]
>   For an officer it's easy to be cocky
>   And yelling at a corporal is a cinch
>   But you get lonely, and never learn anything.
>   You come home on leave and go to her
>   And brace yourself to ask . . .
>   But it never gets said and it never gets done.
>   That's the way it is—
>   Nothing ever comes of anything.

MISS ATTIE:

>   Once I had dreams
>   About home and love.

MR. AMBERGRISS:

>   Me too! But all I have are friends.
>   Three days at a hunting lodge, another at a tavern.
>   Let's be pals, swap hunting stories . . .
>   Comrades! Here's to the King!

God save the King!
I'm talking about *men*. Mostly it was *men*
And later, in the woods, loneliness took their place.
They're not really enough ... friends ... men ...
Between men, there's nothing to remember or to miss
Like now, like this—before the battle.

CARL MICHAEL:

How warm the fire is. Say, have you thought
That by another fire on the other side
There are people sitting just like us
Soldiers like us, mostly mercenaries,
Eating the same food and dreaming the same dreams.
And yet we call them enemies ...

CORIANDER:

All right!
More wood on the fire, boys! Quiet!
I heard something.

ELSA:

Where?

CORIANDER:

There in the brush.

RURIKSSON:

Ah, it was nothing!

CARL MICHAEL:

Except the future
Sneaking up on us. Echoes
Of our small skirmishes echoing on,
Doubling and re-doubling a thousandfold
In an echo chamber of tomorrow.

CORIANDER:

Nonsense!
It's time to sleep. Tomorrow the battle begins. [*Pause.*]

ABRAHAM:

It's hard to sleep.

WILLY [*To* MRS. CORIANDER.]:

Tell us a story to make us sleep!

MRS. CORIANDER:

Most of my stories are evil!

ELSA:

Let's hear one anyway!

[*They lie down in the "grass" to listen to* MRS. CORIANDER. CORIANDER, MR. AMBERGRISS, *and* SHERIFF PLOUGHMAN *light up cigars.*]

CORIANDER:

Tell one anyway. Willy, you're fire watch!
How beautiful it is tonight, bright and clear.
The stars nearly sting.

SHERIFF PLOUGHMAN:

In one way
Not so beautiful. The clearer the morning
The sharper the aim and the surer.
They have many more rifles than we and more cannon
And many more men . . .

CORIANDER:

Quiet!
That's a military secret, for officers only.
Keep it quiet, for God's sake.
Begin, Mama. Legends, whether evil or good,
Bring us comfort, bring us sleep.

MRS. CORIANDER:

Then I'll tell the legend
About The Man Who Wanted to Murder Time.

MISS ATTIE:

Murder time?

WILLY:

How does it go?

MRS. CORIANDER:

He was an idiot, the man who wanted to murder time.
A regular Silly Ass with great big ears
Flapping in the breeze, and
Bright little pig eyes watery blue.
That's the way he looked, the Silly Ass
Who wanted to murder time.

WILLY:

I can see him clear as day!

CARL MICHAEL [*Sourly.*]:
>   So can I!

MRS. CORIANDER:
>   He went to the Owl—she looked like me—
>   And said: "Dear Mother Owl,
>   I want to murder time." "What for?" said Mother Owl.
>   "You see, I'm awfully, awfully scared
>   Of dying," said Silly Ass.

CORIANDER:
>   Why, that's not so silly! Aren't we all?

ELSA:
>   At least on a night like this . . .

MISS ATTIE [*Sighing.*]:
>   Yes.

MRS. CORIANDER:
>   Maybe the Owl didn't think so either,
>   For she cocked her head and said,
>   After thinking very carefully, wisely and long—
>   "Murder time, Silly Ass? Well, I see no other way
>   But to murder everything that *measures* time."

MR. AMBERGRISS:
>   Pretty good advice, as far as I can see!

MRS. CORIANDER:
>   That's what Silly Ass thought, too,
>   And he set out to destroy everything that measured time.
>   First came . . .

WILLY:
>   Yeah?

MISS ATTIE:
>   Yes?

CORIANDER:
>   Well, what?

MRS. CORIANDER:
>   First came the *clocks*, naturally!

SHERIFF PLOUGHMAN:
>   Of course!

ABRAHAM:
>   Yes, that's obvious!

MRS. CORIANDER:

> So he destroyed—bang, crash!—all the clocks,
> From the ones with the Swiss-made movements
> To the bell clocks in the cathedral towers.

RURIKSSON:

> In the cathedral towers?
> Must that be? Yes, I guess it must.
> It's only logical!

MRS. CORIANDER:

> After he destroyed
> Every single clock on earth
> That apportioned time into seconds, he was tired.
> And truly, that was nothing to be wondered at!

MISS ATTIE:

> When you think about all those clocks!

MRS. CORIANDER:

> He lay down under a tree and fell asleep.
> He thought he deserved a nap, the Silly Ass.
> Suddenly . . . he awoke . . . what was that?
> Peep, peep, peep came from all the trees.
> Peep, peep, peep like the ticking of a clock . . .

WILLY:

> It was the birds!

MRS. CORIANDER:

> Yes, it was the birds, measuring time,
> With a peep for every second
> And a chirp for every hour!
> So he went to work and wrung all their necks.
> It took a quarter of an hour . . . or a year . . . or three.
> He really couldn't tell.
> Now, surely, nothing was left to measure time!
> Mother Owl herself was felled by three shots from his gun.

MR. AMBERGRISS [*Pretending to shoot*]:

> Bam! Bam! Bam!

MRS. CORIANDER:

> Now, surely, nothing was left to measure time!

CORIANDER:

> Yes, the sun, Mama! It gives us day and night
> And weeks and months and years. It measures time!

MRS. CORIANDER:

So he killed the sun. And the stars. And the trees
That announce the winter with naked trunks
And the summer with green leaves!
He chopped down all the trees.
He burned the flowers.
Everywhere he saw or heard the ticking of time,
He destroyed. He burned, trampled, chopped to pieces,
Running wild like a savage.
Until he was alone, the Silly Ass, and a savage.
Everything was cold and black, everything was scorched.
He thought he'd murdered everything that measured time.
He lay down to sleep. He was tired.

WILLY:

He deserved a rest!

MRS. CORIANDER:

He awoke with a—tick.
Tick tick tick tick, what was that?!?
Sounded like a Swiss watch, an alarm clock:
Tick *tick*, tick *tick*, tick *tick!*
What *was* it?

MISS ATTIE [*Whispering.*]:

Yes, what *was* it?

MRS. CORIANDER:

His heart.

ELSA:

Aha!

MRS. CORIANDER [*Very dramatically.*]:

He grabbed his knife and . . . [*She strikes at her breast.*]

ALL:

Aaahhhhhhhhh!

MRS. CORIANDER:

Now he belonged to eternity, the Silly Ass.
And so, he got everlasting life in legend,
He who wanted to murder everything that measured time!
That's what he deserved . . . don't you think?

CORIANDER:

That's what he deserved, and you deserve our thanks,
Thanks for that good story, Mama, even if it was evil.

Cover the fire now! And it it burn down.
We must sleep, everyone.

[*They all follow his suggestion and bed down. Some of them yawn. A long period of silence ensues. The lighting suggests night. A loud clap of thunder sounds abruptly, followed by several more. The lightning of a summer storm flashes outside.*]

MRS. CORIANDER: Thunder!

MISS ATTIE [*Throwing herself into* MR. AMBERGRISS's *arms.*] Ohhh . . . dear Lord . . . thunder!

CORIANDER: Certainly not! *That's artillery! They've caught us off guard!* [*More flashes of lightning and claps of thunder.*] *This is war! It's war! Take cover! War! War!* [*Everyone crawls toward some kind of protection, helplessly bewitched by* CORIANDER's *military voice. Everyone, that is, except* CARL MICHAEL. *He lies on his back near the furniture group, his pale face turned upward.*] *Take cover, Carl Michael! This is that future you talked about!*

RURIKSSON [*Under the big table.*]: *Carl Michael, don't be stubborn!*

[*Another clap of thunder and the sound of heavy rain beating down, pattering. The speakers shout to be heard above the din.*]

CORIANDER [*Bellowing.*]: I am Ulysses Grant, Bismarck! I am Cecil Rhodes!

ELSA: Carl Michael?

CORIANDER [*Sensing something amiss, he speaks in a quieter, more human voice.*]: Carl Michael . . . is something wrong?

[ELSA, *still crouching under the pretense, as if avoiding the claps of thunder, hurries to* CARL MICHAEL's *limp, outstretched body.*]

ELSA: Carl Michael? How do you feel? Carl Michael . . . [*She shakes him gently, as if to awaken him. To the others.*] He's sick! [ELSA's *cry has shattered the spell, and everyone, except* CORIANDER, WILLY *and* MRS. CORIANDER, *rushes to her side.*]

SHERIFF PLOUGHMAN: He's . . . [*He bends over* CARL MICHAEL's

body to listen for a heart beat.] Someone give me a mirror!
[MISS ATTIE *takes out a mirror and hands it to the* SHERIFF, *who puts in front of* CARL MICHAEL's *mouth.*] He needs a doctor!
[*Looking up*] Ruriksson . . . Henry . . . come here and help me!
[*They rush to him, along with* ABRAHAM, *and together they carefully lift* CARL MICHAEL *up.*] Easy now . . . that's it! . . . take it easy now. . . .

CORIANDER [*Bewilderedly.*]: Angelica . . . Angelica . . . how many laps?

[ANGELICA, *confused and frightened, puts up seven fingers.*]

WILLY: Seven!

CORIANDER [*Muttering.*]: Seven laps, Sheriff . . . seven laps. We mustn't break the circle . . . it's not allowed. *Seven laps!*

SHERIFF PLOUGHMAN: But Justus . . .

MISS ATTIE: [*Shocked and confused, she whispers.*]: This is no game now, Mr. Coriander!

ELSA [*With determination.*]: Pay no attention to him! That's it . . . carry him this way . . . that's it!

[*There is collective concern:* "Watch it! Look out! Be careful!"
CORIANDER, *his form crumpled and shrunken, looks old, very old.* MRS. CORIANDER *and* WILLY *remain by his side. They are still bound by the spell.* ANGELICA *has also stayed behind. She stands by the upstage door, literally not knowing whether she is coming or going.*]

CORIANDER [*Muttering.*]: Never break the circle . . . it's not allowed . . .

MRS. CORIANDER [*Pausing, then hysterically.*]: We must go back now, Justus! Seven laps. You mustn't falter! Be strong, Justus!

CORIANDER [*Muttering.*]: It's not allowed . . . no, it's not allowed . . .

MRS. CORIANDER: If you don't do as I say now, Justus, the Sunday Promenade is finished! Forever! [*She looks at him intensely, trying to stare him into obeying, but he averts her glance. A long, tense pause ensues. Then* CORIANDER *breaks down. He weeps quietly. Abruptly, he turns and exits quickly, following the others.* MRS. CORIANDER, WILLY *and* ANGELICA *stare after him for a long, long time.*

Slow Curtain

Act Three

Several hours have passed. Darkness has fallen and the large, pretentious, crystal chandelier has been lighted. It shimmers in many colors.

A kerosene lamp on the table next to the furniture group has also been lighted.

ANGELICA *is sitting in one of the chairs and is attentively leafing through a red scrapbook.*

ELSA *enter through the upstage door and crosses to the big table. She looks around, sighs, and brushes several conspicuous bread crumbs off the tablecloth. When a voice calls to her from within, she quickly exits.*

WILLY *enters from stage left at the same time as* MRS. CORIANDER *appears at the top of the stairs. The old lady is barely visible among the shadows.*

MRS. CORIANDER: Willy!

WILLY: Yeah.

MRS. CORIANDER: How is he?

WILLY: I don't know. He's terribly low. I've been . . . you know . . . getting medicine.

MRS. CORIANDER: Maybe he notices I'm not there. But you see . . .

WILLY: No, Grandma. Don't worry! He don't notice anything. He was un . . . uh . . . unconscious when I left.

MRS. CORIANDER: Unconscious! So it's come to that. I had a feel-

ing something was going to happen! I *knew* it! Ruriksson is
there, isn't he?

WILLY: Oh, sure. And Grandma . . .

MRS. CORIANDER: Yes?

WILLY: It's like the Pastor is . . . smiling!

MRS. CORIANDER: Don't say that, Willy!

WILLY: But he *is*. Why is that? There's no reason to . . . smile
like that, is there? I mean . . . stories like the one about Martin
and the sealing wax . . . they're funny! [*He bubbles over against
his will.*] They could make you laugh your head off. . . . But
this . . . this ain't nothing to smile about, is it, Grandma?

MRS. CORIANDER: Maybe it's because he thinks Carl Michael is
going to Heaven.

WILLY: Well, sure he will. But what's funny about that?

MRS. CORIANDER: Hurry in with the medicine now, Willy. I'm going to my room for a while. Promise you'll let me know if
something happens. [*She exits.*]

WILLY [*Exiting through the upstage door.*]: There ain't nothing
to smile about like that. . . .

[*For a moment there is silence.* ANGELICA *sits in her chair leafing
through her red scrapbook. Then* ABRAHAM *enters through the
stage left door. His hands are red and swollen from pickling
herring. He is returning from an errand to get* RURIKSSON's *black
sacrament case, which he carries in one hand. He starts to cross
toward the door through which* WILLY *has just disappeared. But
then he catches sight of* ANGELICA *by the kerosene lamp, alone
with her scrapbook. He changes his mind and crosses to her
instead. He puts the black case down on the floor in front of
him.*]

ABRAHAM: So, here you are, Angelica. [*When* ANGELICA *first sees
him she is startled and afraid. But she soon calms down and
smiles at him.*] Can I sit down here next to you for a minute?
I think I will. [*He sits down carefully on the edge of the chair
next to hers.*] You're not afraid of me, are you, Angelica? No
one is. No one. It's no wonder. And that's good, I guess. Of
course, it's depressing, too. Just think if everyone was scared of
me, I mean really, really scared . . . [*He laughs a little.* ANGELICA

*stares at him, seriously, attentively, almost lovingly, and tries
desperately to understand.*] Think if everyone said, "Here comes
that . . . oh, here comes that *scary* Abraham!" But no one does.
[*He shakes his head, and she does too, copying his movements.
Her gestures are enthusiastic and expressive, like those of a
child.*] Nope, not a chance! Not a single person would say that!
Least of all you, Angelica! [*He suddenly remembers her mute-
ness, but not in time to check himself. To cover his blunder, he
grasps her hand, but releases it when he notices that she reacts.
Pause. He searches for something to say.*] It's so nice sitting
here talking with you! I could do it all the time . . . yes, I could!
If I was allowed, I mean. Is it all right with you, maybe . . .
is it? [ANGELICA *does not understand. She smiles uncertainly.
Then, in order to do something, she begins nodding affirma-
tively with a nearly hysterical enthusiasm.*] Then I can! But Mr.
Coriander wouldn't like it. Neither would your mother, although she's real nice. They probably scared that . . . Come to
think about it, I don't know why they're scared. Maybe of you?
It could be . . . that you frighten people . . . that's not so strange.
But you don't frighten me. No, not me. They don't know
what you're thinking and feeling, because you're so quiet. Maybe
that's what scares them. But I'm not scared of you! [ANGELICA
shakes her head energetically.] No, just the opposite! Because
with you . . . with you . . . a person can talk about everything
. . . talk about everything. Even something a person is scared to
talk about with somebody else, he can talk about with you! Mr.
Coriander says, "Stay away from her! Leave her alone, Abraham!
She's my blushing rose, so keep your mealy fingers away!" That's
what he says . . . your father. And I don't understand it, because
if it was up to me . . . [*He checks himself for a moment, but
then continues, strongly.*] If it was up to *me*, you'd learn to talk
with your hands, like this . . . [*He flaps his hands about in front
of her face. Because she thinks he wants to hit her or tickle her,
she becomes frightened and knocks his hands down.*] I'm sorry.
. . . Forgive me, Angelica. . . . I wouldn't . . . [*Carefully, he
reaches his hand out again and pats her gently on the cheek. She
lets him do it.*] They say you don't understand anything, but I
think . . . you understand everything! If only I got to talk to
you more often, but . . . [*Intensely.*] I know what they're

thinking. Why do they have to think that way? . . . It's ugly. I'm sure there's nothing wrong . . . there's nothing wrong with wanting someone to talk to, when you're as lonely as I am. When all you do is stand in the store all day . . . weighing out flour and wrapping herring. . . . There's nothing wrong with wanting someone to talk to and think about. Someone . . . someone you like . . . What's wrong with that?!? [*These last words are spoken with such intensity and passion, that* ANGELICA *is startled and quickly draws her legs up under her.*] Nothing's wrong with it! Why should there be!? To me, Angelica is . . . [*For a moment it is as if he has forgotten* ANGELICA'S *presence. He talks to himself, to convince himself.*] . . . a normal girl and I. . . [*He turns to her.*] To me you're a normal girl, Angelica, and I . . . I . . . [*He checks himself again and there is silence. Then, once more he searches for something to say, and finally explodes.*] Damn! *Damn!* They look at you and say, "How sad!" But isn't it just as sad to be forever lonely? Damn! [AN-GELICA, *confused and a little frightened, stares at him. When she sees his agitated expression, she shakes her head violently. Her reaction causes him to change his tone.*] I'm sorry, Angelica. But to have to bow and scrape and listen to him make speeches and carry on . . . Everytime I get my pay he reminds me that I have to be grateful . . . *grateful!* Damn! They might as well have put me out when my mother died, might as well . . . [ANGELICA, *trying desperately to speak, forces a little sound. She shakes her head. Her hand suddenly reaches out, as if to touch his cheek, but settles on his shoulder instead. He grasps her hand gratefully. As he starts to kiss it, she pulls it back.*] That wasn't fair of me. Lots of times I like him. I like everybody here. Mr. Coriander seems to be living in a dream. He can't see how shabby and dirty and ugly life really is. He doesn't *want* to see it. The others—Miss Suleima and Miss Elsa and the Pastor —they seem aware of the shabbiness, like I am, and they live with it. That's why they're wiser and *happier* than he is, because he *wants* to be happy, he *has* to be happy, no matter what! That's why he cries sometimes . . . he cries. Did you know that? Once you realize how . . . shabby everything is . . . then you can be happy in the midst of the shabbiness. Then you're wise, Angelica. Otherwise you're not. But I guess all this is depressing, isn't it? [ANGELICA *shakes her head vigorously in denial.*] I wasn't fair. I like Mr. Coriander . . . sometimes. But why must he always say that everything . . . [*Imitating* CORIANDER.] . . . *is* the way it *is*? . . . Dreaming isn't enough for me, I have to hope, too. I have to be able to *do* something. Things won't always be like this for me . . . will they, Angelica? I have to make something of myself, Angelica, so that you and I, you and I . . . [*He checks himself again, but he is gathering courage.*] . . . can be together, Angelica! To me you're just a normal girl . . . and there's nothing sad about that . . . [*Feebly.*] . . . is there? [ANGELICA *stares at him and smiles cautiously. A long pause. He is uneasy and once again searches for something to say.*] Yesterday . . . yesterday, Angelica, Mrs. Ceder's big black cat came in the store when I wasn't looking. With a . . . swish! . . . it jumped up toward a shelf, but didn't quite make it! It slipped and . . . boom! . . . fell right into the flour bin! Ha ha! You should've seen it, Angelica . . . [*With gestures and sound effects, he does his best to reenact the event. Then he turns eagerly and appealingly to examine her reaction. She smiles and nods.*] . . . Swish! He was gone! Boy, did he get scared . . . and white . . . the flour made him look like a ghost, the little black rascal. . . . [*He bursts into hearty laughter as he remembers the cat's exit. Then he becomes serious again. He realizes that laughter is inappropriate now. Pause. He glances back at the sacrament case standing on the floor.*] That belongs to Pastor Ruriksson. It's his sacrament case. He sent me for it. There's something terrible about black bags like that. First the doctor brings his . . . and then the minister brings his . . . and then the lawyer brings his, if there's anything left. It's really terrible. Don't you think so? [*He looks to* ANGELICA *for a response. She shakes her head. She has not understood.*] Angelica . . . Mr. Justus will take it the hardest if Carl Michael dies. He loves him. They're so different . . . but he loves him just as much as I love . . .

[*The door bursts open and* RURIKSSON *enters.* ABRAHAM, *who has been leaning closer and closer to* ANGELICA, *quickly straightens up.*]

RURIKSSON [*Shouting.*]: Abraham . . . has Abraham returned?!

[*He catches sight of the young couple.*] Well, there you are! Where's my bag?

ABRAHAM [*Rushing to him with the bag.*]: Here it is! I just got back!

RURIKSSON [*Taking the bag and disappearing hastily through the door.*]: Why in God's name didn't you bring it in right away?

ABRAHAM: You see . . . Angelica . . . Angelica . . . Carl Michael . . .

MRS. CORIANDER [*At the top of the stairs.*]: What was that? Who was shouting?

ABRAHAM: It's me! Abraham! Come on down, he's getting communion now!

MRS. CORIANDER [*Shakily, but quickly, she descends.*]: God help us! God help us! [*She disappears through the upstage door. We hear her speak before she closes the door.*] God help us! How is he?

[ABRAHAM *starts to follow her, but he has second thoughts and returns to his place by* ANGELICA's *side. He grasps her hand.*]

ABRAHAM: Angelica . . . come on! Let's get out of here! We'll travel far away! Angelica, I'll help you . . . I'll protect you. . . . Come on! [*He half pulls her up out of the chair. She permits him to embrace her and kiss her, and returns his affection.*] Come on! This is no place for us, Angelica. . . . [*He embraces her again. He takes her hand and she follows, willingly. As they cross to the door, he stops and speaks with difficulty, but with conviction.*] I *love* you. Come on . . .

[*They exit. Some time elapses before the upstage doors opens and admits* ELSA, *followed by* WILLY *and* MRS. CORIANDER.]

MRS. CORIANDER: There . . . there . . . Elsa. There . . . there . . .

WILLY: There, Mama . . . [*He helps her sit in a chair in the furniture group.*]

ELSA: To think that this should happen . . . It's our fault, it's our fault.

MRS. CORIANDER: Justus is not to blame, Elsa!

WILLY: Grandma . . .

MRS. CORIANDER: I know what she's thinking. That it's Justus's fault.

ELSA: We should never have gone on that promenade . . . never
   have gone on that promenade . . .
MRS. CORIANDER: If he hadn't taken the promenade, Carl Michael
   would have suspected something. And you know what the
   doctor said. You and I sat right here and heard him say: "Don't
   let him suspect anything." It was nearly two years ago to the
   day, wasn't it, Willy?
WILLY: Yeah, yeah. Maybe so. But be quiet now, Grandma.

[*It is apparent that* MRS. CORIANDER's *grumbling and anxiety are
part of an effort to hide her sorrow.*]

MRS. CORIANDER: Be quiet? When your mother sits there blaming
   Justus? He who followed the doctor's orders and let nothing
   slip? Do you think that was easy for him to do?

[RURIKSSON *has entered. His hands clasped solemnly across his
chest, he is deeply and demonstratively serious.*]

RURIKSSON: Be quiet, Mrs. Coriander . . .
ELSA: Is he . . .?

[MRS. CORIANDER *and* WILLY *wince. The moment they dreaded
has come. They stare questioningly at* RURIKSSON.]

RURIKSSON: Yes, Elsa, dear. Sorrow has visited this house.

[ELSA *begins weeping quietly.* MRS. CORIANDER *bites her lip.*]

ELSA [*Crossing to the upstage door.*]: Where is Justus?
RURIKSSON: Gone out. He said he had to.
MRS. CORIANDER: Don't stand there looking so . . . so damned
   clerical, Ruriksson!
RURIKSSON: Mrs. Coriander . . .
MRS. CORIANDER: Do you know what Willy just told me?
WILLY: Quiet, Grandma . . .
MRS. CORIANDER [*On the edge of tears.*]: The Pastor is smiling,
   that's what he said. Willy, do you . . . do you deny it? And you
   were smiling for two reasons. First, because you finally got a

chance to drag your God and his communion cup into this house. Now you have God's help against your tormentor, Ruriksson! And the second reason: you think you've destroyed Justus. [*The tension has become too much, and she begins crying quietly.*] And maybe you're right. . . .

RURIKSSON: There, there, Suleima. I understand . . . and I forgive. Don't take it so hard. After all, Carl Michael has gone to his Maker. That's a journey we all have to take. [*He crosses to* MRS. CORIANDER *and ventures a comforting pat.*]

MRS. CORIANDER: Keep your hands away from me, Ruriksson. And keep your God away, too. I don't want to hear about it. Inside there, Carl Michael's body is turning cold. Is that God's justice, Ruriksson? If there was a God, like you say, he would have taken an old lady like me, and not attacked a young boy with his whole life in front of him. That's cowardly, Ruriksson. Cowardly and unjust. [*She rambles into a meaningless, sorrowful muttering.*] I'm the one who's sick in this house. I have stones, I have gallstones big as apples. I have pain, right *here*. It's cancer, I know it, right here. Haven't had a well day in years and years. I'm the one who's sick in this house. Still, He doesn't take me . . . He has to take a young boy . . . a poor little boy . . . [*During her speech, she has crossed to the stairs. Now, sniffling and sobbing, she turns and whispers.*] I'm going up to my room. [*She exits.*]

RURIKSSON: Poor Suleima! Death is a transmuter, and not only of those who die!

ELSA [*Returning.*]: Leave me alone. . . .

RURIKSSON: Here's a pill the doctor gave me. Take it and go and lie down. Willy will help you upstairs.

ELSA: No, I'm staying here. I can't leave Justus by himself.

WILLY [*He crosses to his mother and speaks simply.*]: Do as the Pastor says now, Mama. What good will it do to sit here? Come on . . .

ELSA: Should I?

WILLY [*Firmly.*]: Yeah. [*She rises and takes* WILLY's *arm. She follows him, sobbing softly.*] That's it. . . . Then you can take the pill and get some sleep. That's it . . . Come on . . .

ELSA: What have you spilled on your sleeve, Willy? Not again! Haven't I told you . . .

WILLY: We'll clean it off when we get upstairs.

[*They, too, disappear up the stairs.* RURIKSSON *is alone. He sighs and sits at the dining-room table. He opens his Bible, but closes it again. He rises, crosses to the cupboard, pours a glass of port, and downs it in one gulp. Quickly, he pours another glass and crosses with it to one of the chairs in the furniture group. He sits, taking care not to spill the wine. He begins to yawn, but stops, somewhat embarrassed. He straightens up, clears his throat, and looks around for his Bible. A noise on the stairs attracts his attention. It is* WILLY, *returning.*]

RURIKSSON: Did she lie down?
WILLY: Yeah. I feel sorry for Mama.
RURIKSSON: I feel sorry for all of you.

[WILLY *sits down clumsily. He doesn't know what to do with his big hands. He is moved by the strangeness of the moment.*]

WILLY: I . . . I don't know . . . I don't know if . . . I mean . . . if I have the *right* to grieve. . . .
RURIKSSON: For your own brother?
WILLY: I mean . . . we were so different. . . .
RURIKSSON: Didn't you like him, Willy?
WILLY: Yeah . . . sure. Kind of . . .
RURIKSSON: Just "kind of"?
WILLY: Yeah, that's right! Just . . . kind of . . . I liked him, but I really didn't feel nothing. Kind of . . . Like with Papa.
RURIKSSON: I don't think I understand.
WILLY: No. No one around here understands what I say. Except Mama, maybe. But *I* can understand . . . kind of . . . You know what I mean, Pastor?
RURIKSSON: I know that you do feel sorry, deep down, Willy.
WILLY: Yeah, yeah . . . Although . . . I can't help it . . . but I feel like laughing. Sometimes. There's nothing wrong with that, is there?
RURIKSSON: You feel like laughing? *Now?*
WILLY: No, no no. I mean, sometimes. There's nothing wrong with that, is there? I mean . . . if you can't help it.
RURIKSSON: Occasionally you do laugh at the wrong time.

WILLY [*Babbling.*]: There's an old lady plague every hundred years, and then *one* old lady dies. [*He hops up and down in his chair.*] I mean . . . I think that's *funny!*

RURIKSSON [*Severely.*]: Not now and not here, Willy.

WILLY: Everybody can't laugh at the right time, can they? I mean, a time can be right for some people and a time can be wrong for some people. Even though it's the same time, I mean. [*He gropes helplessly with his hands.*] Carl Michael now . . . I didn't understand him . . . and he didn't understand me. . . . It was even hard to play together . . . sometimes. It was hard . . . I mean . . . and nobody understood. Sometimes I wish I wasn't their son!

RURIKSSON: You mustn't say that, Willy.

WILLY. But that's what I wish! Nobody understands that! Instead of their son . . . I'd rather be a servant. Cause if I *was* . . . Pa would at least care what happens to me. . . .

RURIKSSON: But it's obvious that everyone cares what happens to you, Willy! They like you, you know that!

WILLY: Ma cares sometimes, I guess. About stockings and things like that. And spots. But if I was a servant . . . then Pa would care about how I worked . . . care if I did something useful . . .

RURIKSSON: Surely you don't want to change places with Abraham, Willy?!

WILLY: Yes, I do, that's exactly what I want. You see, Pa watches Abraham . . .

RURIKSSON: Watches him?

WILLY: Yeah, watches! To see that he's doing something. That he's . . . I mean . . . where he's supposed to be. But not me. . . . [*He shakes his head sadly.*] Not me. But now, Pa can watch the moon!

RURIKSSON: What do you mean, Willy?

WILLY: Ha ha! [*Bitterly.*] Watch the moon, 'cause that's where he'll find Abraham. . . .

RURIKSSON: What?

WILLY: I mean . . . Abraham ran away. [*He sings sneeringly.*] Abraham ran away!

RURIKSSON: You're joking, Willy!

WILLY: No, Willy isn't joking. Abraham . . . he ran away. With Angelica!

RURIKSSON: Oh no!

WILLY: Oh yes! And now I'm the only one left! They're gone, I saw them go!

RURIKSSON: Didn't you try to stop them?

WILLY: Oh no, oh no. I mean . . . I'm dumb, sure, but not *that* dumb . . . not that . . .. . cruel. They're gone now and I'm left. They're . . . kind of . . . saved.

RURIKSSON: Saved? Willy, I don't understand. . . .

WILLY: And I am, too! But you wouldn't understand, you old devil. . . .

RURIKSSON: *Willy!*

WILLY: Now Pa is gonna . . . he's gonna have to watch *me*, no matter how little he wants to.

RURIKSSON: Now you *are* cruel!

WILLY: No, 'cause they have it good now. Angelica. Now they have each other, old devil! Now . . . they don't have to . . . sneak around . . . now he can love his Angelica. . . .

RURIKSSON: Willy, listen to me . . .

WILLY: He don't have to sneak around, like *you* and Mama. Now they can . . . hold each other . . . and hug each other . . . I mean . . . whenever they want! Not like you, you . . .

RURIKSSON [*Shouting.*]: Willy!

WILLY [*Bubbling over into hysterical laughter.*]: Hug each other. . . . Ha ha! And Pa, he has to watch *me*, no matter how little he wants to. . . .

RURIKSSON [*Whispering.*]: Oh, dear God, this too. . . . What'll Elsa say . . . and Justus?

[CORIANDER *makes an abrupt entrance. He seems happy, almost high-spirited, but it is mostly affectation. There is a desperation in his happiness. He seems a bit insane. He puts his hat and cane down as he speaks.*]

CORIANDER: So, here you are!

RURIKSSON: Willy, for God's sake, don't say anything. Not today.

[WILLY *shakes his head and disguises a big smile. He rises and crosses toward the steps—with a kind of authority in his carriage.*]

WILLY: I'm going upstairs. [*He exits.*]

RURIKSSON [*Nervously.*]: Yes, yes. Go on. [*He turns toward* CORIANDER, *his manner becoming solemn, but friendly.*] Did you have a nice promenade?

CORIANDER [*Crossing with determination.*]: A man needs to think. He has to, sometimes. Well, I see you took a glass of port. Sometimes it's necessary. I think I'll have one, too. [*He crosses to the cupboard and fills up a glass. He takes a sip and puts it down on the table. He toys with the idea of sitting, but remains standing. Somewhat nervously, he begins pacing back and forth.*]

RURIKSSON: It's a lovely summer evening. A proper time for dying.

CORIANDER [*Wincing sharply.*]: Where's Mother and Elsa? And little Angelica?

RURIKSSON: They've gone to bed. You really should have been here, Justus, to say some comforting words.

CORIANDER: I felt I had to think! And you do that best in the open air, Ruriksson. Are they asleep?

RURIKSSON: I hope so. Elsa took a pill. . . .

CORIANDER: Opium! For dreams! Ruriksson . . .

RURIKSSON: Yes?

CORIANDER: There's something I want to ask you.

RURIKSSON: Tonight everyone wants to talk to me! Tonight no one makes a fool of me!

CORIANDER: Be happy they don't! Ruriksson . . . do you *believe* in God?

RURIKSSON: What a question!

CORIANDER: Now, I don't mean only because that's the way it should be with a minister. I mean—*truly*?

RURIKSSON: I don't quite understand. . . .

CORIANDER: I mean *still*. Do you *still* believe?

RURIKSSON: Still?

CORIANDER: Now don't pretend with me. You know very well what I mean.

RURIKSSON: I don't understand anything, as God is my witness.

CORIANDER: Ah, you're dodging the question. . . . All right. Then I have to speak more plainly. Once God put one over on you, Ruriksson—a *big* one! I'm thinking about your vision—*me*!

RURIKSSON: I don't want to talk about it! You're always . . .

CORIANDER: Me in my white grocery coat, me in my . . .

RURIKSSON: The answer to that is not in this world, Justus!

CORIANDER: Not in this world, huh? But what about in that other world? I mean in your soul, in your innermost being, Ruriksson. You took me for an archangel once. . . .

RURIKSSON: Stop rubbing it in!

CORIANDER: I want to know. That experience shook you. Was your faith shaken, too? *That's* what I want to know.

RURIKSSON: If you want to carry on a theological discussion, choose another time and . . . [*Gesturing toward within.*] . . . another place!

CORIANDER [*Persisting.*]: God betrayed you. Can you still trust him? Since that time . . . have you ever been able to trust God?

RURIKSSON: Not always. I have my doubts, the same as everyone else. But often . . .

CORIANDER: Do you still believe in *miracles*, Ruriksson?

RURIKSSON: Yes, I guess I have to believe in them.

CORIANDER: You *have* to believe in them? What an answer! Do you believe that Jesus walked upon the water? Maybe that was a trick, too, an optical illusion, like the time you thought I . . .

RURIKSSON: Not that again! [*After a pause, without conviction.*] Yes, I believe.

CORIANDER: That He fed thousands of people with two loaves of bread and five fish? . . .

RURIKSSON: There were two fish.

CORIANDER: What's that?

RURIKSSON: I said there were *two* fish.

CORIANDER: Bosh! Do you believe—that's the important thing?

RURIKSSON: Yes. [*At first vaguely, then definitely.*]: Yes . . . I mean, I believe.

CORIANDER: Now comes the most important thing, the real heart of the matter! Do you believe that He raised the daughter of Jairus . . .

RURIKSSON: Justus!

CORIANDER: . . . from the dead, Ruriksson?

RURIKSSON [*Sensing something blasphemous, disagreeable.*]: Jus—

CORIANDER: That she rose from the dead young and hale and hearty again? That she was able to live and work until Death caught up with her at a more suitable and much later time? Do you believe that, Ruriksson?

RURIKSSON: Yes . . .

CORIANDER: Without hesitation?

RURIKSSON: I can't say more than "yes."

CORIANDER: I think you have doubts. But you see—*I don't!*

RURIKSSON: Now I don't understand anything. Why, just yesterday . . .

CORIANDER: . . . you heard me condemn the church. You've got blinkers on, like the jackass that you are! You're right, Ruriksson! But I've been *thinking* . . . ever since Carl Michael died, I've been *thinking*. And I've changed my mind!

RURIKSSON: You're blaspheming, Justus, and worse than you ever have before! [*These last words emerge as a shout.* RURIKSSON *quickly puts his hand over his mouth when he remembers where he is. His voice drops in volume, but remains intense.*] You want me to believe that suddenly you have faith. You . . . faith! You only believe because you need Him. You're a child, Justus . . . a child who only wants to have and have and never wants to give!

CORIANDER: "Suffer the little children to come unto me, and forbid them not." Isn't that what it says in your book? [*He points to the Bible on the table.*] Right there!?

RURIKSSON: Yes, but . . .

CORIANDER: You may forbid me . . . but He won't! With His help, I'm going to raise my son from the dead!

RURIKSSON [*Almost whispering.*]: You're crazy, Justus! You're blaspheming! You have no faith!

CORIANDER: You're the one who doesn't have it! I do! And so much stronger, because I never had it before! It's new to me!

RURIKSSON: Don't you at least have respect for the dead, Justus! This is no Sunday Promenade!

CORIANDER: You wait here and see!

RURIKSSON: What are you going to do?

CORIANDER: I told you—revive Carl Michael! I'm going to pray and pray. . . . Oh, dear God, *help* me! [*He falls to his knees to demonstrate.*] He's not dead, he's sleeping! Let him awaken, dear God! I believe in You, I believe in You! Give me the power, give me the gift to raise him. . . . [*He turns from his position of prayer to look pleadingly up at* RURIKSSON.] You see! It'll work, it *has* to work!

RURIKSSON: You poor creature! This is no time for theatricalism!

CORIANDER [*Pitiably but sincerely.*]: But listen, listen! God, I know he's not dead!

RURIKSSON: Justus, Justus . . .

CORIANDER: God, they say he's dead. That's what they say, God, the doubters, the weak. Not me. I know he's alive. I know I'm right. [*He is nearly hysterical, but he speaks softly.*] God, they say a diamond is a dead thing. But I don't. Because when you turn it in your hand . . . [*He holds an imaginary diamond in his hand.*] . . . ohhh, see how it glitters and shimmers and gleams and burns like fire. Oh God! And Carl Michael, dear God, he's alive, too! He's sleeping, like a diamond embedded in coal, like the last ember in a campfire, deep, deep down in the ashes! Awaken him, God . . . [*He swallows and stares eagerly in front of him as if searching for new words. Then, abruptly, he turns back to* RURIKSSON.] That's how I'll pray! You'll see, Ruriksson!

RURIKSSON: You're crazy, Justus!

CORIANDER: That's what you are, Pastor. You, who have no faith. I'm going now: I'm going in to him. Oh, you doubter . . . [*He strides boldly toward the upstage door but he is breathless. Then he turns about.*] And Ruriksson . . .

RURIKSSON: Yes?

CORIANDER: If my prayers are answered . . . no, *when* they're answered, I'm going to show you . . . I'm going to show you *Outer Mongolia!*

RURIKSSON: Outer Mongolia . . .

CORIANDER: I'll sacrifice everything, Ruriksson! Nothing can stop us! We're going to make a pilgrimage, all of us, a pilgrimage of thanksgiving! Together, we're going to save those souls rotting in Outer Mongolia! You, Ragnar Ruriksson, will have the salvation mission of your life, because through me you'll recover your faith!

RURIKSSON: Through you? Justus, Justus, don't you see that you're bargaining with God?

CORIANDER: Look who's talking! Didn't you once bargain with me!?

RURIKSSON: But you can't bribe God!

CORIANDER: That's right. Oppose me! Opposition is my support!

RURIKSSON: God will oppose you, Justus. And His opposition is terrible. You'll accomplish nothing, but you'll be able to see reality, Justus. And reality will be a corpse, a pale, white, dead young body. It's terrible. He'll destroy you, Justus, destroy you, I say, destroy you.

CORIANDER: Doubter! God shall punish you for your doubt!

RURIKSSON: All right, go then, and meet reality face to face. It'll serve you right, Justus! You'll be destroyed. And then, my friend, then we'll be quits!

[CORIANDER *starts through the door, but turns back for an instant.*]

CORIANDER: See you in Outer Mongolia! [*He exits.*]

RURIKSSON: Blasphemer! [*He is extremely disturbed. He downs the last of the port. He crosses to the cupboard and pours himself another glass. Now and then he glances back toward the door, muttering and shaking his head. He crosses back to his chair and sinks down into it.*] The daughter of Jairus! Hm! The things he thinks of! He will be destroyed! Hm . . . [*As he drinks, his enthusiasm rises.*] Outer Mongolia . . . see you in Outer Mongolia! Ha! It'll be the camel and the eye of the needle. Ha! Outer Mongolia. I should have stopped him . . . but let him go . . . it'll serve him right. . . . [*A movement on the stairs. It is* ELSA *descending, almost a ghostly figure. She is a bit dazed from the sedative she took. On the way down, she extinguishes the chandelier, leaving only the kerosene lamp to light the stage. Startled.*] Who's that?

ELSA: It's me, Ragnar, Elsa!

RURIKSSON: You were supposed to sleep!

ELSA [*At the foot of the stairs.*]: I can't, Ragnar. Can I sit here awhile?

RURIKSSON: Tonight everyone comes to me. . . . Come and sit down. Although you should get some sleep . . .

ELSA: I can't, I said. . . . [*She is wearing a dressing gown, which she wraps around her, tightly and modestly. She speaks drowsily. There are long pauses between questions and answers. As the scene progresses, signs of dawn appear through the window.*

The early morning silence is penetrated momentarily as CORI-
ANDER'S *voice sounds from within, repeating the prayer he said
in front of* RURIKSSON.]

RURIKSSON: But you really should . . .

ELSA: What was that? Who's talking?

RURIKSSON: It's . . . it's Justus.

ELSA: Justus?

RURIKSSON: Yes. He's inside. With Carl Michael.

ELSA: And talking? To himself?

RURIKSSON: To God, Elsa.

ELSA [*Confusedly.*]: To God? Justus?

RURIKSSON: Yes. He's asking God to bring Carl Michael back to
life. I tried to stop him. . . .

ELSA: It's no good trying to stop Justus. [*In her drowsiness she is
almost amused.*] I've never been able to stop him from doing
anything. Leave him alone. [*Half-laughing, half sniffling.*] Hm!
Bring Carl Michael back to life!

RURIKSSON [*After a pause.*]: How you've put up with him! That's
what I admire most about you, Elsa.

ELSA: I'm fond of him, you can understand that, can't you?

RURIKSSON: No, I can't. Tonight I can't understand anything.
Elsa, if you and I . . .

ELSA: Yes?

RURIKSSON: Well . . . oh, I know it's sinful, Elsa . . . but you must
have known how I feel about you.

ELSA: How?

RURIKSSON: Oh, you know.

ELSA: Well, tell me then!

RURIKSSON: You know . . . [*Timidly.*] . . . I'm sure you do.

ELSA [*Sleepily.*]: It's just like you, Ragnar! Never venture anything. . . .

RURIKSSON [*Impulsively.*]: Yes, I guess I am different from Abra—

ELSA: What about Abraham, the poor thing?

RURIKSSON: Nothing. It's nothing.

[*Pause.* CORIANDER'S *voice is heard in the distance.*]

ELSA [*Compassionately.*]: He's going to be so tired in the
morning, poor thing.

RURIKSSON: He's blaspheming, that's what he's doing.

ELSA: Let him tire himself out. Then he'll be able to sleep. It'll do him good.

RURIKSSON: Elsa, Elsa, who are you, where are you? He's swallowed you up! You've let yourself be devoured by a dragon!

ELSA [*Sleepily.*]: There's lots to do inside a dragon.

RURIKSSON: Come out!

ELSA [*Sleepily.*]: No, there's much to do here. Hang up curtains, wash, mend, fix meals, look after the house, see that the children get off to school. Brrrr! I'm freezing. The sun's coming up. It's cold for July . . . [*Nearly asleep.*] Mmmm . . . can I sit like this next to you, Ragnar? You're so warm.

RURIKSSON [*Moving closer to her and putting his arm around her.*]: Elsa?

ELSA: Mmmmmm.

RURIKSSON: If only we were young!

ELSA: Mmmmm. Hold me tighter . . . tighter . . . Justus . . .

[RURIKSSON *reacts sharply, but he composes himself. He does not press the matter. His bitter, woebegone face becomes more clearly visible in the waxing dawn light.*]

RURIKSSON: There . . .

ELSA [*Laughing softly.*]: You'll never believe what Carl Michael did today. . . . Can you guess?

RURIKSSON: No . . .

ELSA: He took his paint set . . . and . . . [*Laughing softly.*] . . . started painting the wall in the nursery, red, green, black . . . across the whole wall! And how proud he was, Justus, you should have seen him! What are we going to do with Carl Michael? He won't listen to anything. . . . You can't hit him. . . . I mean, you can't very well . . . can you?

RURIKSSON: Well, you have to talk to him. Be firm.

ELSA: You'll have to do that. Do you know . . .?

RURIKSSON: What?

ELSA: When a little boy dies . . .

RURIKSSON: Yes . . .

ELSA: . . . there's so little left behind. A toy horse . . . some coloring paints . . . a few blocks, perhaps. And then the streak he

painted on the wall. So little is left behind when a little boy
dies. . . . [*She sobs, then sits up as if awakening, and stares at*
RURIKSSON.] Where's Justus?

RURIKSSON: Inside.

ELSA [*Settling down again.*]: Of course. Inside. [*Her head drops
to one side. She nestles close to* RURIKSSON *again.*]

RURIKSSON: Elsa!

ELSA [*Half-asleep.*]: Yes . . .

RURIKSSON: You were right just now. I am a coward.

ELSA: Don't say that, Justus, it's not true.

RURIKSSON [*Not listening, he stares into space.*]: Justus is right.
I'm such a coward. Take the vision, for instance . . . that
damned, damned vision. Ha! Don't you think I knew . . .

ELSA: You know everything, Justus.

RURIKSSON: . . . that it was Justus standing there, and not God!
Don't you think I knew!

ELSA [*Suddenly wide-awake.*]: You *knew!* [*Frightened.*] But
Ragnar, then . . .

RURIKSSON: Yes, yes, yes. That's the way it is with me! That's the
way I am! I knew it. But I didn't want to know. I wanted to believe, not know. I've always wanted to believe, Elsa, but I've
never been able to. Do you really think I could mistake Justus
for the archangel!?

ELSA: How could we think otherwise? With all the humiliation
you've had to go through . . .

RURIKSSON: I wanted humiliation. If I wasn't capable of faith, I
wanted at least to suffer for it. I wanted to suffer for my God,
even though I can't believe in Him, deep down. Then He'll
have to forgive my disbelief!

ELSA: I don't understand what you're talking about. Poor, poor
man . . .

RURIKSSON: "Poor man." That's all you can say, whether about
Justus or me. You don't understand us!

ELSA: You're all alike, you men, I understand that.

RURIKSSON: That we spill coffee on ourselves . . . that's the only
thing you understand about us! You women . . .

ELSA: Well, what about us?

RURIKSSON: You're . . . another species.

ELSA: What else should we be? God has intended it that way.

RURIKSSON: But you're more than another sex. You're another species, another race, another kind of animal. . . .

ELSA: Animal!

RURIKSSON: Yes, animal—exactly! You talk another language. You're animals, you're birds, and no man can understand what you're singing! You don't understand how man can want to suffer, want humiliation, want to feel the lash of the whip . . . because no matter how much you suffer under Justus, no matter how much you taste his whip, his malice, his evil . . . nothing can humiliate you . . .

ELSA: Ragnar, I don't know you!

RURIKSSON: . . . because you're at home in humiliation. You're yourself, you enjoy it! You bear his children, you wash his clothes. Not only do you put up with him, you *thrive* under the tyranny!

ELSA: I have my life!

RURIKSSON: That's exactly what I'm saying. You have a life somewhere that a man can never reach . . . out on the branch of some tree, like some strange breed of hummingbird. . . .

ELSA: I no longer feel sorry for you, Ragnar! Now you *are* cowardly!

RURIKSSON: I despise you!

ELSA: And I you, Ragnar! Here, in this room, in this house of sorrow, you *dare* to talk . . . like that. . . .

RURIKSSON: Forgive me, Elsa. [*As he sees that she wants to rise.*] No, don't go . . . don't go . . . forgive me . . . I love you I love you. . . . Don't you understand? . . . I love you. . . . [*It is daybreak. A long, yellow beam of sunlight plays in the crystal chandelier. Birds are chirping in the trees outside. From a distance come the pounding sounds of a hammer.* ELSA *has risen. She stares at* RURIKSSON, *who has fallen to his knees, with a mixture of fright and pity.*] Why do you humiliate me?

ELSA: You *want* to be humiliated. You said you come here because you *want* to be humiliated. [*Maternally.*] All right! Stand up now and don't lie there like a poor wretch! Come on! [*They embrace, quite suddenly.* MRS. CORIANDER *is on her way down the stairs. She stops when she catches sight of* ELSA *and* RURIKSSON.]

RURIKSSON: Yes, yes. I shall. Forgive me, Elsa . . .

Mrs. Coriander [*Resoundingly.*]: What is this? And Elsa
in only her night clothes! [*She hobbles stormily down the
stairs.* willy's *sleepy face appears on the second-floor landing.
He has either awakened or not slept at all. He shuffles noisily
down the stairs. In his pink and blue nightshirt he presents a
comic appearance.*]

Mrs. Coriander: Well, isn't this cozy!

Willy: What's going on, Mama? Where's Pa?

Mrs. Coriander: Yes, where is . . . [*The upstage door opens
slowly.* coriander *enters. He is worn, silent, and small. He
leans against the wall near the door. He shields his eyes for a
moment with his hands. Everyone becomes quiet; they all stand
as if petrified.*]

Elsa: Justus, what is it?

Coriander [*With difficulty.*]: I . . .

Mrs. Coriander: What is it? Speak up!

Coriander: Here's . . .

Willy: Pa . . .

Ruriksson [*Concerned that* coriander *will fall*]: Justus . . .

Coriander [*Quietly, but clearly.*]: Here's your miracle, Pastor!

[*Through the upstage door comes* carl michael. *He is pale
and shaking a bit. A stir goes through the group. The chirping of the birds grows louder. Then slowly, as if from an infinite distance, the Promenade Song rises: "Everyone, everyone come along, / It's Sunday—Let's sing our Promenade
Song!"*]

Ruriksson [*Sinking gradually to his knees.*]: God . . . God . . .

Elsa [*Drawn toward* carl michael *by an urge to touch him.*]:
Carl Michael . . . my boy . . . it can't be true!

Willy [*On the other side of* carl michael.]: How was it? I mean
. . . how was it?

Carl Michael [*Smiling.*]: What's the matter with you? You
all look so strange. . . .

Mrs. Coriander [*Suddenly bursting into tears.*]: I don't know
I don't know . . . an old lady like . . .

[*The song has become louder. It sounds quite close.* cori-

ANDER's *voice grows almost into a shout as he speaks over the song.*]

CORIANDER: Get up, Ragnar!

RURIKSSON [*Crouching and trembling.*]: God . . . God . . . I'm afraid. . . .

CORIANDER: Ha ha! Come here and let me hold you, Carl Michael! [*He hugs his son.*] It's wonderful to see you up and about. . . .

CARL MICHAEL [*Almost falling in his father's arms.*]: Father . . .

CORIANDER [*Blusteringly.*]: All you need is a little rest. You have to be strong, you see. [*As if to a child.*] In order to be ready for our big journey!

ELSA: Journey?

CORIANDER: We're all going to Outer Mongolia!

CARL MICHAEL: Outer Mongolia . . . [*He cannot keep pace. He laughs.*] When I woke up, I saw Papa lying there. His eyes were popping out of his head. I thought he'd *really* gone crazy. "What are you doing here, Papa?" I said. "Go to bed, I want to sleep." [*He looks around at the others, who have quieted down.*] What's happened here, anyway? [*Shouting.*] Why are you all staring like that?!!?

RURIKSSON [*Whispering.*]: Outer Mongolia . . .

[*There is much shouting and kissing and embracing.* RURIKSSON *remains on his knees, terribly shrunken, terribly alone. He watches all the hugging and the kissing, gesturing weakly toward them, as if he wanted to join in. The next three speeches are spoken simultaneously.*]

CORIANDER: My boy . . . my little boy . . .

ELSA: Think that this could happen . . .

WILLY: How was it? How was it?

RURIKSSON: How wonderful . . . how lovely . . . But now I think we should fall on our knees and thank God! [*No one is listening.*] I think it's time to . . .

[*The song sounds like a hymn of joy. Suddenly,* MRS. CORIANDER *severs herself from the group. It is as if she has regained her reason.*]

Mrs. Coriander: And I think . . . I think we should get ourselves another doctor! [*She trails behind the others as they
march out. Only* RURIKSSON *remains, on his knees, alone. For
a long time he is quiet, his head bowed. Then he looks upward,
angrily.*]

Ruriksson: Oh, no, God, now I'm getting up! [*He rises quickly.*]
I'm not lying on my knees for someone like You! You're too
cruel for me. You don't give a damn about me! I'm just a poor,
miserable wretch, who's fought for You, even though there
were many times when I doubted; who's had to suffer ridicule
and scorn and disgrace for Your sake! And still . . . I'm not
good enough for a Master such as You! You don't want to
act through me! You treat me with contempt, although You
talk a great deal about humility and the spiritually poor and
"suffer little children to come" and camels and the eyes of
needles . . . and everything they pertain to in the gloomy darkness of Your Holy Scriptures! You scorn me! You shove me
aside as You'd push away a chair! Yes, and then, when You
exert Your much vaunted power, it has to be through a
blasphemer like that . . . a doubter like that . . . a puffed-up
red balloon of a man like Justus Coriander! He's good enough
for You! He'll . . . he'll do! But not me, not me—Your faith-
ful servant! No, it has to be a betrayer!
     Thanks, God!
     Thanks a whole lot, God!
     Well, now I'm through with You!
     And I'm going to tell You something, frankly, God!
     I've always hated people in authority!
Others may look up to them as if they were apostles, staring
in awe at their stern, commanding, upright faces, so vain and
ambitious, their eyes fiery like eagles'. But as for me—I hate
them! I hate the generals, those who fight against You as well
as those who fight for You . . . the whole brawling lot, the
whole mess of them!
     I love those who are weak enough to decide for themselves!
     I love those who are weak enough to live not for You, but
          for themselves!
     There You have it, God! [*He becomes hysterical.*]

That's what You get, my Lord Creator! I hope You're satisfied!

That ought to hold You for awhile!

You didn't think I was up to it, did You?

Nobody thought I was . . . You didn't think so, I know
that. . . . You thought You had me like a worm on a
hook . . . like a quail in a trap. . . . I was just nothing . . .
nothing . . . nothing. . . . [*He collapses, falling to his
knees, his head bowed. He whispers.*]

Oh, God, God, Jesus Christ, my Lord . . . what have I said
. . . what have I done? . . .

Forgive me.

Forgive me, Your humblest servant.

Now I understand You, God. Wondrous are Your ways.

You wanted to demonstrate Your power to me through
Justus.

So be it.

And I, I blaspheme.

Oh, forgive me, forgive me, forgive me. Our Father which
art in Heaven, Hallowed by thy name . . . Hallowed be
. . . [*His prayers overflow. For a long while he kneels,
whispering them. Then, the upstage door opens.*]

CORIANDER [*Within, thundering.*]: Ruriksson! [CORIANDER enters.] What in Hell are you lying there for, with your nose in
the floor like a sleepy crawfish! Come on, get up! [RURIKSSON
slowly looks up.] Come on, don't lie there mooning! Breakfast
is on the table! This is a *celebration!*

RURIKSSON [*Dazed.*]: Yes, Justus, I'm coming.

CORIANDER: Herring and new potatoes! Come on now, come on!

RURIKSSON: Sounds wonderful, Justus! I'm coming, I'm coming!
[*He starts trailing after* CORIANDER, *but stops at the door, turns
around and gazes upward.*] Sweet Lord, thank You for what
You are!

Blackout

Epilogue

Seven years have passed. When the light comes up, it finds
MRS. CORIANDER *sitting in her usual place in the furniture
group. Alongside her sits* MISS ATTIE, *now* MRS. AMBERGRISS.
MRS. CORIANDER *is faded and shrunken. She has lost nearly
all of her former bumptiousness. She is withered and small.
Her hair is snow-white and her complexion gray. The rest of
the room around them is shadowed in compact darkness.
When* MRS. CORIANDER *talks about scenes from the past,
they take place in the dim and unreal light of memory. The
pause during the blackout is so short, that when the lights
come up again quickly, the spanning of time comes as a
shock.*

MRS. CORIANDER: So we changed doctors, as I said, Miss . . .
forgive me—Mrs. Ambergriss. Hm! I forget everything nowadays. If we'd left it at that, Mrs. Ambergriss, if only we'd left
it at that. But no . . . well, you know Justus . . . he said Outer
Mongolia and Outer Mongolia it had to be! [*Pause.*] Hm!
It's been seven years now.

MRS. AMBERGRISS: Of course I heard talk about the journey, but
I couldn't believe that. . . . Well, especially not after Carl
Michael died . . .

MRS. CORIANDER: Yes, you must have heard that Carl Michael
died, poor boy. All he got was a . . . short reprieve. A new

doctor didn't help any. Although he was young and knew more about bacilli than old Pettson.

MRS. AMBERGRISS: Yes, I said to Mr. Ambergriss when Carl Michael passed away, that *surely* there couldn't be any talk about that *awful* journey! And after that we moved to Landskrona and there you don't hear anything . . .

MRS. CORIANDER: No, no. That's the way it goes . . . the way it goes. . . . [*She is absorbed in her thoughts.*] It was as if we didn't *notice* that Carl Michael died. . . . He had already died once. . . . Our grief was well . . . all used up. That's it! Our grief was used up, we had consumed it . . . or it had consumed us . . . I don't know which. . . . Bosh! Then Angelica and Abraham came back. . . . That was a joy that soon killed our grief. How miserable they looked when they came . . . the world was too big for them. . . . Everything was bliss—but then they had to travel! They just had to destroy the happiness! . . . Justus, he pushed right ahead, like a fury. . . . You see, for him, it wasn't the poor souls in Mongolia who were important . . . he gladly left them to Ruriksson. And as for his faith, well, he couldn't very well lose what he'd never had. . . . And if Ruriksson had ever had it . . . God only knows! [*Her eyes turn upward sanctimoniously.*] No, Mrs. Ambergriss, it became a matter of *honor*.

[*The lighting around the dining-room table has slowly come up, revealing* RURIKSSON *and* CORIANDER *leaning over a map spread out before them.*]

CORIANDER: My, the world is big, Ruriksson!

RURIKSSON: Ha ha. And yet the table is big enough to hold it.

CORIANDER: Ha! We're going to conquer it, we're going to con- the world! It'll *grovel* at our feet!

RURIKSSON: Pride goeth before a fall . . .

CORIANDER: Ha! Let them think we're falling, Ruriksson. Then we'll do a . . . [*Demonstrating.*] . . . a somersault!

RURIKSSON: Let's keep our feet on the ground. . . .

CORIANDER: That's exactly what we'll do! I have everything planned. Abraham and Angelica will stay here. . . .

RURIKSSON: Why?

CORIANDER: Why? You're not blind, are you? [*He pats his protruding stomach.*]

RURIKSSON: But Justus . . .

CORIANDER: Not a word! It'll be a boy and they'll name him Carl Michael. And it's for Carl Michael's sake, you hypocrite, that I haven't said anything!

RURIKSSON And yet, you let me marry them, before the altar and before God, without telling me . . .

CORIANDER: You asked me no questions, I told you no lies. Besides . . . [*He nudges* RURIKSSON *hard and mischievously in the side.*] . . . you would have married them anyway!

RURIKSSON: Oh, no, I . . .

CORIANDER: Enough of that. He'll be named Carl Michael Justus And his grandfather, my friend, will be that renowned explorer, Justus Coriander! Look here. [*He makes a grandiose gesture.*] Here's the world. Everything is planned. I'll be knighted—like Sven Hedin, the Arctic explorer! Mama stays home, she's too old.

RURIKSSON [*Relieved.*]: Very wise!

CORIANDER: Ha ha! Yes, kitty cat—now you're purring. But soon the cat will be out in the rain and the cold . . . out in the world! You see here, we'll pass over the Siberian tundra. Where the wind roars, the wolves howl, the rain lashes, the thunder rumbles, the wagon rattles, the horses shy. . . . Forty below zero, fifty below . . . we'll be freezing, we'll be shivering. . . .

RURIKSSON [*Frightened.*]: But Justus . . .

CORIANDER: Don't worry! As usual, I've anticipated everything! We won't freeze, because Justus Coriander is taking along heating lamps. Inside the wagon we'll be roasting chestnuts and warming our hands over the hot lamps. . . . We'll be all right in any kind of weather! [*Thoughtfully.*] Maybe we should take a balloon along, just in case!

RURIKSSON: I get dizzy very easily.

CORIANDER: I can believe it! Ha ha! Especially atop the heights of faith, I bet! But you're right, Ragnar. We'll travel by wagon, by wagon it'll be. We'll be able to see so much more, and we're in no hurry. Air is air, it's the same all over, but the earth changes! Ha! I'll become famous, Ragnar, I'll write a book! I'll discover an ocean! I'll get a medal! And you, Ragnar, you and Elsa, you'll be canonized. . . .

RURIKSSON: Heh heh.

CORIANDER: You'll be the saints of Mongolia, that's what you'll be! Look here . . . [*They both lean over the map.*] . . . we'll stop a few days in Omsk. . . . Then we'll continue . . . [*His voice subsides to a mumble.*] . . . along this route . . .

RURIKSSON: It looks like a long trip, heh heh.

The lighting on the table fades and comes up again on MRS. CORIANDER *and* MRS. AMBERGRISS.]

MRS. CORIANDER: That was seven years ago . . . Miss At . . . Mrs. Ambergriss. Hm! He sold almost everything. The house was mortgaged up to the chimney. All for honor. Look at me. Here I am, living on a . . . pittance. But no one thought about that. Oh no, off they went!

[*The table lighting comes up again.* ELSA, RURIKSSON, WILLY *and* CORIANDER *dash about hectically, their arms full of suitcases and strange and unnecessary things: mirrors, a wicker chair, decorative shawls, ladies' hats, and so forth.* MRS. CORIANDER *rises during the scene and crosses to the table to participate.*]

CORIANDER: Is everything ready?

WILLY: We've got everything, Pa!

RURIKSSON: Are the Bibles packed well?

ELSA: My sewing basket . . . yes, it's here! But the spot remover, Abraham, the spot remover?!!?

ABRAHAM: In the bottom of that small bag, Miss Elsa!

CORIANDER: Then, let's go! What's the matter?

[ANGELICA *comes rushing down the stairs carrying a huge can, which she appears to be about to drop.*]

ELSA: Oh, dear Lord, the tooth powder! Thank you, Angelica, dear!

ABRAHAM [*Handing flowers to* ELSA.]: And here are flowers from 'the town square, Miss Elsa!

MRS. CORIANDER [*Intervening.*]: And here's the castor oil, you've got to have that!

WILLY: Hurry up! The horses are getting restless!

ELSA: Goodbye, Angelica. Goodbye, Abraham. Goodbye, Mother Coriander.

CORIANDER: Goodbye, everybody. [*He crosses to* MRS. CORIANDER *and embraces her.*] And especially you, Mama. Take good care of yourself.

MRS. CORIANDER: Goodbye, my boy. Goodbye, my darling little boy. When will I see you again?

CORIANDER: Soon, I promise you. Mama, I've been a dreamer. Now, I'm going to face reality. It was Carl Michael who gave me the courage. He told me I didn't dare behold it. Well, now . . . now I do dare. And I know that reality, Mama, is lovelier than any dream.

MRS. CORIANDER: It's dangerous, Justus. It can hurt you, my boy. Why do you have to . . .

CORIANDER: All right, Mama! Now, don't start crying. One day I'll walk through that door . . . and I'll be famous, a credit to my country, a man laden with honors. . . . And what's more—I've made amends. I've settled differences with all that I offended in my thoughtlessness. I can look life in the eye. I can shake hands with reality as I now shake your hand, Mama.

MRS. CORIANDER: Goodbye.

[*Farewells are taken amid much embracing, sniffling and laughing.*]

CORIANDER [*At the door.*]: Wherever I go in the world . . . there'll never be a road that won't lead home!

RURIKSSON: God bless you!

[CORIANDER, ELSA, RURIKSSON *and* WILLY *leave, followed by* ABRAHAM *and* ANGELICA, *who are waving wildly. Outside is heard the murmur of parting voices, and above them,* CORI- ANDER'S *shouts of: "Farewell! Farewell!" The lights around the table dim again. Meanwhile,* MRS. CORIANDER *has crossed slowly and falteringly back to the furniture group to reoccupy her seat next to* MRS. AMBERGRISS, *who has remained silent and inconspicuous during the scene.*]

Mrs. Coriander: No one could stop them. Least of all Elsa. Elsa agreed to everything! . . . Hm! Some letters came. Then, there were fewer and fewer. A year went by . . . then two . . . [ABRAHAM *enters through the upstage door, dressed in his white grocery coat. He removes it and hangs it up by the door.*] Can you guess who's here, Abraham?

Abraham [*Coming forward.*]: No . . . why, hello Miss Attie!

Mrs. Coriander: Mrs. Ambergriss now, Abraham. So, you've been working, even though it's Sunday.

Abraham: Like Mr. Coriander in the old days. How are you, Mrs. Ambergriss?

Mrs. Ambergriss: Fine, thanks. And how's Angelica?

Abraham: Well, I guess you know we have three children now. So, she has a lot to keep her busy.

Mrs. Ambergriss [*Showing her curiosity.*]: Are they . . . [*She checks herself.*] . . . are they cute?

Abraham: Yes. But they scream a lot.

Mrs. Ambergriss [*Relieved.*]: Oh, that's . . . that's nice.

Mrs. Coriander: I was just telling Mrs. Ambergriss about . . .

Mrs. Ambergriss: Yes, what happened?

Mrs. Coriander: We don't know. We don't know anything. There were no more letters.

Abraham: Suleima, why pretend . . .

Mrs. Coriander: Abraham, you mustn't . . .

Abraham: I can't pretend any more . . . not after seven years!

Mrs. Coriander: I'm not *pretending*, Abraham! I'm hoping!

Abraham: Not one word in five years . . . how can you go on hoping? And we've made inquiries . . .

Mrs. Ambergriss: Really?

Abraham [*To* MRS. CORIANDER.]: Don't you understand that it's impossible to find anyone out there? It's too big, I tell you, it's too big!

[ANGELICA *enters carrying a large picnic basket.* MRS. AMBERGRISS *first notices the girl when she reaches the table.*]

Mrs. Ambergriss: Oh, here's Angelica . . .

Mrs. Coriander: Welcome Mrs. Ambergriss now. [ANGELICA *curt-*

sies for MRS. AMBERGRISS, *like a girl, although she has become
significantly more robust.*] Oh, yes . . . heh heh . . . the picnic
basket. . . . Well, you see, Mrs. Ambergriss, it's Sunday and on
Sundays we usually . . . oh, but you know what we used to do
on Sundays when Justus was home . . .

MRS. AMBERGRISS: The Sunday Promenade! [*She laughs.*] Of
course I remember, I went along! As a matter of fact it was
on one of those Sunday Promenades that Mr. Ambergriss
and I . . .

MRS. CORIANDER: Yes, yes. Heh heh. And on Sundays we still
. . . well . . . as a remembrance . . . But of course, not today . . .
not when you're here . . .

MRS. AMBERGRISS: Why not?! Come on, let's go. How was it we
sang:

> Everyone, everyone come along,
> It's Sunday, let's sing our Promenade Song . . .

MRS. CORIANDER [*Rising.*]: Heh heh. We don't usually go more
than several laps. And we don't sing.

ABRAHAM [*Taking* ANGELICA's *arm.*]: Of course we do! [*He and*
ANGELICA *take the lead, followed by* MRS. CORIANDER *and* MRS.
AMBERGRISS. *Everything seems awkward and pitiable.*]

EVERYONE [*Singing out of key and maching out of step.*]:

> Everyone, everyone come along
> It's Sunday, let's sing our Promenade Song!
>> The North Wind roars,
>> The North Wind roars,
> It's strong and brisk, through we march indoors!

MRS. CORIANDER: Heh heh. My poor old legs. I think it's time
to sit down. [*The door opens suddenly and* WILLY *is standing
on the threshold. Everyone but* MRS. CORIANDER *sees him and
they are dumbstruck.*] Take out the coffee now, Angelica. Don't
stand there staring! What is . . . [*She turns to see what has
captured* ANGELICA's *attention and catches sight of* WILLY *at
the door.*]

WILLY [*In a low voice.*]: Hello, Grandma.

MRS. CORIANDER: Oh, my! Well, don't stand there Willy, Come
in! [WILLY *slowly crosses over to her. She embraces him and
begins weeping.*] Oh, Willy . . . Willy . . . Willy . . . [*They
stand together for a long time. Then* WILLY *pushes his way*

forward to embrace ANGELICA *and* ABRAHAM. *Scarcely a sound is uttered.* MRS. CORIANDER's *tears turn to laughter.*] Well, have some coffee, Willy! We can't stand around jabbering like this all day!

ABRAHAM: Here, Willy . . . [*He pours out some coffee from the pot in the picnic basket.*] Take this . . .

WILLY: The Sunday Promenade . . . I see you still . . .

MRS. CORIANDER: Oh, just for fun, Willy. Get the cookies, Abraham. See that he has some cookies.

WILLY: Thanks . . .

ABRAHAM [*Quietly.*]: Are you alone, Willy?

WILLY: Yes.

ABRAHAM: . . . the others?

WILLY: Well . . . there's so much to tell. I mean . . . I don't know where to begin.

MRS. CORIANDER: Justus?

MRS. AMBERGRISS: I'd better go.

MRS. CORIANDER: No, stay. Justus, Willy?

WILLY: I mean . . . he was crawling. I mean . . . it was just like he said. The wind blew . . . it was cold, Grandma. I mean . . . sixty below. Then we tipped over. The wagon, I mean.

MRS. CORIANDER: Well?

WILLY: There were some friendly Mongolians who took care of me. I could've . . . I mean . . . I wanted to stay with them. But then I thought that you . . . that . . . but they were friendly, those Mongolians. . . . I mean . . . once you got to know them.

MRS. CORIANDER: What happened to Justus?

WILLY: I mean . . . he died, Grandma. Yeah. [*Pause.*] He died. I'm sure . . . I mean, almost . . . that he's dead. Right before they took me with them. I mean . . . he was lying in the snow. And he said: "I didn't know." That's what he said: "I didn't know the world was that big." I mean . . . he said "I didn't know the world was that big." That's what he said. [*He nearly chokes.*] There was snow in his hand. And the moon . . . it was shining on the snow, so that the snow was shining in his hand. I mean . . . it was like a . . . like a jewel in his hand. Although it was melting. It was melting because his hand was hot. Pa was so hot; he had fever. And it was melting, but it was shining. It was like a jewel . . . I mean . . . like a

big diamond that was melting. And then . . . *I think they cut his tongue out, Grandma, Grandma* . . . And the others . . .
MRS. CORIANDER: Bosh, Willy! you're just talking nonsense!

[*During* WILLY'S *monologue, the lighting has dimmed gradually. The people sitting in the furniture group have become silhouettes. On* MRS. CORIANDER'S *last line, the lighting on the dining room table swells magically up.* CORIANDER *is giving instructions to his little group, although none of his words are audible.* ELSA *and* RURIKSSON *are there, as well as* CARL MICHAEL. CORIANDER *gestures, speaks and points. The others listen to him, carefully. From a great distance, the song begins to rise again, very faintly. The lighting becomes quite intense and then sinks down, slowly, to a* BLACKOUT *and a slow*

Curtain

THE CURVE

A One-Act Play

Tankred Dorst

Translated by James L. Rosenberg

CHARACTERS

ANTON

RUDOLPH

KRIEGBAUM

THE TIME: *The present.*

THE PLACE: *In the mountains.*

A charming little Alpine hut standing before a sharply-jutting, fissured rock ledge. Flowers in front of it, in a tiny garden. Not far from the hut, a level area of ground enclosed by a low white fence. On the other side, a shed—a sort of workshop.

RUDOLF [*Wets his forefinger and holds it up, testing the wind.*]: A warm South wind.

ANTON [*Sitting in the grass, under a parasol; looks up from his reading.*]: What did you say?

RUDOLF: South wind.

ANTON: Terrible.

RUDOLF [*Studying the sky.*]: Cloudless bright blue sky.

ANTON [*Following his gaze.*]: Looks like a storm brewing over there, though.

RUDOLF: A single cloud. And it's been breaking up behind the ridge since before noon.

ANTON: Before noon!

RUDOLF: The sun is directly in the south now.

ANTON: Horrible!

RUDOLF: It's warm—like summer. A day for swimming, for picnics, for vacations.

ANTON: Horrible! Stop it.

RUDOLF: Everything is as it should be. What's the matter? You're as nervous as a schoolgirl.

ANTON: I simply can't understand how you can be so—so devoid of feeling.

RUDOLF: Look—do I make the weather? The lovely weather? This vacation weather? The south wind? That lone, dissipating cloud over there? The sun in the south? Did I arrange all that?

ANTON: Well, at least don't call it *lovely* weather.

RUDOLF: That's what they called it in the forecast.

ANTON: And so you just throughtlessly repeated it.

RUDOLF: I'm sorry—I don't have time to sit around thinking all day, like you.

ANTON [*Hurt.*]: Rudolf!

RUDOLF: I've never had a fine education, you see.

ANTON: How often do I have to explain to you that this is not important?

RUDOLF: And I say what I mean, without any fancy talk, that's all. "Lovely weather"—well, it *is* lovely, isn't it? Tremendous. And deadly. No, no, don't close your eyes like some insulted old maid. I know my place in the world, my dear brother, and I know what I'm worth.

ANTON: Every man does his own work. Who can say: "This man is more valuable than another"?

RUDOLF: I support myself by my work. I could support a family, if I had to. I make a contribution to society, don't you forget it.

ANTON: Are you going to start telling me again that I am useless?

RUDOLF: Well—aren't you? Have you ever done an honest day's work in your life?

ANTON: When I look at you, believe me—I wish I could work as thoughtlessly and as carefree as you do.

RUDOLF: All you do is plant flowers.

ANTON: You know perfectly well we need the flowers.

RUDOLF: And then you lie here in the grass all day—I feel that, you know, when I'm standing there in the workshop—I feel these things, they bother me.

ANTON: You're very unfair, Rudolf. You know I'm working as hard as you are. Here—take a look, if you don't believe me. . . . [*Shows him a manuscript.*]

RUDOLF: What's that?

ANTON: The essay.

RUDOLF: The old one?

Anton [*Reading.*]: "Once again it has happened. Once again we find ourselves . . . "

Rudolf: Always the same. I know this one already, just from hearing all the others.

Anton: Then you don't hear very well. I've revised the text six times now. Out of twenty-four different cases.

Rudolf: The opening is always the same.

Anton: Naturally. It always happens the same. Just different people each time—the poor devils. That's where the problem begins for me. But you don't even notice the difference.

Rudolf: Well, it all goes to show you that your work doesn't do any good.

Anton: Such work is its own reward. Can't you understand that? Besides, I now have a new theme.

Rudolf [*Uninterested.*]: Oh?

Anton: A tremendous theme: Inevitability.

Rudolf: That's always good.

Anton: I have considered, maybe it might be the best thing for a man whose thoughts were concerned only with himself, only with his career, or with a villa on Lake Como, with building up his fortune, with his inheritance—I've worked all that in here.

Rudolf: I hope you're not going to be disappointed again.

Anton: It all depends. . . . In any case, I don't intend to revise a word.

Rudolf: Listen! You hear something?

Anton [*Listens.*]: Do you?

Rudolf [*Listening.*]: A heavy bus. Diesel.

Anton: You've got ears like a lynx.

Rudolf: It'll be coming around the curve just about now.

Anton: Now I hear it, too.

Rudolf: A bus.

Anton [*Terrified.*]: Oh, my God! [*They stare upward, breathless, following with their eyes the path of the approaching bus. It moves slowly along the serpentine highway overhead.*]

Rudolf: Now!

Anton: Thirty people, thirty people, thirty people.

Rudolf [*Calculating, cold-bloodedly.*]: Fifty, at least. It's full up.

Anton: Dear God! Fifty people—happy travelers—lovers, children, newlyweds, mothers . . .

[*The noise of the bus fades away, disappears.*]

RUDOLF: Past.

ANTON [*Exhausted.*]: My forehead—look—drops of cold sweat.

RUDOLF: They were lucky. The sun wasn't quite in the right place.

ANTON [*Bursting out.*]: Lucky! Why doesn't someone do some-thing about it? This can't go on! I can't bear it! I'm sick of it, I tell you—sick at heart!

RUDOLF: We are doing something about it.

ANTON: [*Eager to hear the answer.*]: What are we doing?

RUDOLF: Well—there are your petitions to the Bureau of High-way Construction.

ANTON [*Echoing mechanically.*]: My petitions to the Bureau of Highway Construction.

RUDOLF: Twenty-four.

ANTON: Twenty-four—every time that it happens, another one. But nothing changes. No one hears.

RUDOLF: I keep thinking, some day someone *will* do something.

ANTON: Some day! Every day is dangerous, particularly now—at this season—the glaring heat, the sun in the south . . .

RUDOLF: The Secretary of Highways 'can't picture what it's like up here. If *you* were sitting down there in his office, with Venetian blinds, air conditioners, and pretty secretaries, then you wouldn't know what it was like up here either. And you wouldn't care.

ANTON: Secretary of Highways Dr. Kriegbaum can't imagine it. And why not? Because I haven't described the situation prop-erly, I haven't made it dramatic enough. There he sits at his desk, Secretary of Highways Dr. Kriegbaum, and pays atten-tion to the office routine. Official stamp: curve. Famine in India, official stamp, O.K. Executions in Cuba, official stamp, O.K. Mine disaster in Belgium, official stamp, O.K. Juvenile delinquency . . .

RUDOLF: That has nothing to do with highway construction.

ANTON: We are all concerned with highway construction. But no, Secretary of Highways Dr. Kriegbaum sits in his swivel chair and forgets about it, because I am a bad writer. A clumsy writer. *I* am guilty.

RUDOLF [*Pacifying him.*]: Well . . . know what *I* think? I think

Secretary of Highways Dr. Kriegbaum doesn't even read your petitions. Official stamp, wastebasket! I know that type.

ANTON [*Hopefully.*]: You think so?

RUDOLF: Absolutely. The more I think it over, the more I'm convinced of it. This damned Secretary Kriegbaum is just that type, you mark my words. Stiff neck—he doesn't look to the right or to the left, or up or down, and all of a sudden one day he's the new Secretary. I know that sort.

ANTON: You're just saying that to make me feel better.

RUDOLF: It's so. I know him, I tell you.

ANTON: You don't really know him at all.

RUDOLF: No.

ANTON: Well, then . . .

RUDOLF: But I know his type.

ANTON: You don't understand. You refuse to understand that we too are guilty. I have failed, I have written badly—so badly that no one is even interested.

RUDOLF: Well, send them a new petition.

ANTON: Yes, yes—I'll write movingly this time, powerfully. "Secretary of Highways Dr. Kriegbaum," I'll write, "I don't know you at all, but I know that you are a man and that, no matter where you fly, no matter how high your position in the world, you cannot escape the responsibility of being human. The highway, as you know, must be rebuilt. Just picture to yourself an automobile mounting the grade, the sun in the driver's eyes, his head aching with the heat, but the mountains are bright as glass and the driver drums with his fingers on the steering wheel. What a beautiful day, how wonderful it is to be alive! Just picture it, Mr. Secretary . . . "

RUDOLF [*Interrupting.*]: A car!

ANTON [*With averted eyes.*]: Can you see it?

RUDOLF: Not yet, Now he's behind the rocks, on the next to the last curve. Now I see it!

ANTON: How many in the car?

RUDOLF: Only one, I think.

ANTON: Thank God!

RUDOLF: And driving like a damned fool—much too fast!

ANTON [*Without looking.*]: We've got to have warning signs placed all along there: Drive Slow! Slow! Slow!

RUDOLF [*Watching.*]: The last short stretch—it's a dove-blue coupe, white sidewall tires—beautiful! With a radio antenna! [*Noise: shifting gears.*] He's shifting into low!

ANTON: What's the matter, isn't he going fast enough, the idiot! He's going to smash! He's bound to! It serves him right! [*Screams.*] It's his own fault!

RUDOLF: The last curve! Look out!

ANTON: It's his own fault . . .

[*Crashing, the shattering noises of an automobile wreck.*]

RUDOLF: Number twenty-five. [*Exits, toward the wreck.*]

ANTON [*Quickly, staring forward.*]: What have I said? It's his own fault? He's crazy? He didn't pay any attention to the high-way signs? Did I say that? No, no, I am the guilty one! It's *my* fault! I have failed, I have not made my voice heard. He was riding along happily, drumming on the steering wheel, whistling some popular tune, carefree . . . no, it is I who am guilty. Why shouldn't he be carefree? Maybe he had been drinking. Maybe he was going to a rendezvous with a mistress, while his family waited unsuspectingly at home. Such a man deserves . . . No, no, I am guilty that he has crashed! Rudolf! [*He runs off toward the wreck.*]

[*A long pause. One automobile rolls into the stage. Then a second. Then* RUDOLF *enters. He is dragging a piece of the wrecked automobile.*]

RUDOLF [*Calling back offstage.*]: Over there! More to the right! Yes, there by the rocks, in the rhubarb patch! [*He drags the automobile part into the shed, comes out again, looks offstage.*] Fine! Keep up the good work! Right! Grab him by the feet! I'm busy here with the car. [*Calls, hand to mouth.*] By the feet! [*Exits into the shed.* ANTON *enters, dragging the accident victim by his feet.*]

ANTON [*To the body.*]: I'm sorry—excuse me. I'm doing my best, believe me. You're so heavy. The dead are always heavier than the living. I know—this is the twenty-fourth time I've done this. Oh, God—dead! [*He goes back out, returns with a briefcase.* RUDOLF *comes out of the shed.*]

RUDOLF: Well, now. nothing is as bad as it seems, once you take a good look at it. Actually, he was rather lucky. Broken axle, naturally. And the body is pretty badly smashed up. But give me two weeks, and the thing will be standing here as good as new, I give you my word—dove-blue, polished, beautiful. You can bank on it.

ANTON: He's dead.

RUDOLF [*Busy.*]: Tragic.

ANTON: Motionless—a lifeless lump of flesh.

RUDOLF: We are all mortal—you, me, even our Aunt Elsa.

ANTON: When was the last time you were up on the curve?

RUDOLF: I don't know. why?

ANTON: I've got a feeling there are no more warning signs up there.

RUDOLF: Children take them down sometimes.

ANTON: I'm going to report this whole business, down to the last detail. We bear the responsibility, if nobody else will. We do! Us!

RUDOLF: Now wait a minute! What are we supposed to do? Blow up the rocks? Paint warning signs and stock them up along the side of the road? There are laws against that, for one thing. Or are we supposed to stand up there and yell to everyone who drives past: "Be careful, old boy"?

ANTON: We must do something.

RUDOLF: We bury the dead, don't we? Isn't that something? We maintain the cemetery, we plant flowers, we keep up the gravel paths, the fences, the wooden crosses—who does more these days?

ANTON: Not enough, not enough.

RUDOLF: Now, now, now—don't get started again. Just get hold of yourself for a minute. Your funeral sermons, for example —I suppose those are nothing? How many priests or preachers in the big cities can take time for that sort of thing, or do it so impressively, for that matter? Those aren't any dime-a-dozen sermons, I can tell you. You don't hear those just everywhere. They go right to a man's heart. They're religious experiences, for anyone who has ever heard them! And without a penny in salary!

ANTON [*Moved.*]: Rudolf—when you say such things . . .

RUDOLF: No, no, we do our duty and a little bit more besides besides—*basta*. All right?

ANTON: There's such a thing as conscience.

RUDOLF: Furthermore, we're men—that's all—neither cattle nor saints. Just men.

ANTON [*Lapsing into a preacher's tone of voice.*]: "When an accident occurs anywhere in the world, and it comes over us in our day-to-day existence in all its horrible absurdity, then we feel ourselves called, we see a curtain torn away from an abyss. Up till now we have concealed it with reassuring words and a comfortable, easily-lived morality. But now an accident has happened again. This man, who stood in the midst of life . . ." [*Breaking off.*] What about his identification?

RUDOLF [*Looking through the man's jacket.*]: Nothing in his jacket. [*Feels it.*] Leather.

ANTON: He had a briefcase.

RUDOLF: I'll take a look. [*Opens the briefcase, riffles through some papers.*] Letters. A photo—a woman—blond, pretty . . .

ANTON: Give it here!

RUDOLF: Easy, easy.

ANTON: I've got to have it. Where's his passport?

RUDOLF: Look. A yo-yo.

ANTON: His passport!

RUDOLF: A piece of ginger—with a bite out of it. [*Takes a bite.*]

ANTON: Give it here!

RUDOLF: A piece of string, pills, three monkeys: see no evil, hear no evil, speak no evil—hmm—the things you find on a man when he's dead!

ANTON: Give me the papers!

RUDOLF: Here they are. [*Reads through them.*]

ANTON: Age?

RUDOLF: Forty-eight.

ANTON: Name?

RUDOLF: Alpha Romeo.

ANTON: Identification marks?

RUDOLF: 12-13-21.

ANTON: That's the automobile registration! I mean, his personal papers!

RUDOLF: Ah. Here we are.

ANTON: Name? [RUDOLF *is silent*.] Name? [RUDOLF *is silent*.] What's the matter?

RUDOLF: Kriegbaum.

ANTON: Kriegbaum?

RUDOLF: Doctor of Jurisprudence, Erich, Secretary of Highways, married. Special mark of identification: two webbed toes on the left foot.

ANTON: Take a look.

RUDOLF [*Takes off the shoe and sock of the victim, looks.*]: Right.

ANTON: Secretary of Highways Dr. Kriegbaum.

RUDOLF: Apparently. What's he doing here?

ANTON: Is there anything else in the briefcase?

RUDOLF [*Looking.*]: Papers. Prospectuses.

ANTON: Nothing else?

RUDOLF: Here!

ANTON [*Excited.*]: What?

RUDOLF: Look! You've written the whole briefcase—twenty-four petitions.

ANTON [*Triumphantly.*]: So they *did* have an effect! You see? They weighed upon him, they gave him no peace, they awakened his conscience, torturing him—until he decided at last to come and see for himself . . . [*Stops.*] And now—dead!

RUDOLF: Well—now someone else will take over the case.

ANTON: Someone else . . .

RUDOLF: Every man is replaceable.

ANTON: Replaceable—interchangeable . . .

RUDOLF: The only question is: Who will be next?

ANTON: Who knows?

RUDOLF: Should we wait?

ANTON: Let's wait until we know who the next man will be.

RUDOLF: I'll get started on the car. [*Starts out.*]

ANTON: Help me here first.

RUDOLF: How?

ANTON: We've got to get this man into the garden.

RUDOLF: Haul him by the feet again.

ANTON: He's a Secretary of Highways! [RUDOLF *takes hold of the body unwillingly. They carry it a step, then* ANTON *stops.*] Hey!

RUDOLF: What?

ANTON: Maybe he's still alive.

Rudolf: No. He's cold as a mackerel.

Anton: Let's put a leaf on his mouth.

Rudolf: Bosh! [*He picks up the body again.*]

Anton: You're completely insensitive. Wait. Let's try it just once with the leaf. [*He tears a leaf off a bush and lays it on the dead man's mouth.*]

Rudolf: I give up. [*He starts to go.*]

Anton: Rudolf! Rudolf! [**Rudolf** *stops.*] I think the leaf moved! Yes—it's moving!

Rudolf [*Irritably.*]: Count me out on this! [*Crawls under the car.*]

Anton: He's moving. He's breathing. Come here—it's really true— I'm not making it up!

Rudolf [*Working.*]: He'd be the first one!

Anton: Yes, he *is* the first!

Rudolf [*Under the car.*]: You'd better give him a shot of whisky or something, hadn't you?

Anton [*Pleadingly.*]: Mr. Secretary! Mr. Secretary! [**Kriegbaum** *moves.*]

Kriegbaum [*Weakly but firmly.*]: I don't wish to be disturbed.

Anton: Rudolf, he spoke! Please, Mr. Secretary . . .

Kriegbaum [*With feeble irritation*]: Yes, yes, document number CF 735, please . . . !

Anton: Wake up!

Kriegbaum: No, not that. The other. The one with the conference report and the opinions of the ministers. You know . . .

Anton: [*Shaking him.*]: Wake up, Mr. Secretary! Wake up!

Kriegbaum: What are you doing to me?

Anton: Oh, Mr. Secretary, I'm delighted to hear you speak!

Kriegbaum: Where am I?

Anton: In the land of the living, Mr. Secretary.

Kriegbaum [*Sitting up.*]: [*Flinching in pain.*] What do you mean, living?

Anton: Wake up!

Kriegbaum: Wake up?

Anton: You had a bad wreck.

Kriegbaum: Ouch—my arm!

Anton: You were driving along up there on that curving highway.

Kriegbaum [*Groans.*]: Where is my car?

ANTON: I'm sorry to say it's pretty well smashed up, Mr. Secretary. But my brother is already at work repairing it.

KRIEGBAUM: A terrible business.

ANTON: Calm yourself, Mr. Secretary. It will look as good as new. It's true, my brother doesn't have a degree in engineering—he's more or less picked up everything he knows—a sort of tinkerer, as you might say, but you needn't have the slightest worry. He's a better mechanic than most of them in the garages in the big cities. You can trust him.

KRIEGBAUM: How did this happen?

ANTON: Oh, Mr. Secretary . . .

KRIEGBAUM: Certainly no one can claim that I was driving recklessly.

ANTON: No, no, certainly not.

KRIEGBAUM: Or perhaps that I was in—as they say—exceptionally high spirits—eh?

ANTON: No one could accuse you of that, sir.

KRIEGBAUM: I have no spirits. Not the slightest hint of carelessness, no dereliction of duty, no letting up . . .

ANTON: Of course. Everything strictly correct, Mr. Secretary. Nevertheless . . .

KRIEGBAUM: Good. You can testify that I was not exceeding the speed limit.

ANTON: Precisely, Mr. Secretary. But unfortunately . . .

KRIEGBAUM: What?

ANTON: Unfortunately, there *is* no speed limit on that curve. *Most* unfortunately, if I may say so.

KRIEGBAUM: That's got to be changed.

ANTON: I agree with you entirely.

KRIEGBAUM: Yes, yes, now I remember—that damned highway! Curve right, curve left, sepentine, then suddenly the rocks, the sun in my eyes . . .

ANTON: Ah!

KRIEGBAUM: And why was I driving up there? Why? Because I wanted to personally inspect that stretch of road? Right?

ANTON: I assumed that was what it was, yes. No doubt someone had described these dangerous conditions to you.

KRIEGBAUM: Yes. There were some petitions—

ANTON: Twenty-four of them.

KRIEGBAUM: Quite right. However, to tell the truth, one does not always pay close attention to handwritten petitions—you know, it may be a peasant whose cows are made nervous by the automobiles, or some fellow who wants the newsstand concession at a certain intersection. Oh, I tell you, my friend, you have no idea of the things that come across my desk.

ANTON: Those twenty-four petitions were written by my hand, Mr. Secretary.

KRIEGBAUM [*Studying* ANTON *for the first time.*]: Indeed? Interesting. You live here?

ANTON: Yes, my brother and I have a small bit of land here. Very small, but cared for with love.

KRIEGBAUM: The main thing is that a man is happy, right?

ANTON: True. And we have no grounds for complaint. Of course, the ground is very hard, quite stony—so it's difficult digging. But we do our best.

KRIEGBAUM: And why did you send these complaints to the Bureau?

ANTON: Not complaints, Mr. Secretary. Please don't think that. Merely petitions.

KRIEGBAUM: Are you often bothered up here—[*Gestures.*]—as I am bothering you now?

ANTON: Twenty-five times—counting your own—er—appearance today. And we always take care of the—necessities. You can see the mounds over there.

KRIEGBAUM [*Uncomfortably.*]: Ah, yes. The mounds.

ANTON: You can inspect the cemetery a little later. It's a capital walking place for convalescents. Pleasant narrow paths of white gravel, no weeds, no tasteless plaster of Paris headstones. Simple crosses—my brother made them.

KRIEGBAUM: He seems to be a very handy fellow.

ANTON: He does wood-carving, too. Personally, I'm completely inept when it comes to working with my hands. Hand me a knife and, I promise you, I'm liable to cut off my finger.

KRIEGBAUM [*Cheerful again; laughs.*]: I know what you mean— I'm like that, too! You should have seen the woodworking projects I did as a child for my four aunts: Zodiacs with transparent paper and the calendar with sawed-out fretwork—I hit myself in the nose once, I remember, and brought tears to my eyes. Nevertheless, I managed to turn out all right, as you can see.

ANTON: I can, indeed, Mr. Secretary. And I, too, can find a certain satisfaction with myself, although on a far more modest scale. I refer to my own special talent; and bringing this to its fullest development I regard as my most important mission in life. I mean my talent as a writer.

KRIEGBAUM: You don't say so.

ANTON: Oh, it's a very modest talent, I know—very modest! But I can honestly say that I have spared no effort to perfect my art, down to the smallest nuances of expression.

KRIEGBAUM: Aha, you have a market for your writing! A sweet-heart, perhaps?

ANTON: No, no, you don't understand me. Reality, if I may say so, is my goal as a writer.

KRIEGBAUM: Ah, a poet! Respect! Respect! I assure you, when a man is in government work, as I am, it's not every day that he comes in contact with an artistic soul. A pity—I've often thought so. So—the opportunity to grasp your hand today is even more of a pleasure, eh? What are you writing these days?

ANTON: Speeches.

KRIEGBAUM: Speeches?

ANTON: Yes. [Pointing toward the cemetery.] The first one was rather crudely done, like a school exercise, divided into sections, A, B1, B2, C, with transitional passages and formal conclusion. You know what I mean.

KRIEGBAUM: Well, a man's got to start somewhere, doesn't he?

ANTON: From the third one on, I became more skillful in my con-struction, more precise in my expression. I found my true style. Can you picture that—how it frees a man, inwardly, to find at last the right tone, the exact word?

KRIEGBAUM: Practice makes perfect. And now?

ANTON: What do you mean—"And now"?

KRIEGBAUM: I mean, what do you live on now?

ANTON: That's a rather painful question.

KRIEGBAUM: I can understand that it's not easy for you here. But do you work part-time somewhere else?

ANTON: I am completely occupied with my writing, Mr. Secretary.

KRIEGBAUM: Admirable, my dear fellow! A man ought to give himself to something completely—head, hand and heart, as it were. But who pays for—er—if you'll forgive the question. I merely ask out of interest.

ANTON: My brother.

KRIEGBAUM: Your brother?

ANTON: He labors there in his workshop ten hours a day.

KRIEGBAUM: Hmm. Not many like him nowadays.

ANTON: He gets so restless when there's no work to be done. Then he doesn't know what to do with himself.

KRIEGBAUM: Ah, yes—a grave social problem. I've had some experience with that.

ANTON: Most of the time though we are fully occupied.

KRIEGBAUM: Aha. [*Silence.*] And so your brother . . .

ANTON: We help each other, you understand. Each in his own way.

KRIEGBAUM: I want to try standing up.

ANTON: Don't be too hasty, Mr. Secretary. In your present condition, that can only do you harm.

KRIEGBAUM [*Stirring himself energetically.*]: I've got to be moving.

ANTON: Recuperation takes time, Mr. Secretary. You need to rest for a few days. That's the only answer. Rest and more rest.

KRIEGBAUM: You know, I am happy—really happy—that this has happened to me. It was a shock, but, mark my words, some good will come of it.

ANTON: What do you mean?

KRIEGBAUM: The highway.

ANTON: You shouldn't be thinking about your job now, Mr. Secretary.

KRIEGBAUM: I can't help it. In my position—you understand—I'm always on the job.

ANTON: If I may give you a bit of advice: Forget about your work, leave it to your successor. You have a successor?

KRIEGBAUM: Successor?

ANTON: A suitable personality to fill your place.

KRIEGBAUM: Fill my place? That's good! [*Laughs.*]

ANTON: The work must go on, though, even without you.

KRIEGBAUM: Enough of that! Naturally, I have a deputy—a successor, as you call him. But what a successor!

Anton: Isn't he qualified? Isn't he correct? Incorruptible?

Kriegbaum: Listen, if I don't do everything myself . . .

Anton: What's his name?

Kriegbaum: Kirstein, Dr. Kirstein. [ANTON *writes down the name.*] Why are you writing that down?

Anton: I was just thinking . . . about the petitions. . . .

Kriegbaum: Don't bother. I'm going to take charge of the whole affair.

Anton: What do you intend to do?

Kriegbaum: It's perfectly clear what I intend to do.

Anton: The highway . . .

Kriegbaum: Naturally.

Anton: But—can we be sure of that?

Kriegbaum: Evidently you don't know me very well. When I tackle something and throw all my energy into the work—the job is done!

Anton: You will start on it immediately?

Kriegbaum: The minute I am back at my desk, I will start giving the necessary orders. The first thing will be the placing of several warning signs up there: Dangerous Curve. That's the very least we can do, just to start with.

Anton: There used to be some, but they were apparently torn down by children.

Kriegbaum: Then certain regulations will be adopted which will prevent this in the future.

Anton: In case of emergency, too, the highway could be closed to normal traffic.

Kriegbaum: Right!

Anton: What else?

Kriegbaum: What do you mean—"What else"? Next, the whole plan must be officially approved. But there will be no problem there, don't worry! The Minister will give his O.K. to any plan that *I* am sponsoring!

Anton: Good! When?

Kriegbaum: Next week, perhaps. And with at least five work gangs.

Anton: Everyone will work on the highway. And someone—the foreman or the architect or the overseer, or even you, Mr. Secretary—someone somewhere has a clear picture in mind, through it all, of just how the highway will someday be!

KRIEGBAUM [*Patronizingly.*]: Right.

ANTON: How *will* it be?

KRIEGBAUM: Magnificently strong.

ANTON: Asphalt?

KRIEGBAUM: Nowadays we know how to make road surfaces much stronger than in the past. For example, we have no more pot holes from frost. No. Our roads can be made smooth as a board —yet not slippery.

ANTON [*Fascinated.*]: Beautiful!

KRIEGBAUM: But, naturally, this is by no means all. By no means. We will have warnings placed at every curve—particularly that last one. The middle of the road will be marked with a white stripe. We will build parking areas here and there so that any-one who wants to stop—perhaps to view the landscape at his leisure—will not slow down the traffic or create a danger poin' What do you say to that?

ANTON: Beautiful! Look, there's a fresh color mounting in your cheeks, Mr. Secretary!

KRIEGBAUM: The best is yet to come. Reflectors on each of the white posts bordering the highway, so that even in the dark the curves will be clearly visible in the reflections of the headlights. And at the top, on the last curve . . .

ANTON: The rocks! . . .

KRIEGBAUM: Will be blown up. Yes, up there we will make it a divided highway—one part will lead up over the crest, the other down through the rock wall, via a tunnel.

ANTON: Beautiful!

KRIEGBAUM: There's absolutely no other way. For now it's possible that two cars, rounding the curve at the same time, unseen by each other, could . . . eh? . . .

ANTON: Actually, that's never happened, Mr. Secretary. Up until now, fortunately, there has not been much traffic on this stretch of road.

KRIEGBAUM [*Impatiently.*]: But it *could* happen! It *could*! Then what?

ANTON [*Shame-faced.*]: You're right—it could happen. I didn't think before I spoke, Mr. Secretary.

KRIEGBAUM: And what about at night? Doesn't that ever happen?

ANTON: Very rarely. Out of our first twenty-four, there was only one—about 2:00 A.M. But he was drunk, in any case.

KRIEGBAUM: What difference does that make? This one man: didn't he want to live, like all the others? Didn't he have a wife and children, like all the others? I tell you: the fate of this one man concerns us all!

ANTON: I'm sorry. Naturally, I quite agree with you, Mr. Secretary. I only thought—well, there are some things the Bureau of Highways simply can't do. . . .

KRIEGBAUM [*Interrupting.*]: "Can't!" "Can't!" What kind of a word is that? Of course, I can do it! Ultimately, it is a question of individual initiative!

ANTON: What will you do about the night?

KRIEGBAUM: The night will be done away with.

ANTON: That would be wonderful.

KRIEGBAUM: Have you ever heard about such things as neon lights? [*With mounting excitement.*] Just picture to yourself: As night falls, a sudden cascade of light, streaming upon the highway, on all the curves, light upon light—every night, sitting down here, you will look up and see it! And then a man can forget the highway, he can forget that it is night, forget the rock wall on his right and the abyss on his left—he will drive on, happy, safe, through a rush of pure light—forever!

ANTON [*Enthralled.*]: Wonderful! Wonderful!

KRIEGBAUM: No more fear of the unexpected, the unknown. The men of the future will drive in perfect safety.

ANTON: Wonderful. No more families waiting at home in vain. No more sorrow.

KRIEGBAUM: Traffic will flow unhindered, night and day.

ANTON: Traffic, as one might say, between man and man.

KRIEGBAUM: Yes. Well put!

ANTON: Wonderful! Wonderful!

KRIEGBAUM: For, basically, no man can live alone—we all need each other. No man can remain indifferent to his fellows. This is a necessity of life, in the most literal sense of the word. My own personal code of ethics.

ANTON: Yes, we all need each other. We will all love each other.

The world's sorrow will be destroyed. [*Suddenly dejected.*] Too
bad . . .

KRIEGBAUM: What do you mean?

ANTON: It suddenly occurred to me that . . . that . . . [*Stops.*]

KRIEGBAUM: What?

ANTON: That this would never be.

KRIEGBAUM [*Sobered.*]: But why on earth not?

ANTON: It's too beautiful, that's all—too beautiful.

KRIEGBAUM [*Uncertainly, with attempted joviality.*]: But, my dear
fellow, you've got to have faith.

ANTON: Oh, I have faith—but that has nothing to do with it.

KRIEGBAUM: Look at me! Do you have faith in my initiative?

ANTON: Yes. Yes. But I don't know . . .

KRIEGBAUM: Ah, you mean because previously I—er—But that
was quite a different matter. Don't forget—a shock, such as I
have just had—that can change a man.

ANTON [*Murmurs.*]: "When an accident occurs . . ." [*Breaking
off.*] Really?

KRIEGBAUM: Believe me. From the ground up. If you are still
skeptical, I can let you in on a small secret. Do you know why I
was traveling along that highway?

ANTON: You said—the petitions . . .

KRIEGBAUM: In the briefcase, my dear fellow, in the briefcase! But
we are all only human—you know what I mean? I have a friend
— a very pretty little blond friend—living some twenty miles
from here, in a small hotel at the edge of a forest. You understand? And that's why I was driving along up there.

ANTON: So it was mere chance, then? Hmm.

KRIEGBAUM: But a lucky chance, as it now appears.

ANTON: Or an unlucky one.

KRIEGBAUM: Or an unlucky one, depending on how you look at it.

ANTON: There are various ways of looking at it.

KRIEGBAUM: Enough of this! All that is in the past, I promise you.
As of this day, I am a new man. Just let me get back to that
office! Here—let me try to walk again. [*He rises, with* ANTON's
help.] Thank you, thank you. You see, I'm much better already.

ANTON: Careful!

KRIEGBAUM: There! I'm doing splendidly, don't you think?

ANTON: Nothing goes fast enough for you, Mr. Secretary. Back to the office! Really, don't you think that your successor, Dr. Kirstein . . .

KRIEGBAUM: There you go again with that word "successor."

ANTON: It seems to be on the tip of my tongue. Sorry.

KRIEGBAUM: I'm going to walk a few steps now.

ANTON: But you're still unsteady on your feet! You could stumble and fall! Tell me, why are you so opposed to your . . . to Dr. Kirstein's taking over your work?

KRIEGBAUM: He's unreliable! Totally unreliable! I guarantee you, your petitions will lie on his desk for five years before he even looks at them. No, no, let me walk by myself! [*Walks about.*] Mmm, it still hurts a little, here and there. I can't walk very far. Just a little more, over that way. Thank you, my dear fellow. [*He exits.* ANTON *gazes after him, then goes quickly through the papers in the briefcase, selects some, and stuffs them in his pockets. Pause.* RUDOLF *enters.*]

RUDOLF: Where is he? [ANTON *points.*] He's leaving?

ANTON: He's taking a walk. He can get around pretty well already.

RUDOLF [*Suspiciously.*]: He can get around pretty well already?

ANTON: I have nursed him back to health, so to speak. After you had given up on him. Wrecked, dead, finished—that's what you thought.

RUDOLF [*Irritably.*]: Where's he going?

ANTON: He's coming right back. He's just trying his legs.

RUDOLF: So—he's coming right back.

ANTON [*Pointing.*]: You see him? There he is. Now he's sitting down. He's still a bit weak in the knees.

RUDOLF: Mmm—he's still a bit weak in the knees. But he's getting stronger by the minute.

ANTON: We don't want to be too optimistic. An automobile wreck is nothing to laugh at. At first, he really seemed to be as good as dead. No motion, no breath.

RUDOLF: Yes, he was as good as dead. He *was*.

ANTON: And now? It's like night and day. He's fairly bursting with activity.

RUDOLF: Hmm.

ANTON: The accident naturally was a terrific shock to him. [*Quoting from his speech.*] "When an accident occurs anywhere in the world, and it comes over us in our day-to-day existence in all its horrible absurdity, then we feel ourselves called.. .." [*Drawing his manuscript from his pocket.*] ". . . We see a curtain torn away . . ."

RUDOLF: Stop it.

ANTON: It's a good beginning, very good.

RUDOLF: Look: he's doing some setting-up exercises.

ANTON [*Looking.*]: So he is. [*Carefully folds up his manuscript and puts it back in his pocket.*]

RUDOLF: Now he's trying an endurance run.

ANTON: You don't understand me. You have never understood me. You see only what you see, you hear only what you hear. You are a very dull man.

RUDOLF [*Quarrelsome.*]: I hear autos coming, that's what I hear. A Fiat . . . a bus . . . a Rolls Royce.

ANTON: Secretary Kriegbaum would have understood me—my slightest word . . .

RUDOLF [*With hate.*]: So. You like him?

ANTON [*Uncertainly.*]: In a way, yes—as a man.

RUDOLF: Look! He's climbing up the rocks!

ANTON [*Horrified.*]: Stop him! He's getting away from us!

RUDOLF [*Looks at* ANTON.]: What do you mean—"getting away from us"?

ANTON: He—might hurt himself.

RUDOLF: He was just picking a flower.

ANTON: What happens now?

RUDOLF: I don't know. I'm a man who repairs automobiles. The rest is your business.

ANTON: The rest?

[*Pause.* KRIEGBAUM *returns; he looks very happy; he is holding a flower in his hand.*]

KRIEGBAUM [*Entering quickly.*]: Aha! I astonish you, eh?

ANTON: This is my brother.

KRIEGBAUM: Just what I thought to myself, as I saw you two standing there: the two brothers! I am delighted to make your acquaintance. [*Gives him his hand.*] If you hadn't been down here, you two, if you hadn't seen the accident and hurried to help me as I lay there among the rhubarb—I was just taking another look at the place—well, I wouldn't be standing here now. Thank you.

ANTON: You can thank your unusually strong constitution, Mr. Secretary.

KRIEGBAUM: No, no, credit where credit is due. Anyway, I just missed by a hair being hurled onto those sharp rocks up there.

RUDOLF: That's where most of them land.

ANTON: You see! You must have a good-luck charm, Mr. Secretary.

KRIEGBAUM: Yes, I've always been lucky, if I do say so myself. Look what I have here.

ANTON [*Looking.*]: A columbine.

KRIEGBAUM: I took the liberty of picking one. It's not against the law?

ANTON: Oh, no, no!

KRIEGBAUM: Incidentally, you've done a very tasteful job of arranging the garden—the paths, the flower beds.

ANTON: We've worked hard to insure a constant supply of flowers. Without flowers [*Indicating the graves.*], all that is too sad to contemplate.

KRIEGBAUM: May I take this columbine with me—as a memento?

ANTON: Please do!

RUDOLF: As a memento.

KRIEGBAUM: I'll put it in the flower holder in my car. By the way, how *is* my car?

RUDOLF: Almost finished.

KRIEGBAUM: Splendid! Then I can drive it back?

RUDOLF: The seats still need to be remounted.

KRIEGBAUM: No hurry—the main thing is that no trace of the accident remains.

RUDOLF: None of my customers has complained yet.

KRIEGBAUM: Naturally not, naturally not—er—that is—please don't misunderstand me . . .

RUDOLF: Every car I turn out looks as though it had never been in an accident.

ANTON: There will be nothing to remind you of your terrible accident. You will get in, wave gaily to us, and drive away.

KRIEGBAUM: Beautiful.

Rudolf: Beautiful.

Anton: Beautiful.

Kriegbaum: And then, I promise you, we'll get the project started. At once. [*The two brothers look at each other.*] You can be sure of that. How much do I owe you for the repair work?

Rudolf: Forty dollars.

Kriegbaum: Isn't that a little high?

Rudolf: I've been offered forty-five.

Kriegbaum: Offered?

Rudolf: By the junk dealer. He knows what cars are worth.

Kriegbaum: Junk dealer?

Rudolf: That's what we live on.

Kriegbaum: Oh, yes. I forgot.[*Silence.*] All in all, a difficult way of life, eh?

Rudolf: It varies from season to season.

Kriegbaum: Mmm—yes, that *would* make a difference.

Anton: ". . . a curtain torn away . . ." Or: "a curtain ripped aside . . ." Or: ". . . a curtain . . ." No, "curtain" isn't right.

Rudolf: Stop it.

Kriegbaum: What did he say?

Rudolf: Nothing—of any importance.

Anton: Very often, Mr. Secretary, when I hear my brother working, or when I hear you say, "You can be sure of that"—it seems to me like—like the signing of a solemn treaty—and when I see how efficient you are . . .

Kriegbaum [*Modestly.*]: Now, now—

Anton: Yes, yes, I see it: there is a morality in your work. You are a happy man, a choice spirit—you have a job which comes easily to you, you have a mission in life. . . .

Kriegbaum: But so do you, my dear fellow! How often must I assure you of that?

Anton: I am overcome by the crippling shame I feel at the senselessness of my own actions. The uselessness of it all . . . I don't mean in the material sense, don't misunderstand me. I can truly say that I am not interested in material success. No, what I mean is: who pays any attention to my work?—And it *is* work, laborious, crushing work, trying to find the right word, the right tone, the right conditions for the expression of reality—but who finally pays any attention to this? [KRIEGBAUM *starts to speak conciliatingly.*] No, don't answer hastily. I know what you're going to say: my work is not for the masses, and it is enough if *one* man in the world knows how to value it.

KRIEGBAUM: I, for example, value it very highly.

ANTON: Value it! That's only a surface judgment. Don't you see that? What worries me, you see, is the awareness that my work, with which I struggle so painfully, has no meaningful connection with life, with reality. Don't you understand that?

KRIEGBAUM: I'm trying to.

ANTON: My brother fixes cars. And, as a result, people can travel, right? You build highways—and that, too, has a tangible value and a meaning. But I . . . [*Draws his manuscript from his pocket.*] What kind of sense does this make? It has no value nowadays, my brother tells me. We are very different, my brother and I.

KRIEGBAUM [*Mediatingly.*]: You complement one another.

ANTON: Good. Yes. But somehow we always come to the precipice. [*He reads.*] "Suddenly a curtain is torn away . . ." You alone can understand that.

KRIEGBAUM: Yes indeed. It has, you might say, a special meaning for me.

ANTON: Help me.

KRIEGBAUM: How can I help you?

ANTON: With my manuscript . . .

KRIEGBAUM: Well, I'm not exactly a literary critic.

ANTON: All you have to do is listen. React to every nuance—suggest improvements where you feel that the truth is not being expressed.

KRIEGBAUM: Well—if I can help you in any way . . .

ANTON: And give me your opinion—without prejudice!

KRIEGBAUM: Oh, come now! Tell me, what is the theme of your essay?

ANTON: You.

KRIEGBAUM: I?

ANTON: Basically, we know each other scarcely at all. Help me to correct my impressions.

KRIEGBAUM: This is a very comical idea.

ANTON: ". . . Suddenly a curtain is torn away; the abyss becomes visible—the abyss which we have concealed with comfortable words and an easily-lived morality."

KRIEGBAUM: It reads very smoothly.

RUDOLF: The beginning has already been well-tested.

KRIEGBAUM: Aha.

ANTON: "This accident has happened once again. A man, who stood in the very midst of life, now suddenly lifeless—mute—"

KRIEGBAUM: Please! May I point out that I am . . .

RUDOLF: This is still just the introduction.

ANTON: I'm sorry, I had forgotten that you had . . . I must revise that part. "A life of dutiful performance . . ."

RUDOLF: Can you say a thing like that?

KRIEGBAUM: Yes, there is such an idiomatic phrase. However, I don't feel it is quite appropriate as a means of praising me.

RUDOLF: You hear that, Anton? That's very impressive. Go on—ask him some more of the questions.

ANTON: It is your duty, for example, to build highways, Mr. Secretary. But would you perform that duty faithfully, even if there were danger for you involved in it?

KRIEGBAUM: What kind of danger could there be for me?

RUDOLF [*With veiled threat.*]: Someone could say to you: "Don't do this thing." That could happen.

ANTON: Something which otherwise your sense of duty would impel you to do.

KRIEGBAUM: I'm afraid I don't quite understand.

RUDOLF: And then they might point a pistol at your head.

ANTON: Figuratively speaking.

RUDOLF: When a man's afraid, he'll promise anything.

ANTON: He'll leave the important task undone.

RUDOLF: A man wants to live. That's understandable.

ANTON: And then, shortly after, you return home . . . assuming, say, you were on the road when this thing happened to you. You go back to your office, you have nothing more to fear—it has all passed like an Alpine dream.

RUDOLF: Then will you forget your promise? Will you still perform your duty?

KRIEGBAUM [*Uncertainly.*]: I'm sorry, I don't quite understand. I can only say that I have always striven to act according to the dictates of my conscience and will continue to do so.

ANTON: A life of dutiful performance! But let us not begin with that.

RUDOLF: It makes no difference where you begin. No one will pay any attention, anyway.

ANTON: ". . . And now we stand here, at the end of a life, and we ask ourselves . . ."

KRIEGBAUM [*Uncomfortably.*]: But—just a minute!

RUDOLF: Let him speak.

ANTON: "What was the meaning of this life? I've got to find a transition in here, Mr. Secretary. "I suspect we can only answer this question by surveying the life of the man in its entirety. In the main, it was a happy life."

KRIEGBAUM: What do you mean, "was"?

ANTON: I mean, up to this point, Mr. Secretary. Everything moves toward this point. Before it and after—two different worlds.

KRIEGBAUM: You are straining my patience a bit, I'm afraid.

RUDOLF: You see, Anton? We're boring him.

ANTON: "His life was devoted to service, his days were filled with tireless labor, even in his later years he consistently put in more hours at his desk than many of his younger colleagues."

KRIEGBAUM: Kirstein, for example.

ANTON: "But it was not only at his job that he did his utmost, not only in the bosom of his family that he sacrificed himself self-lessly. As he was so fond of saying: 'That goes without saying.' "

KRIEGBAUM: True. What else do we live for?

ANTON: "No, his service, his devotion was directed toward society at large—toward, in the broadest sense of the word, the family of mankind."

KRIEGBAUM: One has examples, of course: Albert Schweitzer, Gandhi.

ANTON: "He was beloved by his colleagues. Some of them could be said to have idolized him. Once a woman in his employ had to be dismissed because of . . ."

KRIEGBAUM: Let us speak no more of that affair. Give me the photo!

ANTON: "Every morning, regular as clockwork, a fresh bouquet of roses stood on his desk. Also, a stick of ginger, on which he loved to nibble."

KRIEGBAUM: How do you know that?

ANTON [*Producing a letter.*]: It's all in this letter.

KRIEGBAUM: What are you thinking of? That's a completely private letter.

ANTON: It is precisely privacy which interests us, Mr. Secretary. It is the private part of a man's life which gives it color and interest. "He was extraordinarily skillful in dealing with men, because he himself was first and foremost a man—not a moralist, not a mere time-server, nor a narrow-minded bureaucrat."

KRIEGBAUM: Right!

ANTON: "He loved sports. As a mere stripling of twelve, he won a medal in broad-jumping." [*Takes a medal out of the briefcase.*]

KRIEGBAUM: Fifteen feet, ten inches—if I remember correctly.

ANTON: "And even later, one could truly say that, even in his advancing years, he kept himself in tip-top physical condition. *Mens sana in corpore sano.* Within this noble body there dwelt a noble spirit! In his early school days, he made his first uncertain intellectual trial-flights—not wholly directionless, it is true; interested in everything, trying everything, yet wavering still, uncertain of which path in life he would eventually follow . . ."

KRIEGBAUM: I was no teacher's pet, though! I had a "D" in Religion—in a class where it was necessary not to argue with the teacher.

ANTON: "Youth wants everything, and as a result achieves but little. But it is only the yoke of restriction which teaches the spirit to blossom fully."

KRIEGBAUM: That was the subject of my speech as class valedictorian!

ANTON: A speech that attracted great attention. "It was later that he discovered his legalistic abilities."

KRIEGBAUM: Yes—during a political debate concerning rearmament. The nub of the problem was: "Is one justified in killing in defense of one's way of life?"

RUDOLF: I don't understand that.

ANTON: "Is one justified in killing . . ."? Mmm. Which side did you take?

KRIEGBAUM: I said no. Of course, it was important for me to win the sympathy of my acquaintances at that time.

ANTON: "Finally, after years of searching, he chose his political allegiance. It was this that brought him to . . ."

KRIEGBAUM: I was not an opportunist!

ANTON: "No, it was to free himself from the isolation of individualism, which, as he clearly saw, must always remain unfruitful. To serve something greater and more complete than himself. Shortly thereafter, he became Secretary of Highways."

KRIEGBAUM: *Before* my party came to power!

ANTON: "A rich, successful, fully developed life lies spread before us now, a life lived to the fullest, right to the very end."

KRIEGBAUM [*Starts to go.*]: Let's stop all this nonsense.

RUDOLF [*Flatly.*]: Sit down and be quiet.

ANTON: "But who was he? What was hidden behind that mask of the public personality? Who is it really who is dying here at this moment?"

[KRIEGBAUM *starts up as though to protest.*]

RUDOLF: Don't move. It would be bad for your health.

ANTON: "He was a happy man, a man capable of fun and jokes, even at times when his work was not going well. . . ." [*He takes the yo-yo from the briefcase.*]

KRIEGBAUM: There is a time for everything. But now I really must be going. [*Turns.*]

ANTON [*Playing with the yo-yo.*]: This is very calming to the nerves.

RUDOLF [*Holding* KRIEGBAUM *by the arm.*]: Why are you trembling?

KRIEGBAUM: Trembling? Me?

RUDOLF: Now you have clamped your teeth together to keep them from chattering. My hearing is very keen, isn't it?

KRIEGBAUM: Nonsense.

RUDOLF: I do believe you're afraid.

KRIEGBAUM [*Trembling.*]: Afraid? Of what?

RUDOLF: Of what? That's good! Of what? [*Laughs.*] You hear that, Anton? The Secretary says: "Of what?" [*Laughs.*] Maybe of you, do you suppose? [*To* KRIEGBAUM.] He won't do anything to you. All he can do is write and talk—that's all. Look, isn't he comical? [KRIEGBAUM *and* RUDOLF *laugh at* ANTON'S *playing with the yo-yo.*]

ANTON [*Shouts.*]: No! [*Then, more quietly, taking a jackknife out of the briefcase.*] "This memento of boyhood days, of summer nights by the campfire, of hikes along the river, cutting a walking stick from a hazel branch, or carving a flute from the rushes. This little knife . . ."

RUDOLF: Isn't he good, Mr. Secretary?

KRIEGBAUM: I want nothing to do with all this.

RUDOLF: And now he opens the little blade—click! My hearing is very keen, isn't it?

KRIEGBAUM: My knife!

RUDOLF: You sound like something has you by the throat.

ANTON: "He carried it with him for years. Once he had used it to carve a certain young lady's name in the bark of an oak tree— a name which he later forgot."

RUDOLF: Just think of that! With his little knife!

KRIEGBAUM: I don't know . . .

RUDOLF: You think he's going to do something to you?

ANTON [*Searching the briefcase.*]: And pencils! Sharpened pencils! Look—who put a colored pencil in here? Do you mean to poison me?

RUDOLF: Sounds good, eh? Real terror, right?

KRIEGBAUM: The little blade is to sharpen the pencils!

ANTON: And the big one to peel apples!

KRIEGBAUM: You wipe them off with a paper napkin!

RUDOLF: You carry them with you, eh?

KRIEGBAUM: Or . . . with your handkerchief, if no one is looking!

ANTON: "He had his eccentricities. His passion for order in little things. The most touching of his qualities, it would seem, though, was his love for flowers. Yes, the Secretary loved flowers. Even as he died, he held a columbine in his hand."

KRIEGBAUM [*In panic.*]: Stop this! Let me go!

RUDOLF [*Hauls him back brutally.*]: But, Mr. Secretary—!

KRIEGBAUM: What are you doing? What are you doing to me?

RUDOLF: Why, I'm a prince of good fellows.

KRIEGBAUM [*With mounting panic.*]: I think you are splendid men! We understand each other! You saved my life!

ANTON: "What, we ask ourselves now, was the value of this life? What was the meaning of this experience—was it sheer accident, nothing more?"

KRIEGBAUM: I am grateful to you for everything! There has been a fundamental change in my attitude toward life. Thanks to you, my friends, I have come for the first time to an understanding of myself . . . [*He tries to break free.*]

RUDOLF: Just sit nice and still. No need to be so nervous.

ANTON: "The value of this life lay, then, in the insight which the man himself achieved through its final episode. . . ."

KRIEGBAUM [*Breathless with terror.*]: . . . myself and myself and the things I am guilty of, through carelessness, through thoughtlessness . . . please, you must understand me. . . . [*Tries weakly to escape, but* RUDOLF *stands before him, hands in pockets, legs spread apart.*] You must understand what I am trying to say, my friends.

RUDOLF: Quiet!

ANTON: ". . . achieved through the beautiful, heartwarming words . . ."

KRIEGBAUM: We must help one another . . . help . . . [ANTON *stabs* KRIEGBAUM *with the knife.*] My friends . . . [*He dies.* ANTON *wipes off the knife with his handkerchief. Pause.*]

RUDOLF: It had to happen this way. Take hm away.

ANTON [*Suddenly terrified.*]: He's dead! He's dead! What shall we do?

RUDOLF: Start sending in petitions again. He has a successor, right?

ANTON: Yes. Dr. Kirstein. Yes. I've got to write him at once. But he has a fault, Rudolf—remember?

RUDOLF: Every man has some fault. The car will be ready tomorrow. Clear this thing away. [ANTON *starts to lift the body.*] By the feet! [ANTON *takes* KRIEGBAUM *by the feet, drags him out.*] No more work today.

ANTON [*Returns.*]: But what if another one?

RUDOLF: That would be very annoying. [*Wets his forefinger, holds it up.*] No wind.

ANTON: No sun either. It's evening.

RUDOLF: Time to rest. [*Gathering up his tools.*]
ANTON [*Moved.*]: Evening silence.
RUDOLF: Evening peace.
ANTON: Peace.

[*They fold their hands.*]

Slow Curtain

THE LAUNDRY

A Play in Three Acts

David Guerdon

adapted from the French by Howard Richardson

CHARACTERS

MADAME YVONNE, a laundress
LENA, her daughter
LAURENT, Lena's husband
ESTELLE, the maid
DANIEL, Madame Yvonne's son
SENOR ARMANDO, the owner of a circus

SYNOPSIS OF SCENES

ACT ONE

The drying room of a public laundry. An evening in the present.

ACT TWO

The same scene, later that night.

ACT THREE

The same scene, early the following morning.

Act One

Inside a public laundry. Drying sheets are hanging from cords, giving the entire stage the appearance of a mystical labyrinth. The furniture consists of three stools and high stepladder.

It is evening. MADAME YVONNE, *a middle-aged woman, enters followed by her daughter,* LENA, *a woman in her early twenties who is obviously pregnant, and* ESTELLE, *the maid, who is in her teens. The women are followed by* LAURENT, *a young man of about twenty-three. All four have just come from the funeral of* MADAME YVONNE's *husband and are in deep mourning. The women in their black dresses and heavily veiled faces stand for a moment motionless, silhouetted against the white sheets.*

YVONNE: There you are. One counts for little in this life.

LENA: It goes by so quickly.

YVONNE: Everything is erased—like a dream.

LAURENT: You wake up and it's gone.

ESTELLE: When you realize it, it's too late.

YVONNE [*With sudden irritation she turns to* ESTELLE.]: Estelle, heat the coffee. There's a little left over from last night.

ESTELLE: Yes, Madame . . . Oh, I'm exhausted! A cup of coffee is just what I need.

YVONNE: I did not ask your opinion.

ESTELLE: Very well, madame.

YVONNE: Run along! Don't stand there gawking at me like an owl.

ESTELLE: I loved him too, you know . . . Papa George.

YVONNE: And I suppose we didn't? Go ahead—say it. We're cold and heartless.

LENA: Oh, Mama, don't argue with her. You know she's an idiot.

YVONNE: Of course! I keep forgetting! [*She looks at herself in a mirror she takes from her purse.*] I've aged a hundred years!

LENA: There should be no such thing as death!

YVONNE: My poor husband. At least he has no more worries. He always used to say, "When I die I'll finally be able to sleep the clock around."

LENA: He was a hard worker!

YVONNE: How he loved his laundry!

LENA: Poor Papa!

YVONNE: It's frightening. Everything is so quiet now! We'll never again hear him stoking the boilers and whistling, "There's a monkey in the grass with a beetle up his . . . " I can never remember the words of that song!

LENA: Already we miss him!

ESTELLE: That's just what I said.

LENA: Mama, she's still here!

YVONNE: What about our coffee? What are you waiting for, my girl?

ESTELLE: I'm no longer waiting for anything, Madame Yvonne! [*She leaves.*]

YVONNE: And I took her in off the streets! I'm too kindhearted.

LENA: Mama, I think she isn't all there. Have you ever heard her talking to herself when she's alone—just like Hamlet?

YVONNE: Oh—she's not so bad.

LENA: Yes, but—

YVONNE: Not everybody can be intelligent.

LAURENT: The medal of honor of the Cordel family! The mind of the Cordels!

LENA: Laurent!

YVONNE: Oh, I simply must get out of these shoes. For a while there at the cemetery I thought I wasn't going to be able to take another step. [*She removes her shoes with a sigh of relief.*] My bunion! It didn't help at all, putting that willow leaf in my shoe.

LENA: The Monthiers were there. I was amazed—the whole tribe of them showed up. The stuck-up prigs!

YVONNE: They can't say we didn't do everything in the best of taste—and it certainly cost us enough!

LENA: I never could stand her—with her stomach stuck out like a whale's belly.

YVONNE: She used to be Papa George's mistress before the war.

LENA: Impossible! Madame Monthier—that worn-out old frump?

YVONNE: Try to understand men, my dear. He was absolutely wild about her. And she had no shame whatsoever. I even think she was the cause of all that unfortunate trouble.

LAURENT [*In an offhand manner.*]: You mean those two years he spent in the clink?

YVONNE: Well, yes, if you want to put it that crudely. My husband was an adventurer.

LAURENT: An adventurer with a crowbar.

YVONNE: Be quiet! How can you understand?

LENA: I like the way he talks. Everything he says sounds so— so romantic.

YVONNE: He has no respect for the dead! Poor Papa George!

LAURENT: That for the dead! [*He makes a vulgar gesture with his center finger.*]

YVONNE: You see! He has no respect for anything! He's a brute, a beast, a wild animal—like those gypsies from the circus who showed up at the graveyard. They insulted our tears!

LENA: It's true, Mama. They laughed at us—the riffraff!

YVONNE: You did nothing to stop them—or your husband here. You let him lead you around by the nose. If I weren't here, he'd sell the laundry and go off to the races, drinking with his fancy friends.

LAURENT: Ah, yes—the Laundry of the Future! What sort of business is that for a man?

YVONNE: It allows you to steal the food out of our mouths.

LENA: Mama! Laurent! Stop it!

YVONNE: All right, but remember—I'm boss now, so please be good enough to light the furnace. The sheets have to be boiled. Don't forget, our customers are not in mourning.

LAURENT: I'm like Estelle. Sorrow makes me sick.

YVONNE: You loafer! No-good, worthless loafer! That's all you are. Now that poor Papa George has deserted us, you'll make the most of it, won't you? The small-town sport! But I'm not like Lena here. I'm on to you!

LAURENT: You—on to me?

YVONNE: My poor husband put it well. "Laurent is the type that ends up in jail."

LAURENT: He had the background to judge.

YVONNE: Poor Papa George—looking down at us from the sky. He's probably throwing up. He loved us so much.

LAURENT: If he's in Heaven—St. Peter can give him a bucket.

YVONNE: You will not insult my husband! He was worth a dozen of your kind! He was awarded the medal of honor—and he won it by hard work.

LAURENT: They gave me a medal for the breast stroke.

YVONNE: I can still see his hands—the hands of a laborer, strong and calloused—not like those of a girl!

LAURENT: That's from breaking all those rocks.

LENA: Mama, mama, Laurent—please! Can't you see what you're doing to me—in my condition?

LAURENT: Come on, Lena, Let's leave her to her tantrum. I know what it is she really misses.

YVONNE: And what do I really miss?

LAURENT: I beg your pardon.

LENA: All right, Laurent. . . . Go change into your work clothes and light the boilers. [*She exits.*]

YVONNE: He doesn't dare say what it is I miss.

LAURENT: I'm not afraid to say it, my darling mother-in-law, but you wouldn't understand.

LENA [*Calling off.*]: Laurent! Come on!

LAURENT: In a minute. First I must have some coffee. Funerals always give me a chill.

LENA [*Off*]: We'll drink it in the kitchen.

LAURENT [*Calling after* LENA.]: Admit that I'm right. She wanted to humiliate me!

YVONNE: You take advantage of me because you know I'm only a weak woman.

LAURENT: Yes, you are a weak woman—but I'm a strong man— even if I have the hands of a girl—and I'm not blind. There's

something going on here that I don't know about, and I want
to be counted in on it.

YVONNE: Counted in—on what?

LENA [*Off.*]: Come on, darling.

LAURENT: I'm talking about the trips you take in the middle of
the night to the hidden room.

YVONNE: What hidden room? You're babbling.

LAURENT: I'm not a fool, you know. I hear you crawling around
up there.

YVONNE: I don't crawl around up there, and there is no hidden
room.

[ESTELLE *comes on with a cup of coffee and stands waiting to
hand it to* MADAME YVONNE.]

LAURENT: Oh, don't give me that crap! I've seen you. [*With a
glance toward* ESTELLE.] We'll talk about it later.

YVONNE: You've been drinking too much.

LAURENT: I want what's coming to me—and I plan to get it!
[*He exits.*]

YVONNE: Imbecile!

[ESTELLE *hands her the cup of coffee.*]

ESTELLE: Here's your coffee, Madame.

YVONNE: Now get back to your ironing. If Lena has told him anything, she'll regret it.

ESTELLE: Madame, I wanted to . . .

YVONNE: What?

ESTELLE: When death comes, a word of comfort . . .

YVONNE [*With sudden disgust.*]: Ugh! This coffee isn't hot. . . .
It's dreadful!

ESTELLE: They turned off the gas.

YVONNE: Always a new excuse.

ESTELLE: I—I wanted to . . .

YVONNE: Well—you wanted to what?

ESTELLE: I wanted to thank you.

YVONNE: Thank me?

ESTELLE: Yes, for everything you've done for me.

YVONNE: Hmm . . . I'd rather not talk about it. There are times when I regret it.

ESTELLE: Without you, Madame, I would have been less than nothing—a creature. You saved me from worse than death— a death that would have lasted every day, every hour.

YVONNE: Well—I'm glad to find you grateful. You're less stupid than you seem.

ESTELLE: Oh, yes . . .

YVONNE: Then try to remember it—at least while you're working. Yesterday there were scorch marks on one of Doctor Ludovic's shirts. I don't know whether you fully realize that you hold the honor of this laundry in your hands.

ESTELLE: Oh, but I do!

YVONNE: It's quite obvious that you have no roots. You don't know the meaning of a dynasty!

ESTELLE: It's true. I'm afraid I have no roots.

YVONNE: We date back to the Revolution, my poor Estelle! Think of it! We bleached under the emperor!

ESTELLE: Under the emperor!

YVONNE: Look upon this medal! It's our Legion of Honor. Ours! We must all be worthy of it! The Laundry of the Future! One day it will be handed down to Lena's son.

ESTELLE: Yes, Madame.

YVONNE: A spotless dignity. He must inherit a laundry unsoiled and without a stain.

ESTELLE: The poor little baby. He'll be so cute!

YVONNE: You understand me then. You don't want to hurt him in any way before his birth, do you?

ESTELLE: Me, harm that little treasure?

YVONNE: Then just keep your mind on your work.

ESTELLE: I'll try to, Madame.

YVONNE: You can't even heat a cup of coffee—and you know very well lukewarm coffee gives me heartburn.

ESTELLE: I'll put it back on the stove.

YVONNE: No, I'll drink it as it is. It will be your fault. One must learn to suffer in this life. . . . Well, what are you waiting for now?

ESTELLE: I want to show my gratitude. In sorrowful moments . . .

YVONNE [*Breaking in and finishing* ESTELLE's *sentence.*]: Solitude is necessary!

ESTELLE: I'd like you to know that you can have absolute confidence in me, Madame. I'll never betray our secret.

YVONNE: Well—I should hope not!

ESTELLE: Last night I surprised Lena's husband trying to force the door to the little stairway that leads to the attic. I didn't spy on him. I was on my way to pay my respects to Papa George.

YVONNE: That's no good. . . .

ESTELLE: He had a bunch of keys on a chain and he was trying them all. He was very upset and kept cursing! His language made me blush.

YVONNE: What did he say?

ESTELLE: He tried to force me to talk. Then he said he knew that every night someone carries things upstairs. I told him I didn't know anything—and it's true. Well, he believed it was true.

YVONNE: As long as he believed you.

ESTELLE: He frightened me so! He acted just like Dracula!

YVONNE: I'm glad you told me. I'll clear up this whole situation. [*She leaves.* ESTELLE *turns suddenly to find that* LAURENT *has appeared from the white sheets. He is dressed in his work clothes—a tight T-shirt and blue jeans.*]

LAURENT: Congratulations! So this is the way you sell your friends.

ESTELLE: I haven't sold you.

LAURENT: And I trusted you!

ESTELLE: I didn't know . . .

LAURENT: You didn't know I was listening.

ESTELLE: I hope I did nothing wrong.

LAURENT: Oh, no—of course not. Everything with a clear conscience! All for the honor of the laundry! But what about me —hmm? [*He pulls her to him.*] That's a beautiful necklace. Who gave it to you—you haven't forgotten already?

ESTELLE: Let me go!

LAURENT: And I suppose if I were to twist the necklace—like this. What would happen to you then—hmm?

ESTELLE: You're hurting me!

LAURENT: You poor girl—I pity you.

ESTELLE: They'll see us.

Laurent: What if they do?

Estelle: Think of your little unborn baby!

Laurent: That's exactly what I'm thinking of—and I don't want some slut like you to harm him.

Estelle: Me—harm that little treasure?

Laurent: Then tell me who's hiding in the attic!

Estelle: Your wife knows. Ask her.

Laurent: That bitch—she lies as much as her mother.

Estelle: I've told you all I know—really. . . .

Laurent: You can't be that dumb. My God, if I'd lived here as long as you, I'd have a good idea of what was going on. You won't be sorry, I promise. I can be generous. And you know, the climate here is so sultry. I've been thinking of taking off for the Riviera.

Estelle: The Riviera—where the rich people go?

Laurent: Yes, I'll dip my feet in the sea and smoke cigars.

Estelle: I've always longed for the sea. It must be very beautiful.

Laurent: If you're a good little girl, I'll take you with me. I'll buy you a castle, but you must obey me.

Estelle: That's my job, sir—to obey—everybody.

Laurent [*Embracing her.*]: I love you when you're obedient, Estelle.

[MADAME YVONNE *enters.*]

Yvonne: Please, don't let me disturb you! And under my own roof!

Laurent: I was telling her the plot of a movie.

Yvonne: While I have you both here, Estelle, would you kindly repeat what you saw last night?

Estelle: Who? Me? What I saw?

Yvonne: Yes, you! You just swore to me . . .

Laurent: She was joking, this little thing . . . [*He goes to the ladder and climbs up a few steps.*]

Yvonne: Let her do her own talking.

Laurent: With you browbeating her she'll say anything.

Yvonne [*To* ESTELLE.]: Are you going to repeat what you told me—yes or no?

Estelle: Well, it seemed to me that . . .

Yvonne: What do you mean—it seemed to you?

LAURENT: Let her speak. You're scaring her.

[LENA *enters*.]

LENA: Have I missed something? What's she done now?

YVONNE: She's pretending to be struck dumb.

LAURENT: Come on, Estelle, say something. Be reasonable.

LENA: And what is that supposed to mean?

LAURENT: Go ahead, Estelle—tell us what you know.

YVONNE: If you don't answer immediately, its back to the streets.

LAURENT: That's an argument that has no answer.

LENA: Say something, Estelle!

ESTELLE: Oh, leave me alone—leave me alone! [*She runs off.*]

LENA: Well, there you are!

YVONNE [*To* LAURENT.]: You threatened her. I'm sure of it.

LAURENT: Who? Me?

LENA: Him?

YVONNE: Last night Estelle caught him trying to break down the attic door.

LAURENT [*With mock surprise.*]: No!

LENA: Is that true, Laurent?

LAURENT: If your dear mother says so.

YVONNE: You see!

LAURENT: Am I one of the family—yes or no? Well then, why do you hide things from me?

YVONNE: Nobody's hiding anything.

LAURENT: I had to go to a bar to learn that Papa George had done time. But you wouldn't tell me!

YVONNE: That's not the same thing.

LAURENT: So you admit there *is* something! [*He climbs down from the ladder.*] Why won't you trust me, my dear little wife?

YVONNE: Don't let him fool you, Lena. He's putting on an act. When I came in, he was kissing Estelle.

LENA: That's not true—is it?

LAURENT: Yes, it's true. So what? I was learning from her what goes on in this house. I was using the psychological approach.

LENA: Psychological?

YVONNE: That's his word for it.

LAURENT: I was forcing myself, I assure you.

LENA [*Sweetly, believing him.*] : I'm sure you were.

LAURENT: You know I think only of you, my darling.

LENA: Ah, my Laurent!

LAURENT: My little sweetheart.

YVONNE: What a touching sight! But let's get down to business, Laurent. You're living here now since Papa George's death. We need a man in the house, so it's only right you should be told what goes on here.

LAURENT: Now you're talking sense.

YVONNE: I couldn't tell you about it before. . . . These last few days we've been through so much.

LENA: Those painful hours . . .

YVONNE: Please—don't interrupt! Can't you see I'm suffering? Well, to come to the point. There's something I must confess to you, Laurent, because as you say, you have a right to know our secret—a shameful secret that must be kept among us.

LAURENT: My God—then's it's not Papa George?

YVONNE: Prison is nothing, Laurent. There are shames that hang on, shames that live . . .

LENA: Shames that grow.

YVONNE: Yes. Laurent, the heavy hand of Destiny gives each his cross to bear. Oh, it's true. . . . Sunshine and showers, the greatest joys are mixed with sorrow. . . . A long time ago when poor Papa George was given this gold medal—it's been twenty years, Laurent, yes—after I had Lena, I bore a son.

LAURENT: A son?

YVONNE: Yes, a son. We had wanted him so long, George and I. He would carry on the laundry. We could die in peace. We called our laundry The Laundry of the Future! We're so proud of it—you can't imagine.

LAURENT: But I can—oh, yes, I can.

[*Softly from outside the music from a traveling circus can be heard. This hurdy-gurdy theme repeats itself throughout the play, underlying parts of the action.*]

YVONNE: It was winter—a very cold winter. Snow was on the rooftops. And there in the emergency ward of Our Lady of the Bleeding Heart I bore my son. . . . When I woke up, my baby wasn't beside me, and the doctor didn't want to show him to me. I was burning with fever and I wasn't allowed to see my child. I cried out for him—and they wouldn't show him to me!

LENA: You'd have to be a mother, Laurent, to understand.

YVONNE: Then poor George came to me and kissed me. There were tears in his eyes. I'd never seen him cry before. I said to myself, "Little Daniel must be dead." I turned pale and I thought I'd die, too. We held hands for a moment, not speaking. Outside the snow went on falling . . . falling. Finally George shook his head and told me. Little Daniel wasn't dead. He was worse than dead.

LAURENT: Worse than dead?

YVONNE: They showed him to me the next morning, bundled up in his little white nightshirt—bursting with life and raising his tiny, trembling hands to heaven. He was alive, Laurent, and I loved him in spite of everything.

LAURENT: In spite of what?

YVONNE: In spite of his defect, in spite of the stain. He could never be a normal child, never run and play in the school yard with the others.

LENA: His condition was most unusual.

YVONNE: And so I raised him in secret in the little room above. Our poor little angel. We cared for him like a child. He still is a child.

LENA: And he didn't die. That kind of creature has his soul nailed to his body.

YVONNE: Yes, Laurent—there you have it, our sad secret—our stain. Now you understand my sorrow.

LAURENT: Of course. It can't be much fun for you.

YVONNE: And I hope you realize why it has to remain a secret.

LAURENT: Poor kid. You should have sent him to camp.

YVONNE: I've never wanted to be away from him.

LENA: He's well cared for—I promise you.

YVONNE: He has a very good appetite.

LENA: Three meals a day.

YVONNE: You see he eats as much as we do.

LENA: He's cost quite a bit.

YVONNE: And in the end he's been happier than we.

LENA: He doesn't even know the dfference between good and bad.

LAURENT: How nice for him.

YVONNE: He doesn't know what sin is—our sin—like a worm in a bud.

LENA [*Glancing at her mother.*]: The memory of sin!

YVONNE: I feel scared by it. It's like a burning wound!

LAURENT: You must be uncomfortable.

LENA: You wanted to know everything, didn't you? Well, now you're guilty, too.

LAURENT: Guilty?

LENA: You're in on it.

LAURENT: Stop it! Keep your dirty little secrets to yourself. You make me sick! I'm sane . . . I'm normal.

YVONNE: The finger of fate, Laurent! Beware of the finger of fate!

LAURENT: But I haven't done anything.

YVONNE: And I deserved it. . . . Go on Laurent, say it!

LAURENT: I didn't say that.

YVONNE: Yes, yes, I did deserve it! I've sinned. I've soiled our beautiful laundry!

LENA: Mama!

YVONNE: But how I've paid since! Look at me, Laurent! Let me be a lesson to you. . . .

LAURENT: It's never too late to make amends.

LENA: My son will continue the laundry, Mama.

YVONNE: Yes, my daughter. There's always a little ray of hope.

LAURENT: He'll be a blockbuster—I guarantee it. You have only to look at his father.

YVONNE: Yes, you're right. We must look to the future, to the child who is to be born. Life must continue.

LAURENT [*Pressing* LENA *to him.*]: It always does.

YVONNE: That's why you must work, Laurent. It's a simple question of will power.

LENA: You'll get used to it.

YVONNE: It's your duty to your child to remove the stain.

LAURENT: But I'm not responsible for it!

LENA: I told you. You're in on it.

YVONNE: The laundry must continue.

LENA: The Laundry of the Future!

LAURENT: The medals.

YVONNE: Ah, yes, the medals, Laurent—and that modest pride in satisfying the clientele.

LENA: Just a little will power . . .

YVONNE: A great deal of will power, Laurent. Be like me. Sorrow doesn't stop me. I'm inexhaustible . . . like Papa George! [*And she leaves.*]

LAURENT: I didn't know your mother was so emotional.

LENA: She's always been unlucky, believe me.

LAURENT: Yes, but that's no excuse for persecuting people. She wears me out with her passion for work.

LENA: She's only thinking of our baby, darling.

LAURENT: Yes, but when I'm pushed, I lose all my drive.

LENA: I understand you, you know. I'm the only one who does.

LAURENT [*Caressing her hair as he passes behind her.*]: Do you?

LENA: Of course. You become so brave when someone has faith in you.

LAURENT: There, you see—you understand everything. You've a sensitive soul—just like mine. I told you that the day of our wedding.

LENA: You were nice that day!

LAURENT: By the way—I hope you weren't upset just now.

LENA: Over what?

LAURENT: You know—what your mother said about Estelle and me, remember? I love only you. You know that, don't you? [*They kiss.*]

LENA: Ah, my dearest. I couldn't live without your kisses.

LAURENT: Sometimes we argue—but no matter what I say, remember I always love you.

LENA: Always?

LAURENT: Always!

LENA: My darling.

LAURENT: Sometimes the blood rushes to my head. It's hereditary.

LENA: I love you like that, my darling. You're just like a lion. You're beautiful.

LAURENT: My kitty-cat.

LENA: My Laurent! [*They embrace again.*]

LAURENT: You do believe me? You don't think I'm a liar—like your mother does?

LENA: You mustn't hold that against Mama. She has dyspepsia.

LAURENT: You told me just now that you trusted me.

LENA: Blindfolded, my darling.

LAURENT: My little wife. I'm lucky to have you.

LENA: My Laurent!

LAURENT: You love me a little?

LENA: My dearest!

LAURENT: You really love me?

LENA: I adore you!

LAURENT: You really want to please me?

LENA: I'll do anything for you . . . darling.

LAURENT: Anything?

LENA: Yes, yes. Just tell me.

LAURENT: Now, can't you guess?

LENA: No.

LAURENT: You must give me the key.

LENA: What key, darling?

LAURENT: Why, the key to the attic.

LENA [*Pulling away.*]: So that's it. You wanted the key.

LAURENT: What's the matter. Now what have I done?

LENA: You don't believe us!

LAURENT: All right—give me the key.

LENA: You put on an act!

LAURENT: You told me fairy tales.

LENA: Mama was right.

LAURENT: Will you give it to me—yes or no?

LENA: Don't raise your voice.

LAURENT: Come on, give it to me.

LENA: Ask me nicely.

LAURENT: Darling.

LENA: Like on our wedding night.

LAURENT: My little sweetheart—give me the key!

LENA: I don't have it. Mama does.

LAURENT: If you're telling me the truth, I don't see why you won't let me have the key.

LENA: You don't seem to realize what we've been living through.

LAURENT: I want to see your monster!

LENA: Shh! Why are you so mean sometimes?

LAURENT: Madame Yvonne and her medals! The whitest wash in

the world! What do I care about the aristocracy of the laundry business?

LENA: You only want to see my brother to make fun of us.

LAURENT: No—but it would do me good. It would make up for some of the humiliation. I could laugh to myself, thinking about it, when your mother puts on her grand manner.

LENA: She shouldn't have told you the truth.

LAURENT: You want me to work my ass off and then you refuse me the family secrets.

LENA: Think of our baby, Laurent.

[MADAME YVONNE *enters carrying a hamper.*]

YVONNE: Well, I see you're working as usual.

LAURENT: I've had enough—I'm warning you. Something tells me I'm going into town tonight to relax.

LENA: Don't drink too much. Remember your liver.

LAURENT [*To* MADAME YVONNE.]: I'm going to light your miserable boilers—and then, three cheers for liberty! Dead bodies make me thirsty! [*He exits.*]

LENA: Now I feel all twitchy inside. It's the blood feeding my child. All of a sudden he moved.

YVONNE: Blood is the symbol of sin. [*She begins to work.*]

LENA: It's like a big, throbbing orange.

YVONNE: You pay too much attention to yourself. You're like your grandmother—no starch.

LENA: He moved. Can't you understand? I felt him move.

YVONNE: So? If you think it's going to be a great joy for us—

LENA: You said there's always hope.

YVONNE: I have a right to change my mind, haven't I?

LENA: You're like me—you have premonitions.

YVONNE: We're victims of a terrible plot, my poor daughter.

LENA: Mama, I had a bad dream last night.

YVONNE: Now don't you get superstitious.

LENA: I dreamed that Laurent and Daniel met. They found each other in a moldy hallway. Daniel was moving like a sleepwalker, with his arms stretched out—and there was a crowd yelling— and we were screaming. . . .

YVONNE [*Trying not to seem distressed.*]: And then?

LENA: Then . . . I've forgotten. But it was horrible.

YVONNE: There, you see? Things always turn out badly.

LENA: I woke up and my hands were icy. And today Laurent asked to see Daniel. . . . You realize that?

YVONNE: We shall never have peace, my poor Lena.

LENA: Now I am afraid, Mama. I wonder . . .

YVONNE: What?

LENA [*Holding her stomach.*]: Suppose—suppose he were like Daniel—my baby?

YVONNE [*Furiously*]: Don't say that! Don't even think it! Are you out of your mind?

LENA: What if it were something that—well, that runs in the family.

YVONNE: Be quiet and don't think about it.

LENA: But it could be hereditary.

YVONNE: No, it was my fault. I alone am responsible for Daniel.

LENA: Even so—what if your fault gets into the blood of my child?

YVONNE: No, no! God would never permit it! I've already paid dearly enough for my moment of fantasy. The washing is over. The stain has been removed. And the laundry is drying white and clean in the sun.

LENA: In the sun . . .

YVONNE: We have nothing more to fear. Your child is saved. . . . It's on Daniel that the wrath of God fell—on Daniel and on me. I sometimes wonder how I've had the courage to go on living. It might have been better if I'd taken my laundry shears and stabbed him through the heart!

LENA: Mama!

YVONNE: I was a coward! I was afraid of what they'd do to me. [*She sinks onto a stool.*]

LENA: Yes, you're right. It would have been better had he died!

YVONNE: But instead we went on living with our wound laid open —and we became used to it. It was a sore, something to caress, to cherish. Now it's almost a luxury. I'd be lost without it.

LENA: But then you'd be independent. You could leave us the laundry and buy the farm of your dreams—and milk cows till the day you died. You told me that was your dearest dream.

YVONNE: I told you it was my dearest ambition.

LENA: Mama, we must get rid of Daniel!

YVONNE: I don't think a little farm is asking too much.

LENA: Oh, if only he would die—if only it were all over!

YVONNE: In this age of progress, all these washing machines are going to ruin us.

LENA: The nightmare would be ended!

YVONNE: If we sold the laundry now, it would bring nothing.

LENA: We could get away—we could travel!

YVONNE: It's the automatic laundries that are ruining our business —you know that!

LENA: To visit the Riviera and see all the elegant people!

YVONNE: Machines ruin the wash. They'll realize that when we're gone.

LENA: We could leave right away, buy your farm where you'd be happy—and get a motor scooter for Laurent!

YVONNE: A motor scooter for Laurent! How will you pay for it— by selling the laundry? You forget that Daniel is still up there!

LENA: He hasn't been well. He's been running a temperature.

YVONNE: He has the grippe. And then there's the carnival in the square—that circus music breaks his heart.

LENA: The circus! Freedom!

YVONNE: Do you know what you're saying? You realize what that would mean to him? He'd be a monster in a cage!

LENA: At least he'd travel. He'd see the country. And little children would look at him all day long with wide, astonished eyes.

YVONNE: Yes, he'd certainly be making a good living—and an honest one. Who knows? He might even like that kind of life.

LENA: I'd love to travel around like that!

YVONNE: It's not good to be shut up all one's life.

LENA: The fanfares of the band!

YVONNE: The road—open road—packing up and on to new places —over and over.

LENA: Perhaps one, day, who knows, in some out-of-the-way spot some girl with unusual tastes might even fall in love with him. It's been known to happen.

[MADAME YVONNE *reacts violently to this remark—almost as if she had been physically struck.*]

YVONNE: Don't say that!

LENA: Mama! What's the matter?

YVONNE [*Trying to regain her composure.*]: Nothing . . . nothing.

LENA: You're ill!

YVONNE: No. . . .

LENA: What is it?

YVONNE: It's this guilt—this shame. I keep it pushed down, but it keeps popping up to the surface, like a cork. Love is a disgusting disease!

LENA: Mama!

YVONNE: Disgusting!

LENA: Mama, if Daniel reminds you of some horrible memory, what should stop us from getting rid of that memory today— right now? He'd be well taken care of in the circus. And he'd enjoy himself, I'm sure of it—seeing all those people passing by.

YVONNE: Are you out of your mind? You want everyone to know that I'm his mother?

LENA: We must think of his happiness, too.

YVONNE: Be quiet. Don't ever mention the circus again. Daniel will stay where he is. My decision is final. And I shall continue to wash sheets to feed him.

LENA: I'm sick of it, do you hear? Sick of the honor of the laundry. Your son turns my stomach. I can't help it, he turns my stomach. I don't have time to lose. I want to live. I want to be happy before I'm old like you!

YVONNE: Daniel is your brother in spite of everything.

LENA: I'd rather take care of my husband.

YVONNE: Oh, yes. He's the one who puts ideas in your head. Well then, go with your husband. What are you waiting for? I'll stay alone here with Daniel. At least he loves me!

LENA: Of course he does! He's never seen anyone else. Laurent chose me from the whole world.

YVONNE: You poor innocent fool. He chose the laundry. He chose your inheritance. It was the Laundry of the Future he was courting. Tell him that we're bankrupt, that we've lost the business, and he'd walk out on you tonight!

LENA: You're jealous of Laurent. You love him yourself. Don't deny it! I've seen you—making eyes at him across the table. And at the cemetery this afternoon you fainted in his arms.

YVONNE: He was behind me when I fell!

LENA: You'd be happy if I died, so you could stay on alone with him. You've never loved your children! You were ready to sell Daniel to the circus! But what about me? Where could you sell me?

YVONNE: Nowhere, my poor child? Who'd want you? Oh, I sighed with relief when Laurent agreed to marry you. I'd have given you to the first junkman who came along!

LENA [*Dissolving in tears.*]: I'm leaving here! I don't want to see you again! You can stay here and—and rot with your monster!

YVONNE: Daniel is no monster! He's your brother!

LENA: Liar! I wonder what it was you made love to on that famous day that caused such a—a—miscarriage!

YVONNE: Get the hell out of here! Do you hear! Get the hell out of my laundry!

LENA: Laurent! Laurent! [*She falls back on the stool.*]

YVONNE: Go on, get out—both of you! I'll find someone else to carry on our traditions. Don't let it worry you for a minute— but I can promise you one thing: You'll never get your hands on the Laundry of the Future! [*She sweeps from the stage in a grand exit.*]

LENA [*Calling after her.*]: Oh, I hate you! I hate you! You're only good for breeding monsters!

ESTELLE [*Speaking to herself, not seeking* LENA.]: Just now I forgot to disconnect this iron. I'm afraid Madame Yvonne is right. One of these days I'll start a fire.

LENA: Go ahead start one—burn this dump down! Burn it down!

ESTELLE: Oh! You scared me!

LENA: Laurent has confessed everything.

ESTELLE: About what?

LENA: You sniff around him like a bitch in heat! But if I ever catch you together, I warn you, I'll tear your eyes out!

ESTELLE: It's not my fault. I can't help what he does.

LENA: You're a tramp! My mother picked you up out of the gutter. We felt sorry for you. Well, we've been well repaid.

ESTELLE: For your baby's sake you shouldn't get angry.

LENA: Let me worry about my baby. It's no concern of yours.

ESTELLE: I don't want him to be sick, the little treasure.

LENA: Don't try to make up to me. I repeat. I forbid you to have anything to do with my husband. You understand? I've seen bedbugs prettier than you!

ESTELLE: That's where we're different. I've never seen a bedbug.

LENA: Will you listen to her?

ESTELLE: Why can't you leave me alone?

LENA: Don't worry. My husband and I are getting out of this dump. We'll be packing.

ESTELLE: You're leaving the laundry?

LENA: Exactly! We'll send you a postcard! [LAURENT *enters, his T-shirt smeared with coal dust.*] You've done it again—look at you. Now I'll have to wash it!

LAURENT: What's the problem? This is a laundry. [*He takes off his T-shirt, stripping himself bare to the waist, and throws it in the direction of* ESTELLE, *who catches it.*]

LENA: Well, this is one laundry where I'm not staying. [*Very grandly.*] My mother has insulted me!

LAURENT: Insulted you?

LENA: We're packing. We're leaving.

LAURENT: Are you crazy? [*Suddenly seeing* ESTELLE, *who stands holding the T-shirt.*] Estelle, when will you stop listening at the door?

ESTELLE: But—there is no door! [*She exits.*]

LENA: Oh, Laurent, I'm so miserable! Mama treated me like a servant!

LAURENT: Your mother goes too far with her nervous stomach.

LENA: I'm the one who's nervous. I'm delicate and high-strung and I'll be damned if I'll put up with her—her tyranny another moment.

LAURENT: Now just calm down, my darling. There's no use losing control. Be like me.

LENA: I refuse to look after my brother for another day. We've got to get out of here.

LAURENT: But you're forgetting something.

LENA: What?

LAURENT: The loot. There's the laundry! You say yourself that our kid will take it over.

LENA: So? That's no reason to put up with everything.

LAURENT: Do you have a job? And do I have a job? I can't even tighten a bolt.

LENA: But you were a mechanic when I met you.

LAURENT: Yes, but in a special way—a very special way. I've never worked on automobiles.

LENA: You never worked on anything. You were the lover of that old—that . . .

LAURENT: Hush. No vulgarity, please. We can discuss this like civilized people, can't we? Now, as I was saying, what will we do without the laundry?

LENA: I can iron. I can mend shirts . . .

LAURENT: And I'll go to the factory, I suppose. Six o'clock. Zing! The alarm. Not for me!

LENA: Wait a minute! I've just had an idea!

LAURENT: You've had a—what?

LENA: The circus . . .

LAURENT: What about the circus?

LENA: Maybe we could both get a job there.

LAURENT: You want to ride bareback in spangles? I'm afraid you haven't taken a good look at yourself lately.

LENA: I could mend the costumes and iron them—and you— you'd look wonderful as a lion tamer!

LAURENT: A lion tamer? That doesn't appeal to me.

LENA: No, really. Think about it. The circus! Doesn't it tempt you at all?

LAURENT: Yes, of course it does. I've always dreamed of such a life. Even as a little boy I remember looking up at the posters of the clowns and elephants. They made my head spin.

LENA: You see, I do get good ideas.

LAURENT: Yes—but what could they do with us? All the jobs are filled.

LENA: Perhaps not.

LAURENT [*Beginning now to consider the idea seriously.*]: As a matter of fact, I've met the director of the circus. I might even call him a friend of mine. We had a drink together yesterday down at the corner.

LENA: Then it's all set. [*Suddenly struck with a thought.*] Say— I've got it!

LAURENT: Another idea!

LENA: A dazzling idea.

LAURENT: What idea?

LENA: You'll see.

LAURENT: Tell me!

LENA: You love your little wife very much?

LAURENT: Of course I love her.

LENA: Cross your heart and hope to die?

LAURENT: Forget it. Keep your idea!

LENA: Please let me tell you. You've seen that sideshow outside the circus—they have one bearded lady, one giant, one dwarf . . .

LAURENT: Well?

LENA: I thought if my brother were willing to leave with us . . .

LAURENT: Your brother? The one in the glass jar?

LENA: The circus might be very happy to get him—and they could hire us to take care of him.

LAURENT: You want to make everybody sick looking at your brother?

LENA: He's not ugly. He just takes a little getting used to, that's all.

LAURENT: What does he look like? Is he a hunchback?

LENA: Oh, no!

LAURENT: Is he made of rubber with arms like drumsticks?

LENA: No—nor three heads exactly.

LAURENT: All right. I give up.

LENA: He's the only one of his kind.

LAURENT: My darling wife, my dearest love—tell me what he's like!

LENA: Mama must have been thinking peculiar thoughts that famous day she . . . After all, she keeps saying it was her fault.

LAURENT: Don't keep me waiting. Tell me, quickly!

LENA: Guess.

LAURENT: Oh, God!

LENA: I've got another idea! Instead of describing him, I'll try to show him to you tonight. But we'll have to hurry, because the circus leaves tomorrow. This way it will be a surprise for you.

LAURENT: And you think your brother will really go along with us?

LENA: He'll be glad to. And Mama won't do anything about it for fear of the scandal.

LAURENT: Let's think this over carefully. I'll invite the director to have a drink with me. He's a very educated man.

LENA: Don't drink too much. Remember your liver.

Laurent: Oh, forget my liver! Come on, let's eat. I'm starved! [*He exits.*]

Lena [*Patting her pregnant stomach.*]: So are we! There, there, we'll have a nice big meal. [LENA *goes out and turns off the lights. The stage is left in a strange, eerie darkness. In a moment a door offstage is heard opening slowly on rusty, creaking hinges and a dim light falls across the stage. The shadow of a man appears and a voice whispers.*]

Voice [*Off.*]: Mama! Mama!

Curtain

Act Two

The same. Later that night.

    The moonlight from outside streams into the room, giving an eerie quality to the set. Drying laundry hangs as before, but the sheets and clothes have been changed in such a way that the effect is quite different from that in the first act. The stools are still visible, but the stepladder is hidden behind one of the hanging sheets.

    ESTELLE *is discovered standing motionless before a sheet.* MADAME YVONNE *enters and comes quickly to her. She seems agitated and speaks in a breathless, nervous manner, betraying an inner excitement. In contrast to her,* ESTELLE *is calm and almost detached, unaffected by the older woman's intense, hysterical attitude. Both women are dressed as they were in Act One.*

YVONNE: Well?

ESTELLE [*Paying no attention to* MADAME YVONNE, *she looks straight ahead.*]: Well . . .

YVONNE: You locked the door, I hope?

ESTELLE: Here's the key.

    [MADAME YVONNE *takes the key from her and puts it in her pocket.*]

YVONNE: Did he say anything about me?

ESTELLE: I don't remember.

YVONNE: Well, my girl, you'd better start remembering in a hurry. What do you think I'm paying you for?

ESTELLE: I didn't entirely understand him . . . I mean, what he said didn't make sense.

YVONNE: Well, repeat it—word for word. Let me worry about understanding it.

ESTELLE: I'm sorry. I've had enough of this. I'm tired of being a spy.

YVONNE: Well—what's got into you? Don't tell me you're developing scruples.

ESTELLE: What I've been doing hasn't been—honest.

YVONNE: Now, just a minute, young lady! Don't forget what I hired you for. You're here to make love to my son. You're to relieve him of all sexual tensions—within reason, naturally— in addition I want regular, detailed reports. You knew what was required when you took the job, so let's not suddenly develop a twisted sense of morality.

ESTELLE: I can't go on lying to him.

YVONNE: But it's for his own good! That's what we're here for, my little Estelle—the two of us—to save him!

ESTELLE: Save him from what? What can he hope for from life?

YVONNE: Perhaps he has nothing to hope for—but he has everything to lose.

ESTELLE: He's as unhappy and miserable as I am.

YVONNE: Misery loves company—so what's your problem?

ESTELLE: There's no future for us.

YVONNE: At least you can get away for a bit—take a walk in the country, see the outside world. You get a day off once a week.

ESTELLE: A half day off.

YVONNE: Selfish! Why not think of him—poor boy? There's nowhere he can go, nowhere he can even see the face of another man.

ESTELLE: I just don't want to hurt him.

YVONNE: Who said anything about hurting him? My dear child, I'm doing my best to explain it to you. I'm not his enemy! Can't you believe me?

ESTELLE [*After a long pause.*]: I don't know.

YVONNE: All I'm trying to do is find a little happiness for him—

I want to preserve him from the outside world. Don't you realize how horrible it would be if he should ever get away, if he should be exposed to the gaping public? Daniel knows nothing of life. He's pure, innocent. So it's up to us to be afraid for him. Until now I've been able to do that. But today something's happened. He's changed—he's even turned against me. He wants to get away—to leave the laundry—and if he does, it would kill him!

ESTELLE: He'd like so very much to walk in the forest, to be a wanderer, living on nuts and berries.

YVONNE: He's talked to you about this?

ESTELLE: He has shared his dreams with me.

YVONNE: Nuts and berries my ass! He's lost his reason. And you've told me nothing about this? You stupid girl!

ESTELLE: He wants me to leave with him. Listening to him made me cry. [*As she speaks, seemingly without emotion, tears stream down her cheeks. She makes no effort to brush them away.*]

YVONNE: Idiot! That's all I need at my age—aggravation and torment.

ESTELLE: There are many kinds of love, Madame, kinds that you can't understand.

YVONNE: I'll tell you right here and now that these conspiracies with Daniel are to go no further. In the future you're to make love to him—period. No more whispered confidences and exchanged secrets!

ESTELLE: Conspiracies? The poor boy! All day long he sits up there in the attic at his sewing machine mending sheets! He's had enough—and so have I!

YVONNE: How dare you? [*With cold, controlled fury.*] All right. Just you wait . . .

ESTELLE: I have a heart, too.

YVONNE: That's enough, do you hear? How dare you speak of a heart—after all I've done for you? . . . Very well, since you no longer wish to take advantage of my charity, get out! Pack your bag and hit the sidewalk tomorrow morning. As for Daniel . . .

ESTELLE: You won't hurt him, will you?

YVONNE: I am his mother!

ESTELLE: Daniel will never agree to my leaving.

YVONNE: I'm the one who'll decide that, young lady.

ESTELLE: Daniel will protect me.

YVONNE: Oh, yes, turn him against me—his own mother!

ESTELLE: You'll never be able to destroy our love.

YVONNE [*Suddenly weakening, she seems undecided.*]: You really mean what you say, don't you?

ESTELLE: He's all I have, Madame Yvonne.

YVONNE: Very well. Now you get to bed. We'll see about it in the morning. I'll have a little chat with him before he goes to sleep.

ESTELLE [*With sudden fear.*]: But he's already asleep.

YVONNE: I said, go to bed! I know what I have to do—so don't worry about it.

ESTELLE: I don't want him to be hurt.

YVONNE: Will you go to bed. If Daniel is hurt, that's my affair! [*With tragic dignity she sweeps from the stage.*]

ESTELLE [*Alone, she begins to look for* DANIEL *among the hanging sheets, weaving in and out of the mysterious labyrinth. She calls to him softly.*]: Daniel! She's upstairs, and she'll find out that you've gone—and that we've been taking walks together in the moonlight! She'll be furious, you know she will. It's true—she's already fired me. But you won't let her send me away, will you? Daniel! Daniel! Answer me! [LAURENT *enters followed by* SEÑOR ARMANDO, *who remains hidden in the shadows.*] Please speak to me! I know you're here somewhere. Where are you?

[LAURENT *turns on the lights. He comes up to* ESTELLE. *It is evident that he has been drinking, and as the scene progresses, the alcohol continues to take effect.*]

LAURENT: Talking to yourself again? You should watch that, my girl. At this hour little girls your age should be in bed. [*There is a pause. Then he speaks to her in a conspiratorial manner.*] I bet you were waiting up for me.

ESTELLE: You've been drinking. You'd better go to bed.

LAURENT: You're the one who should be in bed. Can't you see I'm talking business with this gentleman? Leave us.

ESTELLE: Madame Yvonne is upstairs! She'll be coming down at any moment.

LAURENT [*Turning to* SEÑOR ARMANDO, *who remains in the shadows.*]: Ah—she's upstairs with him now!

[SENOR ARMANDO *comes into view. He is a rotund gentleman with a red face and a hearty, open manner. He is dressed in the flamboyant costume of a circus ringmaster, with bowler hat and riding boots.*]

ARMANDO: We won't be able to see him then?

ESTELLE [*Looking off in the direction where* MADAME YVONNE *left and speaking to* LAURENT *in a worried whisper.*]: She's sure to be right back.

LAURENT [*To* ARMANDO.]: I've got to get my hands on that key! Where the devil did my wife go?

ESTELLE: You're up to something. I can tell.

LAURENT: Go wash the dishes!

ESTELLE: You're up to no good.

LAURENT: That's enough! Go to bed!

ESTELLE: I want to know!

LAURENT [*To* ARMANDO.]: I'm a victim of women.

ESTELLE: He's not from around here. I've never seen him before.

LAURENT: Of course not—he's Santa Claus. Go on to bed!

ESTELLE: Why is he hiding?

LAURENT [*In sotto voice to* ESTELLE, *so* SEÑOR ARMANDO *cannot hear.*]: He's a real gentleman. He's loaded—you understand? He's going to pay for our trip to the Riviera. So you behave yourself.

ARMANDO: Why the wait? I've been working all day and I'm tired. I want to get to sleep.

LAURENT: How about some of my mother-in-law's brandy?

ARMANDO: Just a drop, perhaps—but let's get on with it! I don't want to stay one moment longer than necessary. I'm responsible for eighty artists.

LAURENT: An extraordinary bargain like this is something you can't pass up. Wait for me here behind this sheet.

ARMANDO: Me—hide myself? Never! Always face to face, cards on the table! That's my motto!

LAURENT: I'm going to look for my wife. She's the one who has to get the key.

ARMANDO: Perhaps she's flown the coop with your extraordinary bargain! [*He laughs boisterously.*]

LAURENT: Very funny, very funny, Señor Armando! Wait here.

I'll be right back. [*He goes off.* SEÑOR ARMANDO, *seeing* ESTELLE *across the room, walks over to her.*

ARMANDO: You work here, my dear?

ESTELLE: Yes, sir.

ARMANDO: The maid, I suppose.

ESTELLE: Yes, the maid.

ARMANDO: How can anyone be satisfied with such a lowly position. It's ridiculous!

ESTELLE: We serve a purpose. Rich people needs us.

ARMANDO: I'm afraid you've developed a mediocre soul.

ESTELLE: I didn't do it on purpose, sir.

ARMANDO: The usual excuse—very handy. But as for me, my dear, I won't debase myself. I refuse to wait on others. I'm a self-made man. I've fought my way to the top with the fists of Hercules. Here, let me show you. Just feel that. [*He flexes his muscles and presents his biceps for inspection.*] But of course I must admit that I'm the rare exception. There's always something going on up here. [*He taps his forehead.*] Call me conceited if you will. I'm proud of myself with good cause, you understand? If you'll permit a metaphor—I don't grovel in the dust. I soar through the clouds!

ESTELLE: Oh yes, sir.

ARMANDO: Tell me, my dear. You must know what goes on in this house. Here—with my compliments. [*He hands her a bill. She accepts it with neither thanks nor remonstrations.*] No, I insist. I'm naturally generous by nature.

ESTELLE: Thank you, sir.

ARMANDO: No, don't thank me. I prefer that you answer a question or two. [*Suddenly very intimate and secretive.*] Have you seen the monster? What's he like?

ESTELLE: Monster?

ARMANDO: The one that's going to cost me a small fortune. Why would I be here tonight if I wasn't on the track of some rare and exotic beast?

ESTELLE: There's no beast in this house.

ARMANDO: Now, now, my dear. I'm speaking of an outrageous monstrosity, and abnormal and enormous aberration of nature— over which I can roll my drums and and crash my cymbals. Surely Laurent hasn't been leading me up the garden path!

ESTELLE [*Handing back the bill.*]: Take back your money. I am not a spy.

ARMANDO: Proud, eh—like me? But I like that! Integrity like yours merits an even greater reward. Here! [*He tries to hand her back the bill.*]

ESTELLE: I'm not for sale. I've already been bought.

ARMANDO: My apologies. But I must make a living, too.

ESTELLE: With other people's flesh.

ARMANDO: Now, try to understand! I'm an exhibitor of dancing bears—if you'll permit the metaphor. The public is hungry for new sensations, unusual thrills. They demand the uncensored, the unexpurgated. They want to pry with their fingers into the open wound of life. So—I present them with a kind of strip-tease, only naturally more elevated. You might almost say I'm a philosopher, my child, a philanthropist if you will! Don't get me wrong. I'm no carnival charlatan with shell game for the suckers. I'm an honorable artist—an impresario, responsible for the lives of eighty other artists. And I pay well. Here, take back your money, and here's another bill to go with it. Buy yourself some nylon stockings. [*He pauses a moment, looking at her legs.*] I'm sure you've been told that you're the happy possessor of two exquisitely shaped limbs!

[LAURENT *returns with* LENA, *who is carrying a traveling bag and seems, if anything, more pregnant than ever.*]

LAURENT: Señor Armando—may I present my wife? Here she is! Her bag packed, ready to leave.

ARMANDO: Hold on a minute! First let's have a look at the merchandise.

LENA: I packed my bag to be ready, just in case. But I haven't decided yet on what dress to wear.

LAURENT [*He goes up to where* MADAME YVONNE *exited and returns, speaking in a low, excited voice.*]: The boss is upstairs.

LENA: She's probably giving him one of her lectures—and once she starts that, she can go on for hours. When she juices up, she gives off as much steam as one of her laundry boilers.

[MADAME YVONNE, *unseen by the others, appears and stands*

*hiding from them behind a hanging sheet, listening to the
conversation.*]

LAURENT: She'd be a real attraction for your circus, Señor Armando.

ARMANDO: Thank you, but I don't care for comics. All right now, to business! I want to see your phenomenon.

LENA: I have a surprise for you!

ARMANDO: I hope it's a happy one.

LAURENT: What is it—something you haven't told me?

LENA [*Speaking in a childish, little-girl manner.*]: Guess!

ARMANDO: Really, Madame, I'm hardly in the mood for children's games.

LAURENT: Come on, Lena. Don't joke with Señor Armando.

ARMANDO: I'm responsible for eighty artists, Madame!

LAURENT: Hurry up! The boss will be down any moment.

LENA [*With hurt dignity.*]: My mother has my permission to go to hell!

ARMANDO: Would you kindly come to the point, Madame?

LENA: Very well. Here. It's a photo of Daniel that I found just now in a trunk. I took it secretly to sell to a newspaper. It was an idea I had once when I needed some money. [*She takes from her purse a small snapshot. She holds it in her hand so no one can see it.*]

LAURENT: You never told me about this!

LENA: It was before we were married. Do you think I need you to get ideas?

ARMANDO: Well—show me the picture.

LENA: The paper wouldn't buy it. They thought it was trick photography.

ARMANDO: Give it to me, for God's sake! Really this is getting to be too much.

LENA: Prepare yourself for a shock. [LENA *goes to the exit and looks out expectantly.* MADAME YVONNE *moves out of view so as to remain hidden from* LENA. LENA *returns to* SEÑOR ARMANDO.] I think she's coming down. [*She hands* SEÑOR ARMANDO *the photo. He looks at it and gasps, clasping the picture to him so* LAURENT *is unable to see it also.*]

ARMANDO: Quick—a chair! It's not possible. [*He falls half-fainting*

onto a stool.] Oh, this is too marvelous! At last, my life's search
is ended!

[MADAME YVONNE *chooses this moment to make her appearance.
She enters in the grand manner of a tragic actress and swoops
down upon the startled group.*]

YVONNE: Bravo! What comic scene am I interrupting?

ARMANDO [*To* LAURENT.]: Didn't I hear you mention a drop of
brandy? I think now is the propitious moment to break open a
bottle.

YVONNE [*Noticing* LENA's *bag.*]: You're leaving?

LENA: You insulted me. My dignity as a woman and as a future
mother has been . . .

YVONNE: Good riddance! [*She turns to* SEÑOR ARMANDO.] And
you? Who are you and what the hell are you supposed to be
dressed up to look like?

ARMANDO: Madame, I am Señor Armando, director of the circus
that has been visiting your town. I am responsible for the lives
of eighty artists.

LAURENT: Yes, Mama, he's the director.

LENA: The director of the circus, Mama!

YVONNE: So? I'm supposed to be impressed?

ARMANDO: I, Madame, am the director!

YVONNE: I am not enchanted. Your employees are a bunch of
bums!

ARMANDO: You astonish me, Madame!

YVONNE: They showed no respect for our dead, sir. They made fun
of our funeral. But that's not the question. You had no business
drinking with my son-in-law here. He will soon be the father of
a family and he shouldn't be wasting his money in frivolity and
debauchery. Besides, his income is very limited.

LENA: And whose fault is that? You're his boss.

LAURENT: That's telling her, Lena!

YVONNE: I pay him quite enough—for the work he does. From
each according to his abilities—to each according to his needs.

LAURENT: I'm surrounded by an aura of dignity!

YVONNE: You're surrounded by an aura, all right! [*She sniffs
at him disdainfully.*] The corner bar!

ARMANDO: Please, please. Let's not engage in a vulgar dispute!

Away with petty conflicts of the workaday world. Listen to me
for two minutes, I beg of you. Forget about your idle rivalries,
your worries, your mediocre problems. Ladies and gentlemen,
your kind indulgence for a moment. [*He makes a few dramatic,
hypnotic passes at* MADAME YVONNE *with his hands. The others
look on in wonderment.*] Calm yourself, Madame. Relax! There!
Just let yourself go. Now then, don't you feel better already?
Can't you sense the eternal You slowly dissolving itself and
separating from the transitory physical You of the moment? I'm
a graduate of the Benares School of Psychic Vibrations and
Extrasensory Perception!

YVONNE: Stop it! Keep your hands to yourself! Oh, you give me
the creeps with whatever it is you're doing. [*She walks across the
room and sits.*]

ARMANDO: Shh! Listen to me. Listen to my extraordinary proposi-
tion!

LENA: Listen, Mama, listen to him!

YVONNE: I'm listening.

LENA [*To* SEÑOR ARMANDO.] She's listening.

ARMANDO: Hmm . . . now then—Madame, you should be proud,
because in a moment I shall share with you the greatest event
of my life. Yes, Madame, I do not exaggerate. In a moment,
thanks to you, I shall become the happiest of mortals. You will
see before your very eyes a man to whom you have given joy in
the present and hope for the future!

YVONNE: You're drunk, too.

ARMANDO: No, madame, it's not the blood of Bacchus that dazzles
my brain. The happiness you see is real, tangible—a marvelous
encounter, a splendid discovery!

YVONNE: Get to the point, man!

ARMANDO: Madame, you possess a treasure! No. Let's say rather
that you possess *my* treasure, the ultimate goal of my entire life,
my only ambition as an artist and a leader of men. You control
the unique object of my melancholia! Ah, happy mother of such
a son! [YVONNE *rises in cold fury.*] Yes, Madame, and you hide
him! You treat him as a freak, a pariah, a monster! Ah, Madame,
what an error, what injustice, what a crime! I am here to announce the Great Event, to proclaim the tidings of joy. For who
could forget the mother of such a son?

YVONNE: Get out. I order you to leave my house!

LAURENT [To SEÑOR ARMANDO.]: I warned you she might not be easy to handle.

LENA: What eloquence! A silver-tongued orator!

ESTELLE: I knew all the time that Daniel was a king!

YVONNE: I repeat—out of my house! Have you no shame to trifle like this with the heart of a mother?

ARMANDO: This is what I think of your heart, Madame. [He lifts the hem of her dress and kisses it.]

LAURENT: That's her heart you're kissing?

YVONNE: I don't understand why any glory should be promised me. Daniel, as you are well aware, is a monster, a grotesque creature born through an unpardonable error of creation, a crime against nature!

ARMANDO: Listen to me, Madame!

[During the following dialogue MADAME YVONNE sweeps back and forth among the hanging sheets, often hidden from view. She is followed by SEÑOR ARMANDO, and the two weave in and out in the maze of the laundry. SEÑOR ARMANDO speaks in the rapid salesman-like manner of a street vendor.]

YVONNE: What sort of joke is this? Your tasteless farce has gone quite far enough.

ARMANDO: But there are monsters—and then again there are monsters, dear lady. There are little monsters that actually amount to nothing. They run loose in the streets and likely as not end up behind bars selling stamps in the post office. But then there are the great monsters—those who bring honor to their parents, who move in the salons of the world capitals! History is full, Madame, of these exceptional creatures, who in the realms of art and of politics leave upon their epoch the burning brilliance of their personalities!

YVONNE: None in the image of my son.

ARMANDO: But Madame, that's my point! [He sighs.] One can see that you live an isolated life in the backwash of civilization.

YVONNE: Backwash! I'll have you know, sir, this laundry has been honored with a medal!

ARMANDO: I'm not speaking of your laundry. I'm sure there's

none finer. The point I am making is that, in order to attract attention, one should be distinctive, of an unusual shape. And it follows naturally that the greater the difference between the ordinary and the bizarre, the richer the opportunity for publicity. Don't you ever look at the papers? Your son has a better chance for fame than any of these local notables whose faces appear in the press. His case surpasses any on record, dear Madame. It's transcendental!

YVONNE: No, sir, you're wrong. My son is nothing . . . nobody.

ARMANDO: Infinitely more, dear Madame! He is both tradition and revolution, the past and the future, the transgression and the hope of mankind! Four thousand years of civilization at last reach fulfillment in him! That is why, Madame, your duty is not to hide him under a bushel but to offer him to the adulation of an adoring public!

YVONNE: You honestly believe the public will—er—adore him?

ARMANDO: I shall be his manager, Madame. Trust me. Like the better mousetrap, they'll beat a path to his door. I shall pay whatever is required for his release, for his deliverance, from the bondage of his hiding place—and if I personally haven't enough money, I shall launch a public subscription—with a guaranteed return of three and a half percent a year.

LENA: A fortune, Mama!

LAURENT: A fortune!

ESTELLE: A king! He's a king from a faraway land—like in a story book.

YVONNE: Stop it! Stop it! You're raving mad—the lot of you!

ARMANDO: Oh, the dream of my youth! I've arrived! We're here. [*He rushes about the stage looking for the door behind which he hopes to find his monster.* LAURENT, ESTELLE, *and* LENA *run after him excitedly.*] The Armando Circus opens unto you its portals of salvation!

LENA: Fame and glory!

LAURENT: Ingots of gold!

LENA: Travel and adventure!

YVONNE: Imposter! [*The group returns to her.*] This man is making fun of you!

ARMANDO: I'm offering him a magnificent contract. You must understand I'm an artist—not a business executive. We'll keep

the enterprise in the family. Naturally you'll all accompany him
on his triumphal journey—you'll be his entourage. [*To* MADAME
YVONNE.] You can be called the Queen Mother if you wish.

YVONNE [*In haughty disdain.*]: I—a queen mother? I'm a
laundress.

LENA: What can I be called?

LAURENT: And me? What will they call me?

ESTELLE: What about me?

ARMANDO: I can see it all now—the pennants snapping in the
wind, a hundred-voice choir raised in songs of praise, red bal-
loons emblazoned with phosphorescent letters, souvenir repro-
ductions in plastic—even his picture on chewing-gum wrappers!

LAURENT: Don't forget—I'm the one who told you about him!

LENA: I'm the one who first had the idea!

ARMANDO: Madame, why do you hesitate? What false sense of
modesty, what fraudulent shame allowed you to bury this talent?
Of course it's fortunate that you kept him hidden until now so
that I, the great Armando, could have the distinction and honor
to discover him, to present him to a grateful people! The masses
await him, Madame. They demand his appearance! This is his
hour—indisputably, this is his hour! He will heal us of our rage
to live. In this era of bombs and fusion, here at last is he who
lifts high the torch of the lost light. Here at last is the return of
him for whom the world has been waiting! And we shall receive
him unto ourselves with humility, with compassion! Just as has
been foretold in the prophesies of Nostradamus! [*He falls to his
knees and kisses* MADAME YVONNE's *feet. As he does so he takes
from his pocket a folded contract.*] I understand our international myth is still a minor. Therefore I'll need the slight detail
of his mother's signature.

[*There is a long pause.*]

YVONNE: And you think you've turned my head with all this high-
flying talk? I told you I was a laundress—that and nothing more!
But laundresses all the same are not fools!

ARMANDO: A laundress you may be perhaps, but mother of a new
superbeing you are without a doubt! We may well—you and I
—be the founders of a new system of philosophy, of a new

religion even. But first things first. For the moment, while we're waiting, the only thing needed is a little signature at the bottom of this page.

YVONNE [*Indicating* LENA *and* LAURENT.]: Look at those two—would you—with their eyes gleaming with greed and selfishness! You've got them snapping at your bait all right!

LENA: Mama, please! I beg you! I've wanted a mink coat and a motor scooter for so long! Mama, please say yes! You can buy all the automatic washing machines you want—and driers, too. Think of the customers you'll have! [*She breaks down and weeps.*]

YVONNE: Washing machines tear sheets!

LENA [*Weeping.*]: It's not true!

LAURENT: I want a fishing yacht for the Mediterranean, and cigars, and a pair of binoculars to follow my horse at the race track!

YVONNE: I will not sell Daniel.

LENA: Mama—you can't do this to us! This is our one chance in a lifetime.

LAURENT: It doesn't happen often, you know.

LENA: I want a baby-sitter for my child!

YVONNE: That's enough! Just look what you've done to them with all your fancy stories. Well, as for me, my fine fellow, count me out on your balloon ride! You'll not get Daniel! Perhaps he's not happy where he is, but at least no one is going to ridicule him.

YVONNE: Unfortunately no one is waiting for him—neither children nor adults. He remains what he's always been—a disgrace to creation.

LENA: Think of his happiness, Mama. He's so bored and lonely up there!

ESTELLE: He'll have his own temple where he'll be protected!

LAURENT: And his picture on chewing gum!

ARMANDO: Think of the joy he'll bring to little children!

YVONNE: No, no, no. I shall not relent! I refuse!

ARMANDO: Madame, I—what can I say? Before such scruples I am left defenseless. Such idealism is incomprehensible.

YVONNE: Incomprehensible perhaps—but irrevocable!

ARMANDO: Listen. I'll come back again tomorrow. It's late, and the night, as the poet says, brings its own counsel. Also, when I'm tired my psychic powers of magnetism are somewhat diminished. Think about what I've said, and you two—[*He turns to* LENA *and* LAURENT.]—do your best to persuade her to see reason. This is going to be a completely new revelation for humanity. We shall found a new doctrine that reaches back to the cradle of civilization. We shall reunite with the Greeks.

YVONNE: I never let Greeks mix in our family affairs! [*She haughtily leaves the room.* LENA *follows her out.*]

LENA [*As she goes.*]: Tomorrow you must say yes. It would be too stupid to let this chance slip by.

LAURENT: I'll walk back with you. I haven't forgotten the drink I promised you.

ARMANDO: Oh, I'm exhausted! I've never used up so much nervous energy.

LAURENT: We'll have just one little drink.

ARMANDO: I've drained myself completely, you understand.

LAURENT: All the more reason for a refill!

[LENA *reappears.*]

LENA: I'll go with you.

LAURENT: Oh, no—really! Get to bed!

LENA: You're always like this—and I'm fed up with it!

[YVONNE *reappears.*]

YVONNE: Haven't you spies finished your plotting? The secret meeting is adjourned! You're burning my electricity. And tomorrow Estelle will be dozing off while she's supposed to be working.

ESTELLE: You just fired me, remember?

YVONNE: I've been reconsidering. . . . Besides there's something I want to talk to you about, you understand?

ESTELLE: I know, Madame Yvonne. [*She leaves.*]

LENA [*To* LAURENT.]: Now don't get drunk, you hear? I've decided not to put up with a sot for a husband.

LAURENT: Naturally—the sister of such a grand personage!

YVONNE: Show more respect for womanhood. The female body is a cathedral!

LENA: A place of worship!

ARMANDO: Come on, come on! I haven't got all night. Good evening, dear lady, and think of all I've offered you. Until tomorrow! [*He kisses her hand.*]

YVONNE: Don't bother to come back! [*But it is obvious she is flattered by his attention.*]

LENA [*To* LAURENT.]: I won't go to sleep until you get in.

LAURENT: What's the point? The cathedral is closed for additional construction. [*He leaves with* SEÑOR ARMANDO.]

LENA: He's so vulgar, Mama.

YVONNE: Well—that's the husband you picked for yourself, my poor Lena! What a joy for the family.

LENA: At least my husband knows how to run our business. I hope you weren't serious just now when you were talking to Señor Armando. He offered us a bridge of gold. We don't get the chance to turn that down every day.

YVONNE: He said he didn't have the money himself.

LENA: But he'll find it!

YVONNE: I didn't quite understand the details of how he plans to operate.

LENA: I didn't either—but it's worth thinking about.

YVONNE: In any case, in business matters one should never close a deal on the spur of the moment. Always say no the first time. That makes the price go up.

LENA: I'm proud of you, Mama!

YVONNE: If Daniel is worth so much, perhaps it would pay us to shop around—look over the whole field.

LENA: What do you have in mind?

YVONNE [*Draping herself against a sheet like a movie queen.*]: Cinerama!

LENA: Mama!

YVONNE: I shall never sell my son—for peanuts!

LENA: You're so clever!

YVONNE: I want him to be well situated, my little boy. I want to live to see him really established. Then I could die in peace.

LENA: Naturally.

YVONNE: Of course in his condition he might have trouble running a laundry, but he could certainly manage Western civilization! . . . Ah, well, it's late! After such an exhausting day, it's time we were asleep. Go to bed!

LENA: I think I'll wait up for Laurent.

YVONNE [*In commanding voice.*]: In your room!

LENA: I'm too excited to sleep, Mama.

YVONNE: Then knit your layette. You haven't even finished one pair of booties.

LENA: My son will be able to buy his own booties.

YVONNE: Get your head out of the clouds—and knit!

[LENA *shrugs her shoulders and starts to leave. At the door she turns back into the room.*]

LENA: You're not coming?

YVONNE: I want to check and make sure the front door is locked. What with all the emotion tonight I can't remember what I've done. [*There is a silence.* LENA *stands in the doorway looking at* MADAME YVONNE.] Besides I don't like to be spied on! [LENA *leaves.* MADAME YVONNE, *alone, looks about her, turns off the electricity, and then stands immobile in a shaft of moonlight. She lights a cigarette. In a moment* ESTELLE *returns and, after a worried glance toward the labyrinth of hanging sheets, walks up to* MADAME YVONNE.] Well—I'm waiting. . . .

ESTELLE: Madame Yvonne . . .

YVONNE: You lied to me!

ESTELLE: I wanted to tell you everything as soon as you went upstairs. . . .

YVONNE: Where is Daniel? And how long has this been going on behind my trusting back?

ESTELLE: For two years now. On a night like this—when the weather is nice—he walks in the country. He breathes the air of the fields and runs with the animals through the forest.

YVONNE: And what if someone should see him? Do you realize the scandal? We might all land in jail. . . . Well, I don't know any more. All that's been changed since tonight. I can't seem to find the strength to be angry.

ESTELLE: Yes—everything will be different after tonight!

YVONNE: When will he get back?

ESTELLE: Before the sun rises. He's very timid, you know. He's afraid of people.

YVONNE: I want to talk to him as soon as he comes in. You've behaved very badly, the two of you. Estelle, you really should have kept me informed.

ESTELLE: I love Daniel, Madame.

YVONNE: It's true then. . . . You really love him? And what about him?

ESTELLE: I don't know.

YVONNE: You never know anything! You have no feeling for me, for my wishes. . . .

ESTELLE: Madame . . .

YVONNE: Go on, go on—satisfy your sordid appetites! You're like the rest of them. Oh, yes, don't deny it! [*There is a pause. Then* MADAME YVONNE *speaks with quiet and deep emotion.*] I understand, my dear—all too well! I know how such a sentiment is possible. . . .

ESTELLE: You don't understand.

YVONNE: Go on—get to bed; I shall wait the return of my son while I knit his pullover. That's the role fate has designed for us, my poor girl—to knit and wait! [*She starts to leave, then turns.*] Go to bed. I want to be the one to speak to him first. [*She leaves.* ESTELLE *goes to the hanging sheets and calls softly.*]

ESTELLE: Daniel! Yes, he must have left. He's no longer here. The drying room is empty. While I wait for him, I shall be praying. [*She leaves. The stage is empty for a moment. Then the sound of the outside door can be heard opening and* LAURENT *enters slowly and stealthily. He is more obviously drunk than he was earlier and it is with uneven steps that he makes his way to a stool and sits down.*]

LAURENT: Ooo! the floor is reeling! I'm not at my best. A cup of black coffee would pull me together, I'm sure. But my wife has gone to bed, and just when I need her, for once. And Estelle— do you think she'd wait up for me? She's sleeping while I suffer and probably dreaming about swimming on the Riviera. I'll give her a Riviera! Can't even take care of a sick man. [*He lights a cigarette.*] Señor Armando—there's a fine gentleman. A lot of learning and temperament just like mine. He understood me. We'll get rich together and we'll see the world. We'll roast in the sun like a couple of bankers. When the chips are down, only men understand each other. [*Calling loudly.*] Estelle!

Estelle! My coffee, or I'll crack your skull! She's sleeping. She's left me, like the others. Alone in the dark . . . and there's a monster in the house. [*A strange grating noise is heard which makes him start with fear. He turns around and examines the the hanging sheets around him as if looking for someone.*] All alone. I'm all alone. [*He seems somewhat reassured.*] Well, when it comes down to it, everybody is always alone in this life.

DANIEL [*His voice is heard speaking close to* LAURENT.]: You're not alone, Laurent. You have a brother near you!

LAURENT [*Completely shattered by fear.*]: No! No! Don't do this to me. I have a weak heart. Where are you?

DANIEL: I'm among the sheets—so white and fresh.

LAURENT: Please . . . I—I have a headache.

DANIEL: For a long time I've wanted to know you.

LAURENT [*Starting to leave.*]: I think I'll go to bed.

DANIEL: No, Laurent. You and I should have a talk.

LAURENT: At least let's turn on the lights. [*He clicks the switch, but no light turns on.*]

DANIEL: I've pulled the master switch.

LAURENT: You—you're trying to frighten me. But I warn you—I can defend myself.

DANIEL: But I don't want you to be hurt, Laurent. It's the other way around.

LAURENT: You don't think I want to hurt you? Really, I'm very gentle. I just put on a front sometimes, like this, so that they'll respect me.

DANIEL: You said just now that you're all alone. Doesn't anyone love you?

LAURENT: Of course. Lena loves me! Estelle loves me! The girl who works for the butcher loves me! Every woman loves me! I'm irresistible!

DANIEL: And you're all alone!

LAURENT: I'm alone because I want to be that way! I have a right to be, haven't I? Are you going to come out and show yourself— yes or no? It's not polite to hide like this!

DANIEL: Look for me—you'll find me!

LAURENT: I'm going to get mad in a minute.

DANIEL: Fine. Let's see what your real self is like.

LAURENT: You're making fun of me. You're not showing me the

proper respect. [*He walks among the hanging sheets, pulling at them. Suddenly he pulls one which falls to the floor, revealing* DANIEL *sitting on top of the stepladder. He is a young man, whose resemblance to the Minotaur is a matter of question.* LAURENT *refuses to look up at him and falls to the floor, his face hidden in his hands.*] No! No! Don't frighten me! I don't want to see you!

DANIEL: Little country butcher!

LAURENT: I'm not a butcher—I'm a mechanic.

DANIEL: Look at me then.

[LAURENT *turns slowly and looks up at* DANIEL. *The scene between the two men takes on an unrealistic, dreamlike quality.*]

LAURENT: Oh, God—no! You—you can't be . . .

DANIEL: You know me?

LAURENT: Of course. You've been following me for years. We've played this scene before. You crush me between your arms like a walnut smashed in a nutcracker!

DANIEL: I've been following you? I crush you? Why?

LAURENT: In this labyrinth of sheets—in this unending maze of millions of drying sheets . . .

DANIEL: I didn't even know you existed until seven months ago, when you married my sister.

LAURENT: Don't try to trick me! Admit that you've been hunting me for years. You've been lying in wait, biding your time for the moment when you could spring upon me and trip me up!

DANIEL: You mean we met somewhere in your dreams? But I've never seen you in my sleep.

LAURENT: All the same it's your fault—it's because of you that this streak of bad luck has been hounding me—that I'm afraid every time I go to sleep!

DANIEL: You have confused me with some one else.

LAURENT: No, no—it's you all right. Listen! When I was twelve, I ran away with Tony. We escaped together. He was my pal. We walked for miles and miles. . . .

DANIEL: I don't want to hear about it.

LAURENT: No! No! Listen to me. You've got to listen! You might be able to give me the answer. Now that you're here, you must

save me. Now at last I'll be able to break the spell, escape from
the chains that have been strangling me. Finally I'll be free of
you—I'll be free by screaming to you my disgust!

DANIEL: Yes, perhaps you're right. Speak the truth, Laurent! Yell
it at the top of your voice! It's probably the same truth as mine.

LAURENT: I had no father—never knew who he was. My home was
the orphanage. When I was twelve, I ran away with Tony—a
real tough guy. One night we had an argument—and we fought.
We loved each other too much—can you understand? My hand
came upon a large stone in the road, and in the middle of the
freezing night, a red star appeared on his forehead. It grew larger
and larger. Then I started running. I could never stay long in
one place. One night I was sleeping in a cabbage patch and the
lady who owned the garden found me. She was a little touched.
She'd never been able to have any children of her own—and
since I was by a cabbage, she claimed it was a sign from heaven.
I stayed there three years, and then I had enough—and I ran
away again. . . . Well, that's it.

DANIEL: And your mother, your real mother—don't you remember
her at all?

LAURENT: Yes. I can still see her clear eyes smiling over me. She
was a woman in red among the enchanted lights of the town.
. . . The cover of my cradle was draped in lace. I can see it.
I can touch it. I'm able to unwind it from my mouth like a
fisherman's twine, yellowed by age. I unroll my earliest memories
from inside myself. I chew them in my mouth. They pile up in
my mind like in a store window—lighted for the final Christmas,
spangled with gold streamers and red holly berries.

DANIEL: And you think you've suffered more than I?

LAURENT: All this old blood came back up into my mouth when I
saw you! [DANIEL *comes down from the stepladder and walks
behind* LAURENT, *who is kneeling on the floor.*] I'm afraid,
Daniel! At night while I'm sleeping I sometimes start to cry and
I wake up feeling awful. Then when I get to sleep again it's even
worse and I begin screaming. Lena has to wake me up, she feels
so sorry for me. Yes! Now I know—I suddenly remember! It's
just like this—the way it is now. You're following me down a
hallway and the walls are all moldy, like these. I'm afraid. You
hold out your hand—and then suddenly there's—nothing left.

[DANIEL *places his hands on* LAURENT's *shoulders. The two figures sway slightly back and forth as* LAURENT *continues speaking, as in a dream.*] Yes, that's it—you catch me in the middle of the hanging sheets, and instead of killing me, you hold me in your arms and rock me gently back and forth. I discover a terrible joy, a horrible happiness, and I'm a little boy again. I'm a little boy and I'm back with Tony.

DANIEL: I give you this peace?

LAURENT: You erase everything. You wash everything clean. It's like the waves of the ocean washing the shore.

DANIEL: We're about to fall asleep.

LAURENT: We're not dreaming now. I'm here and you're here, too. This is no dream, I tell you. I'm even sick to my stomach because I drank too much. It was all that brandy I drank with Señor Armando. But you—you haven't been drinking. Do you feel all right?

DANIEL: I'm going to try to make some movement in order to escape this nightmare.

LAURENT: Yes, try to if you can. Tell me—do you think it would be possible to wash everything away and start over again—like in my dream? Could you wash away my fear?

DANIEL: Not wash it away exactly, but forget it—yes, it should be possible to forget.

LAURENT: Be like the animal in my dreams! Destroy the dead body, drink up its blood, blot out my crime! Save me, Daniel! Save me!

DANIEL: Shh! Be quiet—try to forget.

LAURENT: I know you're talking to me—but somehow I can't hear what you're saying.

DANIEL: Try to forget!

LAURENT: If you don't want to save me, it's because you don't love me.

DANIEL: I don't love you.

LAURENT [*He is now completely prone on the floor. Pause.*]: Then I'm all alone?

DANIEL: Shh. Be quiet.

LAURENT: I can't. My head hurts. I'm sick to my stomach. Don't leave me like this. Have pity on me!

DANIEL: Shh. Be quiet. And forget. [*He bends over* LAURENT.]

LAURENT: No, no, I can't! We could both die of this! Save me, Daniel. I'll do anything for you! I'll obey you! I'll be your slave. [*He breaks down and is sobbing bitterly.* SEÑOR ARMANDO *enters.*]

ARMANDO: It is true. I have not been deceived.

[MADAME YVONNE *enters.*]

YVONNE: Señor Armando!

ARMANDO: Forgive the intrusion at this late hour, but I bear with me tidings of great joy. When I left you a short while ago, I decided not to put off till tomorrow what could be accomplished tonight. I held an audience with the mayor, and he is now arranging the details for the ceremony which will take place tomorrow in front of this very laundry. An eager public awaits its salvation!

YVONNE: Ah, Señor Armando, you were right. God is great! look what Daniel has accomplished!

ARMANDO: I see. Tears roll from the strongest rock!

LAURENT [*Sobbing.*]: But I'm not crying!

ARMANDO: Yes, he weeps. Your son worked this miracle? He creates springs from the rarest of sources. He transforms toads into skylarks, wolves into sheep.

DANIEL: Mother, who is this man? He thinks I'm some sort of saint.

ARMANDO: Not a saint, dear boy—but something even more wondrous.

DANIEL: I don't understand. . . .

ARMANDO: Understanding is not necessary. It is enough that you have faith.

YVONNE: That's right, Daniel, Just put your trust in Señor Armando.

ARMANDO: A wise counsel, dear lady. I have never been known to be wrong! Your son holds the key to our happiness! [*Indicating the prostrate* LAURENT.] There's proof before your eyes!

YVONNE: Yes, God is great and His goodness in infinite. I'm sure that right now up in Heaven Papa George . . .

ARMANDO: Let's not worry about Heaven. We have our work laid out for us right here on earth. If Daniel proves to be an apt pupil, we will soon have the world at our feet!

DANIEL: I'm afraid I won't be able to do much . . .

YVONNE: Listen to the dear child—modest and shy, as radiant in happiness as in misfortune. Here is the reason for all my suffering! And I don't understand! There were times when I was even cruel to him.

DANIEL: No, Mama, no, you weren't.

YVONNE: Yes, yes, I was, my son. I punished you unjustly—you, a worker of miracles.

DANIEL: But I don't work miracles.

ARMANDO: Look at Laurent. He's your first convert.

YVONNE: Yes, Daniel. He was a savage brute, and you've transformed him into a lamb!

DANIEL: I haven't transformed him into anything. He's just passed out.

YVONNE: When Laurent drinks, he never gets down on his knees, Daniel. No, when he's drunk, he breaks everything. He insults and abuses us.

ARMANDO: You mustn't permit yourself to doubt your capabilities, my boy. That way lies disaster.

YVONNE: He's right, Daniel! Only tonight I was meditating while knitting your sweater. I said to myself, "I hardly know my own child." I've been ashamed of you, and all the while you were interceding for my salvation. I've locked you up in the attic and made you darn and sew—and you were worthy of a pedestal! No, don't protest, my son. It's true.

ARMANDO: While you were washing sheets, he was washing away your sins. He has only to stretch out his hands and everything will be washed away.

YVONNE: My son. My son! You can save me! I haven't been drinking. I must confess all the miseries of my life so that I can be delivered from the shame of my iniquities.

ARMANDO: Lay your hands upon your mother, and though her sins be as scarlet, you will wash them white as snow. You cannot refuse your mission!

YVONNE: My son, my son! [*She starts to fall upon her knees, but* DANIEL *holds her up. She calls.*] Lena! Lena! Come here quick!

Wake up! A miracle has befallen us! Laurent has been saved! Come and see him.

LENA [*Off.*]: What is it?

YVONNE: Come and see! You must see it to believe it!

LENA [*Off.*]: He's drunk.

YVONNE: He's praying. I tell you, he's praying.

LENA [*Off.*]: I don't believe it! I'll be right there! Don't let him move!

YVONNE: And Estelle—we'll need her too! It's good to humble yourself in front of the servants. Estelle! Estelle! Come quick! [*Turning to* SEÑOR ARMANDO.] I'm glad you're here to see that we do this right. I'm going to tell everything! It's the hour of judgment! [LENA *and* ESTELLE *enter.*] Come in, my daughters, come in unto the manger of the Lord!

DANIEL [*Embarrassed.*]: Mama!

YVONNE: I'm going to tell them everything!

DANIEL: I forbid you, Mama! I forbid it. Please—I won't let you go on like this!

ARMANDO: Too late! This is the moment of truth!

LENA: Mama, Laurent!

ARMANDO: Take off your shoes! You're standing on holy ground!

ESTELLE: It's a miracle!

YVONNE: Yes, my daughters, a miracle! Look at this pig down on his knees, and look at me, burning with the inner flame of truth.

LENA: It's your dispepsia! Mama, I told you not to eat that third tart. Try to burp—you'll feel better.

ARMANDO: Silence! Be quiet, all of you, and listen to me! The hour of revelation is at hand, when the lame shall walk, the dumb shall shout, and the blind shall see. [*He turns to* YVONNE.] Sister, you must unburden yourself of all sin.

YVONNE: Oh, yes, I must confess. I must confess the origin of my sin—the sin that has soiled our beautiful laundry!

DANIEL: Stop, Mama!

LENA: Perhaps he's right. Do you think you'd better let Estelle and —er—this gentleman know about it?

ARMANDO: That's the whole point. We must bear witness in front of strangers. [*He turns to* YVONNE.] Continue, dear lady.

YVONNE: Nineteen years ago a circus passed this way—a beautiful circus. [*She turns to* SEÑOR ARMANDO.] Much bigger than yours.

It was the first circus I ever saw. My first circus! My first fanfare! The golden spangles of the trapeze artists! How could my young heart fail to yield to such new beauty?

ESTELLE: The golden spangles!

LENA: The trapeze artists!

YVONNE: It was then, my children, that I committed the sin—the unpardonable sin—in spite of my innocence and my youth.

DANIEL: I don't want to hear about it!

YVONNE: It's the hour of repentence, my son. Let's all purify ourselves together!

LENA: Mama, your courage is superhuman!

YVONNE: In the sideshow among the freaks there was a golden cage —and there he was, sitting on his circus stool, waiting for me— my beautiful wild beast—waiting for me, motionless, his arms crossed like a wrestler, in rose-colored trunks—and a barren emptiness that drew me to him as one is drawn toward death. They called him the Cretan—I don't know why.

LENA: I want to confess everything, too!

YVONNE: It's not your turn. I haven't finished the recital of my shame. There he was, so handsome, so strong, so impassive—that I kept coming to see him every day, consumed by the fever of love. I couldn't sleep. I had frenzied nightmares. I suffered the tortures of the damned.

LEAN: It's my turn! My turn!

DANIEL: Be quiet, both of you!

ESTELLE: Daniel, you've already cleansed me—of everything.

DANIEL: Tell them to be quiet. Tell them, please!

LENA: I want to speak. I want to confess all the wrong I've done.

YVONNE: It's nothing compared to my crimes. I even tried to drown Papa George in a laundry tub—so I could follow him.

LENA: No, listen, Mama! Listen to me! What I did was worse!

YVONNE: Impossible! Little people can never commit great sins.

DANIEL: I won't listen. I don't want to hear any more!

YVONNE: Finally the Cretan noticed me in the crowd. Every day I'd stand in front of his cage—with tears in my eyes. He had to notice me. His sad, black eyes met mine and he consented to the moment which bound us forever. When the circus finally left town, Daniel, I was carrying you under my heart, with love and anxiety.

DANIEL: Please stop! Haven't you any shame?

LENA: We've hated you from the beginning.

YVONNE: Don't believe her! I always loved you! You were my favorite and she was jealous of you!

LENA: Liar! You said that if you were rid of him, you'd be able to lead a happy life.

YVONNE: I might have said it, but I didn't mean it.

LENA: Oh, we were monstrous, Daniel—monstrous!

YVONNE: Yes, we were the monsters—not you!

LENA [*Falling on her knees.*]: But you will save us!

YVONNE: You won't forget us!

ARMANDO: Yes, he's so close to God! He'll save you!

ESTELLE: Daniel will save us!

LENA: Amen, Lord, amen!

DANIEL: No, no, I wont! I won't. [DANIEL *runs from the room.*]

ARMANDO: He's found his mission. You thought he was worthless. Now all the world waits for him!

[*The scene builds to a collective hysteria.*]

ESTELLE: Daniel! My darling Daniel! Everybody needs him!

LAURENT [*He seems suddenly to be revived.*]: Oh, the past comes back to me! And here I am—the same as before—with my fear!

ARMANDO: Welcome, my child. You're redeemed!

LENA: You're blessed, Laurent, you're blessed!

YVONNE: Hosanna, hosanna!

LAURENT: I must have drunk too much. I'm seeing things.

YVONNE: A new era is upon us!

ARMANDO: A new dawn is breaking!

ESTELLE: Thanks to Daniel!

LENA: The honor of the laundry!

YVONNE: The Laundry of the Future!

LAURENT: The monster in the attic. I'm sick! I'm sick to my stomach! It's Daniel's fault. He'll pay for this!

YVONNE: My son, my son! He will save us! [*She calls hysterically, her face lifted in ecstasy.*] Oh, thank you, Papa George!

ARMANDO: Hallelujah! Amen!

Curtain

Act Three

The same. Early the next morning.
The characters are in the exact positions they held at the end of Act Two. All remain motionless in tableau except SEÑOR ARMANDO, *who addresses them:*

ARMANDO: Quiet, everybody and listen—and pay attention! Each of you knows the role expected of him. [*The three women immediately begin a frenzy of activity, rushing on and off stage as they fold sheets, dust furniture and rearrange the scene as if in preparation for a formal reception. Only* LAURENT *remains seated, staring before him moodily.*] In a few minutes I shall meet with our miraculous monstrosity and explain to him his part in the ceremony. The entire town—I might even say the entire country—awaits his appearance. When all is ready, the circus band will blast forth with a fanfare of trumpets, heralding the arrival of the chief of police. The mayor will mount the podium erected outside the laundry and in front of the assembled multitude of townspeople, newspaper reporters, radio, motion-picture and television cameras, he will introduce to the eager public Miraculous Daniel—Minotaur of the Twentieth Century. What an entrance. Daniel will hold out his sacred hands and the crowd will fall to their knees—washed, purified, redeemed! The entire population will be born again—reawakened to a life of love in which the poor smile upon the compas-

sionate rich. The school children will burst into song—"Unto
Us the Minotaur," which incidently I composed myself last
night. Then a little girl will step forward and offer a bouquet of
flowers to Daniel. Picture if you will the moving spectacle as
Daniel takes the child in his arms and plants upon her cheek a
kiss of purity. Kisses always make a hit with the public.

[ESTELLE *leaves*.]

LENA [*As she continues folding sheets*.]: The little girl will be so
scared she'll start to cry.

ARMANDO: Not at all. I've chosen a dairy maid. She's used to cows.

YVONNE: Daniel is no cow! If anything he's a bull—a beautiful
toro!

LENA: And what am I, Mama?

YVONNE: You, be worthy of your brother!

LENA: I'll try, mama. [*She looks at* LAURENT *tenderly*.]

ARMANDO: Everyone will take a percentage. I have eighty artists
who look to me for their daily bread—eighty, of which four
are children and three nursing infants. One must never forget
motherhood!

YVONNE: In honor of my son I shall found the Society of the
International Drop of Milk!

ARMANDO: An excellent idea. I name you director!

YVONNE: The director is above.

LENA: It's Papa George!

ARMANDO: But for the moment I must prepare our Minotaur for
his triumphal entrance.

LENA: I'll go get him. [*She leaves*.]

ARMANDO: I shall take advantage of this moment of intimacy, my
dear Yvonne, and confide to you my ardour—very quickly. An
old bachelor like me who's spent his life among pinheads and
sword-swallowers ...

YVONNE: Careful! Perhaps Laurent is listening!

ARMANDO: No matter. Since last night he's been blind, deaf, and
dumb—as harmless as a puppy. . . . Yvonne, if I dare—if I dare.
I kiss your hands—the care-worn hands of a working woman.
If only I could see them ironing my laundry. Think of being

able to say that my shirts were pressed by the mother of the Minotaur!

YVONNE: Armando, *mi amore!*

ARMANDO: From the moment we met, we've been living a modern fairy tale. We'll continue the legend—Daniel shall be offered a father! Accept my hand in marriage.

YVONNE: But we've only just met! I hardly know you.

ARMANDO: All the better! Let's dispense with the banalities of the bourgeoisie!

[LENA *enters.*]

YVONNE: Ah, Lena, if you only knew what has happened to me. . . .

ARMANDO: A great happiness, little lady.

YVONNE: I have the strangest sensation. I don't know how to explain it. Suddenly I feel—how shall I put it?—good!

LENA: Does it hurt? .

YVONNE: No—but I seem to have lost my strength.

ARMANDO: Enough of romance—down to business! Where's your brother?

[*From outside can be heard the first murmurings of the crowd which has begun to gather.*]

LENA: I don't know. I've looked all over the house and I can't find him.

YVONNE: He's run off with Estelle again—and without my permission!

ARMANDO [*Looking outside the window.*]: He couldn't get far. The crowd outside would recognize him.

YVONNE [*Calling.*]: Daniel! Estelle! Wherever you are, have the courtesy to show yourselves! Everybody's waiting for you!

LENA: They probably climbed out the window. I hope he won't fail to do his duty. . . .

YVONNE: If only Papa George were here!

ARMANDO: They can't escape without passing through here.

YVONNE [*She takes down one of the clotheslines and loops it angrily.*]: Daniel, Daniel! It's your mother! Come here immediately! [*She exits through the labyrinth of hanging sheets.*]

ARMANDO: Where could they be? They'll ruin me. I've tied up all my capital in this affair. [*He looks out the window.*] They're beginning to get restless out there. The crowd can't be expected to wait indefinitely. In matters of this kind everything depends on timing.

YVONNE [*Off.*]: Are you going to make me climb out on the roof after you—at my age? If I fall, it will be your fault.

ARMANDO: Doesn't he realize the opportunity I'm presenting him?

LENA: It's all Estelle's fault! [*She goes over to Laurent, who until this moment has remained impassive, staring at nothing.*] Laurent, please! Stop dreaming and do something! Daniel has run off.

LAURENT [*Speaking in a faraway, dreamlike manner.*]: What did you say?

LENA: Daniel—he's run away with Estelle!

LAURENT [*Suddenly frightened.*]: Run away! He hasn't the right to run away! He mustn't leave me. Daniel! Daniel! [*He runs off calling.*]

LENA: Laurent! Wait! What's the matter with you? [*She turns to SEÑOR ARMANDO.*] Daniel must have put a spell on him.

ARMANDO: I hope he did. It shows his power potential. But I can't understand why he would want to leave. Everything depends on his following my instructions to the letter.

LENA: Don't worry. Mama will see that he does what he's told.

ARMANDO: I'm sure she will. I have confidence in her capability!

LENA: You know, it's funny. All these years there was Daniel— my own brother—hiding in the attic—a monster, something to be kept secret, to be ashamed of. And now . . .

ARMANDO: My dear young lady, we all have monstrosities of one sort or another hiding in our attics. The fortunate ones are those who are wise enough to present their monsters to the public— with dignity and pride.

LENA: I'm a sister of a Minotaur!

ARMANDO: I'll feel better after I've had my talk with him. In show business one can be certain of nothing.

[YVONNE *enters and, with a sort of gentleness, pulls the rope behind her at the end of which is attached* DANIEL, *his hands bound together. They are followed by* ESTELLE, *her eyes lower dejectedly.*]

YVONNE: Now let this be the last time—you understand?
ARMANDO [*He tries not to show his inner excitement.*]: Well, now —where were you trying to go? The crowd is waiting for you.
LENA: Were you playing hide and seek?
YVONNE: Quiet, Lena! Go and get ready for the ceremony. [LENA *leaves.*] You, Estelle—to your room until further word. And you, my dear Armando . . . [*She hands Armando the end of the rope.*] I trust you with our prize. Be nice to him and don't scold him.

[ARMANDO *timidly takes the rope, looking at* DANIEL *with curiosity and fear. The women leave the two alone.* ARMANDO *takes a stool and places it in the center of the stage, making a motion to invite* DANIEL *to be seated.* DANIEL *does so.* ARMANDO *lays the end of the rope gently on the floor. He begins to walk around* DANIEL *cautiously, much in the manner of a lion tamer training a lion in a cage.*]

ARMANDO: Here we are alone at last—face to snout, if you'll pardon the expression. You're quite a specimen, I must admit— not quite as large, perhaps, as I expected, but—that's all right. We'll manage. You gave us all quite a turn there for a moment! [*He wipes his forehead with his handkerchief.*] But now that's all behind us. If we're going to make a fortune together, it's time we understood each other. Alone we are of little value, but together the potential is boundless. You are the stuff of which dreams are made—a combination of the grotesque, the fantastic, the impossible. In short—you are poetry.
DANIEL: The simplicity of a blade of grass . . .
ARMANDO: Ever since I was a little boy I've been interested in biological abnormalities. I used to draw pictures of them in my school notebooks. I had my own little private museum and I collected all sorts of deformities in nature—insects, flowers, fish —oh, yes, there are freaks among them, too. I wanted to give them a place of distinction in their social order.

DANIEL: The wonder of the sunrise . . .

ARMANDO: I came to the conclusion that they were the true heroes of modern times! You understand me, don't you? You, the most perfect of all monstrosities . . .

DANIEL: The clearness of a mountain brook.

ARMANDO: I'm sorry, I don't seem to follow your line of reasoning. A moment ago when I described you as poetry, that was not an invitation to converse in that medium. Let's get down to basic semantics. Are we going to help each other make a fortune and the world find its ultimate salvation? That's my question, and all I want from you is a direct yes or no.

DANIEL: Do you believe in me?

ARMANDO: Of course, my boy. What a question! Everybody believes in you.

DANIEL: You really think I have the power to work miracles?

ARMANDO: Certainly. . . . [DANIEL *makes a sudden animal movement toward* SEÑOR ARMANDO, *who jumps back in fear*.] Now, now, none of your animal tricks! But you've got the idea and you're interpreting your part excellent-ly. The next step is to play it before the crowd. . . . Well then, it's decided. We have your cooperation? And now to meet the public. [*He calls*.] Yvonne!

DANIEL: Leave me to my deep forests, to my drying laundry sheets that hide me from the world. I wasn't born to be an exhibit in a sideshow.

ARMANDO: My dear, little Daniel—my beautiful, delicate flower—calm down, relax! Rest assured, we shall all grow old in making life pleasant for you! You shall have all the artificial forests your heart could desire, dripping with as many drying sheets as you want. We're not tyrants! [*He calls again*.] Yvonne! Yvonne! What can that woman be doing?

DANIEL: Don't be afraid. I'm incapable of killing—even a cockroach!

ARMANDO: Thank you, my son. Everything's going to work out. You'll see. Only you must understand me. This is my last chance, too.

[YVONNE *enters*.]

YVONNE: My darling, has Señor Armando told you our secret?

ARMANDO: Secret?

YVONNE: Our wedding!

ARMANDO: A minor detail to be discussed later. [*He takes* YVONNE *by the arm and leads her away from* DANIEL.] Things aren't going too well. He's decided to be difficult. It's up to you now to play your role. Be the bereaved mother!

YVONNE: I'll try. . . .

ARMANDO [*Going back to* DANIEL.]: A sacred moment, Daniel— the kiss of a mother. [YVONNE *goes to her son.* SEÑOR ARMANDO *remains discreetly apart from the other two as he speaks to himself.*] After all, what is life if not the movies?

YVONNE: What are movies if not life? I hope, my dear, you fully appreciate this blessed day. It's what we've lived for—all those imbeciles outside waiting for their prey and we, at last, taking revenge for the years of humiliation we've both suffered—for the lies and the fear.

DANIEL: I've been happy here, Mother.

YVONNE: Ah, yes, it's beautiful, isn't it—our palace of mirrors! These barricades of damp sheets that never quite dry, this human filth that we've had to purify—the shame of others left in our care . . . always washing, scrubbing, boiling, looking for the stain, the odor, the residue of sin . . .

DANIEL: Our beautiful laundry!

YVONNE: Fairy tales for the customers! It's been a nightmare, yes, with you always in the background—having to hide the fact of your existence in order to keep the good will of our clients. You, the flower of my youth, the living reminder of a wonderful dream . . .

DANIEL: Always my father . . .

YVONNE: The other night, because of you, he suddenly burst into my memory like a barbarian warrior—standing shining and incandescent in the center of a sunburst. There he was, just as you are now, and he has made the same motion to me as he did once before. . . . I'll meet him again one day of my travels with the circus!

DANIEL: Is that why you're marrying Señor Armando?

YVONNE: In this life we cannot live forever in a dream world!

There comes a time when one must put down roots and toil for
one's daily bread. I must confess to you the truth, my baby, so
you can defend yourself against reality. Compared to your father,
you're a pretty feeble substitute—pretty feeble indeed!

ARMANDO: We can't turn back now—can't you see? Even if we
wanted to. The public knows of your existence and they won't
be put off.

YVONNE: If I marry Armando, perhaps he'll be able to protect you.
[*She goes to the window.*] Yes, those imbeciles outside can be-
come dangerous. The square is overflowing. They're waiting for
your miracles—the paraplegics, the stutterers, the tuberculars.
It's not only their bodies, but their hearts that are ill as well!
I know you can heal them!

DANIEL: Maybe so, Mother, but are they worth the trouble?

[ESTELLE *enters.*]

ESTELLE: Is everything all right, Daniel?

ARMANDO: Ah, there you are, my little Estelle. Come in, come in,
dear girl. You're just the one we need. Daniel wants your reas-
surance. The voice of the heart, you know. . . . You must convince him. We haven't a minute to lose.

ESTELLE [*Going over to* DANIEL.]: Daniel! Oh, my darling, what
have they done to your hands? They're all red. [*She turns to*
YVONNE.] Untie him! Can't you see you've hurt his wrists?

ARMANDO: Of course, he must be untied. [*He starts to untie*
DANIEL.] A mere oversight. Come here, Estelle. You haven't forgotten what I told you earlier? You are going to persuade Daniel,
aren't you? It's to his own advantage—to everyone's advantage.
You must keep him from being obstinate. [*He leads* YVONNE
away from the other two.]

ESTELLE: Daniel knows that he must continue to work his
miracles.

ARMANDO: How I envy the two of you, my little turtledoves. What
a future opens before you! But you must hurry. The official dele-
gations are about to arrive.

ESTELLE [*She sits on the floor at* DANIEL's *feet.*]: Daniel, you
understand, don't you, that you're going to be free, that you'll
leave the laundry forever and give up your miserable life in the
attic? Even if you're not completely in accord with everything

Señor Armando wants you to do, you'll be able to travel with me and do good all around you. Daniel, don't make me spend my life in this hovel, in this decaying house. Don't leave me here to mildew and rot, growing old, with my hands scrubbed raw through years of scalding soap suds and icy rinse water. . . . Look at my hands, Daniel. They're red and cracked. In winter I can hardly move my fingers. Take pity on my hands. . . . Daniel —you know I love you.

DANIEL: You pretend to love me—and you only think of your hands.

ESTELLE: I pretend! Ask me to die for you—and I'd kill myself right now.

DANIEL: But would you do something even harder—go on living . . . with chapped hands?

ESTELLE: Why would you want me to, my darling? Today we're being offered our chance—so we can be together—not hidden away in an attic, but out in the world, free and respected! Of course I'm afraid of what will happen to us, but since I'll be with you, everything will work out somehow—because our love will be stronger than anything else!

YVONNE: You're not going to refuse her, are you, Daniel?

DANIEL: To stay in my attic or travel around in a golden cage. In either case, that doesn't leave me much freedom. I want to live in the open, in the country—in liberty.

ARMANDO: But you will, my boy. You will.

ESTELLE: Daniel, I love you. Can't you believe me? I proved it just now when I offered to run away with you—to give up everything for you. And I still would. If you're afraid, Daniel— afraid of what they can do to you—and if you love me—only a little, we could go somewhere, start over again. . . .

DANIEL: They believe I'm some kind of false god! They don't understand me.

ARMANDO: We do understand you—and we know you're a real god!

ESTELLE: I'll do anything you ask, my darling. I'll stay with you here in the attic, or go with you with them—or leave with you if you want. We'll get past the crowd somehow.

YVONNE: And how far do you think the two of you would get—in his . . . condition?

DANIEL: If I could only find the word—the key—that would explain the reason for my being like this. Laurent said I've appeared in his dreams—even before he saw me, before he knew I existed. There must be some reason, some secret formula.

ESTELLE: You'll find it in my love! We'll teach you how to be God Daniel. I can already feel little stars at the tips of your fingers.

DANIEL: I wish I could feel them, too—if I only could!

ESTELLE: You will! We'll help you feel them—your family and I. You'll see. I promise.

DANIEL: Nothing can corrupt us any more. Hide yourself here in my arms. Our night will fall as the snow, and we'll be safe. [*Wrapped in each other's arms, the two seem completely oblivious to their surroundings.*]

ARMANDO: I think we can depend on him after all. Isn't that right?

YVONNE: Daniel, Señor Armando is speaking to you.

ARMANDO: I want to know if we can count on your cooperation?

DANIEL: I—I may not be able to do what you want.

ARMANDO: Of course you can, and you'll never regret it, my boy. I guarantee it!

[*The sound of the crowd outside grows louder.* LENA *enters.*]

LENA: Mama, the crowd outside is getting bigger all the time. They're waving posters and banners. But some of them are whistling and yelling for the show to start. I'm afraid there'll be a riot.

ARMANDO: Mob violence? Well, what could be better? It's just like Rome during the Decline and Fall!

ESTELLE: Don't forget, everybody, I'm the one who's responsible! I made him change his mind.

ARMANDO: Of course, my dear, and we're grateful. For proof, I grant you permission to marry Daniel.

YVONNE: What? Marry the sole heir to the Laundry of the Future?

LENA: Who are you to give permission?

ARMANDO: I'm his future father.

LENA: Mama!

ARMANDO: Where is Laurent? He should be here. I need him for our entrance.

LENA: He's taking a shower to wake up.

[YVONNE *takes* ESTELLE *in her arms.*]

YVONNE: Come to my arms, my little daughter-in-law!

ARMANDO: A touching sight—two women of different status, bridging the class barrier! We'll have to stage it over again for the photographers! . . . All right, my children. It's time to present ourselves to the public. Line up, everybody.

LENA: I'll get Laurent.

YVONNE: Too late. We can't wait for him.

ARMANDO: Daniel, you be the last to make an entrance, after all the rest of us. We'll form a guard of honor for you and each wave a circus pennant. [*He hands each a pennant.*] Estelle, just before you come out, go to the window and open it. That's the signal for the trumpets.

YVONNE: I'm going to faint. I know it!

ARMANDO: No! No! Daniel, catch your mother before she falls!

YVONNE: My child!

ARMANDO [*To* DANIEL.]: Now I'll do most of the talking for you, so there's nothing to worry about. Of course they'll want to hear you say something—so tell them . . . oh, I don't know what, but it should be something they can't understand—something that sounds high-flown and flowery. I have complete confidence in you.

DANIEL: I'll speak to them of love.

ARMANDO: Magnificent—but be careful. We don't want to be cut off by the censor.

[*The sound of the crowd grows louder.* LAURENT *enters.*]

LENA: Laurent! Thank God you're here in time. We were going to start without you.

LAURENT: Daniel, Daniel, where are you? That hairy beast is lying in wait for me. I climb the scaffold. Daniel, don't let me die.

DANIEL [*Holding* ESTELLE *to him.*]: You hear him? And the others outside in the square? From all their aching hearts comes the same cry.

LAURENT: Tony's blood.

YVONNE: What's he talking about?

ESTELLE: He's gone crazy!

LAURENT: Softly, softly I used to hear that voice behind the windows—misty with rain. I'd press my nose against the pane, and my breath would cloud the glass in the shape of a heart. I was waiting for a miracle, for the falling of the snow that would prove to me that everything was still possible, that they were there, protecting me—that they would save me from the chosen moment—just as Tony explained it. The two of us would share our lives together in the delights of the wind. We were waiting for the miracle that never came.

ARMANDO: You're right. He is crazy! Lena, get him back under that shower! We've got to meet our public.

LAURENT: Daniel, you haven't the right to show yourself! You haven't the right to toss them into the boiling water of awakening, only to leave them later to their own mirror! Look at me —at what I've become: a worthless nobody! And I used to have such strength.

LENA: That's right, Daniel. He's changed and it's your fault!

LAURENT: See? Even Lena has contempt for me now. No one looks at me anymore—and they're no longer afraid of me. When you save people, you should save them completely. Otherwise it's better to leave them to their misery!

ARMANDO: Please—keep this discussion for later.

LAURENT: I can still feel the taste of blood in my mouth.

DANIEL: I would like to cure you if I could—I really would.

ARMANDO: We must start the ceremony! Any minute now the crowd will be out of hand.

LAURENT: I remember there was a large oak tree outside the house of the woman who ran the candy store. I hid in it, my knees scraped raw by the rough bark of the branches—and I lay suspended in space, caught up in the blue of the sky—like a drop of water.

DANIEL: Those are your memories. What have they to do with me?

LAURENT: Erase them—erase everything so I can start again from nothing.

YVONNE: A miracle, Daniel!

ESTELLE: Yes, make a miracle! Hold out your hands!

LENA: Convert him!

LAURENT: After I saw that Tony was dead, all that was left for me was to run—to run, run, run. I ran because I was afraid and I was afraid because I ran. I left my sunny country by the sea— and I traveled—I crossed many borders. I wanted to stop and begin to live again, but always a horrible face with a little red star of blood would follow me, would wake me in the night— and so I began to run again. I was looking for peace, for some hidden spot where the face in my dream would not be waiting for me. And finally I thought I found it. It was the laundry. But it was here that it was waiting—the same face with the same eyes, the same taste of blood in my mouth! It was here that I found you.

DANIEL: Stop it! Please! I'd like to help you! I'd like to help all of you—all of them—

LAURENT: Then tell me. I've got to know why I'm living and why I'm running. The key! You have it, Dainel, and you must give it to me. Tell me why I've been tortured all these years by the vision of your face. You know and you're going to tell me!

DANIEL: I know nothing except the four walls of my attic, Laurent —the four walls, a few trips out into the forest in the moon- light, the sound of water in a brook, the smell of a few flowers. That's all I know of life. How could I help anybody?

LAURENT: You can give me your secret.

DANIEL: I have no secret, Laurent.

LAURENT: During all those years it's amused you to make me run. Well, that's over; that's finished. You're my dream become reality—and the reality must explain the dream.

ARMANDO: Ready, everybody! Line up! Forward, march! [DANIEL *starts to leave.*] What's the matter? Where are you going?

DANIEL: Back to the attic. Back to my sheets. I shall disappear into the rushing and bubbling waters of the laundry. And every- thing will be washed clean. I want no part of all this.

ARMANDO: But the public? Think of the public!

DANIEL: I was not made to show myself off on a circus platform.

YVONNE: You can't do this to us! Think of your mother!

LENA: Think of my baby!

ESTELLE: Think of my hands!

LAURENT: You're not going upstairs!

DANIEL: Get out of my way! [*He starts out.* LAURENT *blocks his way. Suddenly he takes out a switchblade knife, which he flips open. The group backs away in horror.*]

YVONNE: We must drag him outside!

LENA: Don't let him leave, Laurent!

ESTELLE: Please, Daniel, please come back!

ARMANDO: Capture him—the sideshow freak! I'll sick my lions on him!

ESTELLE: Don't let him run away!

LENA: Yes, get him! He's a mad dog! Get him!

YVONNE: Daniel! Daniel!

ARMANDO: Get him!

ALL: Get him! Get him! Get him!

[*The crowd outside joins in the screaming with those on the stage.* LAURENT *and* DANIEL *have moved into the labyrinth behind the sheets. There is a sudden silence followed by the joyous blast of a Spanish fanfare.*]

ARMANDO [*Taking off his hat.*]: My song! "Unto Us the Minotaur"!

[*After a moment,* LAURENT *appears, wiping his knife on a sheet. The music outside continues.* LAURENT *moves toward the group, which backs away from him.*]

LAURENT: There—it's finished! The dream is over.

LENA: He's dead. We're ruined!

ARMANDO: Perhaps it's not all lost. We could preserve his body in alcohol. Possibly the crowd would accept that.

ESTELLE: Now I'll never be able to leave the laundry!

LENA: Why did you do it?

ESTELLE: And we let you! We even wanted you to. Why?

LAURENT: When a dream becomes a reality, it must be loved— or destroyed. Nothing else is possible.

YVONNE [*Transfigured.*]: Estelle, my child . . . Lena. It's time to light the furnace. There's still so much laundry to boil. [*She goes to the sheet that is stained with blood.*] And I'm afraid these stains will never wash out. [*She begins to fold the sheet as the . . .*

Curtain Falls